# LATINOS FACING RACISM

◆

# New Critical Viewpoints on Society Series
## Edited by Joe R. Feagin

# LATINOS FACING RACISM

## DISCRIMINATION, RESISTANCE, AND ENDURANCE

JOE R. FEAGIN AND
JOSÉ A. COBAS

Paradigm Publishers
Boulder • London

Copyright © 2014 by Paradigm Publishers

Published in the United States by Paradigm Publishers, 5589 Arapahoe Avenue, Boulder, Colorado 80303 USA.

Paradigm Publishers is the trade name of Birkenkamp & Company, LLC, Dean Birkenkamp, President and Publisher.

Library of Congress Cataloging-in-Publication Data

Feagin, Joe R.
  Latinos facing racism : discrimination, resistance, and endurance / Joe R. Feagin and José A. Cobas.
     p. cm. — (Critical viewpoints)
  Includes bibliographical references and index.
  ISBN 978-1-61205-553-4 (hardcover : alk. paper)
  ISBN 978-1-61205-554-1 (paperback : alk. paper)
  1. Hispanic Americans—Social conditions. 2. Race discrimination—United States.
3. United States—Race relations.  I. Cobas, José A. II. Title.
  E184.S75F43 2013
  305.868'073—dc23

                                                                            2013021795

Printed and bound in the United States of America on acid-free paper that meets the standards of the American National Standard for Permanence of Paper for Printed Library Materials.

18  17  16  15  14    5  4  3  2  1

*En gratitud y a la memoria de mis queridos padres* (José)

*and in gratitude for our colleagues who have*
*assisted us in our research over many years*
(Joe and José)

# Contents

# Preface

The results of the 2012 presidential election forced the Republican Party, albeit kicking and screaming, to confront the reality that US Latinos can no longer be dismissed as an unimportant segment of the electorate. It was clear that Latinos, a rapidly growing demographic, can act as an effective umbrella group when it comes to common concerns such as immigration and social support programs. Since that election, Republicans' proposed solutions to deal with the "Hispanic issue" have included a begrudged reexamination of long-languishing immigration legislation as well as the lionization of Florida's young senator Marco Rubio, the son of Cuban immigrants, as a Republican candidate for the presidency in the near future. Other important issues for many Latinos, such as decent-paying jobs, better health care and housing, more support for education, and bilingualism, were left untouched by this new Republican political concern.

Nonetheless, many observers have adduced that these political developments are clear indications that Latinos are finally on the path to full assimilation and integration into mainstream US institutions, much as European immigrants had done in the first half of the twentieth century. In an article titled "Hispanics, the New Italians," David Leonhardt (2013), Washington bureau chief of the *New York Times*, strongly supports this point of view:

> The German immigrants of the 19th century were so devoted to their native language that Americans wondered if the new arrivals would ever assimilate. The Irish who followed were said to be too devoted to a foreign pope to embrace American democracy. . . . Whatever Washington does in coming months, a wealth of data suggests that Latinos, who make up fully half of the immigration wave of the past century, are already following the classic pattern for American immigrants.

A West Coast journalist, Hope Yen (2013), wrote a similar article arguing that the significant growth in the Hispanic population and associated changes mean that "being white is fading as a test of American-ness." Yen concludes from this journalistic analysis that the speed of contemporary "assimilation for today's Latinos and Asian-Americans is often compared with that of the Poles, Irish, Italians and Jews who . . . eventually merged into an American white mainstream." Indeed, for some time now a few public commentators have insisted that certain Latino and Asian American groups have already been accepted by whites as now fully white (Lind, 1995).

We are not as sanguine as these analysts. Italians first had to become accepted as "white," that is, as the racial equals of Anglo whites, before they could fully integrate into mainstream institutions. The long history of Latinos facing discrimination from whites, including persistent racial profiling and attacks against the Spanish language and Spanish speakers, makes it unlikely that Latinos will be integrated into this society as true equals of Anglo whites anytime soon. Our research shows that Latinos, including those in the middle class, still experience racial discrimination regularly. Indeed, these journalistic commentaries point to a significant part of this racialized reality. Leonhardt, who cites the nativistic social scientist Samuel Huntington, and numerous other journalists seem to assume that the centuries-old white racist system of the United States is no longer a path-blocking problem for full societal integration. As they imply, a major difficulty for this societal integration lies in the group involved giving up its language, important parts of its home culture, and its ties to the home country. Numerous popular analysts do not seem to understand that expecting a group to give up much or most of its home culture is not only a view from a traditional white racial framing of assimilation, but also an expectation that is, in effect, for one-way cultural "cleansing," with its often harmful personal and group effects.

In this book we go beyond this rather unreflective and conventional approach, which can be found in many research studies as well, and interpret our Latino interview data from a theoretical perspective stressing systemic racism and its important white racial framing of society. Only when we juxtapose the racialized experiences of the members of our Latino sample with insights from this systemic racism theory can we fully appreciate that US racism is not just a matter of individual bigotry but a broad phenomenon that penetrates the entire society and is grounded in a foundational racism that has long been maintained by elite and ordinary whites. Without this realization that individual agents of anti-Latino racism are part of a centuries-old institutionalized system of racial oppression, attempts to correct ongoing oppression and its many injustices will be insufficient at best. We hope our efforts here contribute to the ongoing national struggle against this long-standing and pervasive societal evil.*

## Acknowledgments

We would like to thank numerous colleagues for their useful comments and other helpful input in regard to various drafts of this manuscript and for their impact on our thinking and research as we developed this project. We would particularly like to thank Maria Chavez, David Orta, Marisa Sanchez, Hilario Molina, Nestor Rodriguez, Shari Valentine, Zulema Valdez, Louwanda Evans, Glenn Bracey, Rogelio Saénz, and Daniel Delgado. We are especially grateful to Rachel Feinstein for her comments and substantial library assistance. We would also like to express our appreciation to the reference librarians at Hayden Library at Arizona State University and at Evans Library at Texas A&M University. We are especially grateful to our publisher, Dean Birkenkamp, who was always supportive in the gestation and completion of this project. Joe would like to thank José for his yeoman efforts in completing the many interviews conducted for the project and for his long dedication to it, and José would like to thank Joe for taking over completion of the book and first authorship when he was faced with a serious illness and could not finish the first draft. We would also like to express our gratitude to the numerous respondents in our study, who gave their time generously and made this book possible.

In portions of Chapters 2 and 4 we draw on, but heavily rework, earlier versions of our arguments in "Latinos/as and the White Racial Frame" (*Sociological Inquiry* 78 [February 2008]: 39–53) and "Language Oppression and Resistance: Latinos in the United States" (*Ethnic and Racial Studies* 31 [February 2008]: 390–410).

---

*The authors agree with the goals of colleagues who want to affirm the dignity of women by modifying Spanish language terms in English. However, we observe standard Spanish grammar rules in respect to *grammatical* gender. We also adhere to standard Spanish grammar rules on diacritics. Two exceptions are the names of individuals who do not use diacritics and the titles of existing publications.

# 1

# Racializing Latinos

In the spring of 2006, a middle-class Mexican American teenager was viciously attacked and sodomized by two white teenagers yelling "white power" and anti-Latino insults at a party in a mostly white suburb of Houston. Suffering from multiple serious wounds, including a swastika cut into his chest, the young man was hospitalized for months and had numerous surgeries for his severe injuries. He later committed suicide, and his white attackers were eventually imprisoned for the brutal crime (Associated Press, 2007).

While most whites were certainly abhorred by this violent act against a young Mexican American, and while most whites would not shout out extreme white supremacist slogans, they often do hold to significant elements of a widespread anti-Latino perspective. From this white-framed viewpoint, the lives, livelihoods, and cultures of Latinos at various class levels are frequently viewed as having less value than those of whites. Indeed, over the past several decades, the negative racial framing of Mexican Americans and other Latin Americans has increased substantially—framing that is dramatically seen in incidents like this one, in white vigilante groups patrolling the border with Mexico, and in the many whites who support forceful "border security" measures such as vigorous border patrols and big electrified fences on the Mexican border. In numerous areas of the US Southwest, white policing agencies have accelerated the vigorous policing and racial profiling of Latinos of diverse nationality and class backgrounds. Moreover, everyday discrimination targeting Latinos takes not only these more blatant forms but also more subtle and covert forms.

The United States has a very large Latino population, estimated at more than 51 million. This population is larger than that of Spain and second in size, among all countries, only to Mexico's 112 million people. The current breakdown of the US Latino population is about 63 percent Mexican

American, 9 percent mainland Puerto Rican, 4 percent Cuban American, and 3 percent Salvadoran American, with the rest of the Latino population distributed over a large number of national origins in Latin America and the Caribbean (US Census Bureau, 2011). The US Census Bureau (2010) calculated that in 2010 Mexican Americans, by far the largest Latino group today, were about 10 percent of the US population. They also made up large and growing percentages of the population in several important US states: Texas (32 percent), California (31 percent), New Mexico (29 percent), Nevada (20 percent), and Illinois (13 percent). Note that this numerical dominance of Mexican Americans in the US Latino group, to be explained in detail below, ultimately stems from the early annexation of much of Mexico to the United States as a result of the 1840s US war with Mexico.

Although they or their ancestors have come from a number of Latin American and Caribbean countries, US Latinos are increasingly seen by those inside and outside this umbrella Latino category as constituting a distinctive group that shares not only much racialized attention and discrimination from the white Anglo population but also, increasingly, certain distinctive values and perspectives that are shaped by their often similar home-country cultures. This umbrella conceptualization linking together a number of Latin American groups is true for both Latinos and non-Latinos. Also significant is that the growing and influential Latino-owned and Latino-oriented mass media are greatly helping to create a more integrated Latino umbrella group. For example, the two US Latino television networks, Univision and Telemundo, currently have the largest audiences of Spanish-language viewers across the globe, and in numerous areas the local television stations affiliated with them have more viewers than competing English-language stations. With their major coverage of Latin American and US Latino issues, and now with the development of English-subtitled broadcasts for bilingual Latinos, these major networks have expanding influence and help to integrate the diverse national origin groups within the Latino umbrella category (Navarro, 2000; Thielman, 2012).

The US Census Bureau projects that by 2020 the US Latino population will reach more than 60 million, nearly a fifth of the total population. Yet, relatively little systematic attention has been given to the everyday experiences of this large group of Americans with racism and related racialization issues. Most popular and scholarly discussions focus on undocumented and other immigrants from Latin America in regard to their putative impact on crime, government programs, health care, and public schools in the United States, as well as on their supposed failure to assimilate and conform to the core Anglo culture and institutions.

# The Assimilation Tradition and US Immigration

US Latinos are very frequently viewed by media commentators, politicians, and social scientists from a societal assimilation perspective. Such assimilation perspectives mostly conceptualize this process as ideally involving a gradual and orderly integration of a racial or ethnic group into the dominant core culture and social patterns of the United States. Today, both popular and scholarly analysts make extensive use of this concept of societal assimilation in referring to Latino immigrants and their individual and group adaptation, or lack of adaptation, to the dominant culture and institutions of the host US society.

There is a long social science tradition of this generalized and agent-less approach to immigrants. Robert Park (Park and Burgess, 1924), an early white sociologist, focused on assimilation and proposed an ongoing cycle that characterized intergroup "race relations." Initial intergroup contact, often generated by migration from one country to another, was normally followed, sequentially, by competition, accommodation, and eventual full assimilation into a society like the United States. For contemporary societies, Park and most subsequent scholars in this assimilationist tradition envision a long-term societal trend toward large-scale assimilation of immigrant groups. Even those who are racially subordinated are often viewed as eventually assimilating substantially into the core culture and institutions of the United States (Park and Burgess, 1924: 735–760; Gordon, 1964). Presumably, the core culture and institutions they have in mind include US legal, political, economic, and educational institutions.

More recent social science analysts, especially sociologist Milton Gordon (1964), have presented a detailed perspective on societal assimilation. Gordon emphasized specific dimensions of this racial-ethnic assimilation (for example, primary group assimilation, marital assimilation, civic assimilation) in which the outcomes for various groups can occur at different rates. Gordon and other analysts in his tradition have often focused rather substantially on European immigrant groups and their subsequent generational processes of assimilation. For Gordon there are three possible outcomes for groups in the process of societal assimilation—a blending together in a melting pot, a cultural pluralism where groups remain distinctive, and a substantial conformity to the white-Anglo culture and institutions. Examining the relevant history of the United States, he accurately concludes that the reality has mostly been one of *Anglo-conformity* assimilation. Historically, all immigrants and their descendants have abandoned much of their home-country heritage and conformed substantially to important aspects of the dominant Anglo core culture. For European immigrant groups, thoroughgoing assimilation to the core culture has typically been completed in a few generations. Assimilation analysts have understood that racial bigotry impedes full assimilation for non-European Americans but tend to be optimistic about (especially middle-class) members of groups of color eventually being fully assimilated into the dominant culture and institutions.

Contemporary assimilation analysts such as Richard Alba (2009) have argued that numerous racial-ethnic identities are weakening significantly. Increasingly, especially for European American groups, ethnic identity is mostly symbolic and decreasing greatly in importance (Gans, 1979). According to Nee and Alba (2009), the sociocultural mainstream to which immigrants and their descendants assimilate includes US institutions that substantially weaken their national origin identities. Not just contemporary white ethnic Americans, but also the descendants of immigrants of color over time will be fully assimilated into what Nee and Alba present as a relatively unproblematic sociocultural mainstream without significant racial barriers. Their reasoning includes the idea that, as the contemporary white baby-boomer generation retires, new economic opportunities are opening for people of color. They seem rather optimistic that whites' racial views and discrimination targeting people of color will greatly change, thereby allowing them to integrate fully into mainstream sociocultural institutions. The assimilation analysts continue the optimistic tradition of mainstream social scientists and media analysts who view these white-dominated core institutions as essentially inclusive and receptive to ongoing emancipation of non-European Americans from major racial barriers.

## Serious Flaws in Assimilation Perspectives

In our view, such optimism about this adaptation process is problematic for a number of conceptual and empirical reasons. One problem with these aforementioned assimilation perspectives is that they typically view assimilation from a substantially individualistic perspective and/or give too little attention to the societal structures that hamper or prevent the immigrant adaption processes. Thus, several researchers focusing on Latino and other immigrants of color (for instance, Portes and Zhou, 1993; Telles and Ortiz, 2008) have accented significant structural barriers and developed important concepts like "segmented assimilation." From their empirical studies, they have demonstrated that various immigrant groups have significantly different paths to assimilation as they adapt to the host society within structurally different socioeconomic sectors and with divergent adaptive patterns—including downward mobility in the case of certain Latino immigrant generations. For instance, contrary to optimistic media reports (see Anonymous, 2000), the children and grandchildren of Mexican immigrants frequently do not move up the US education and socioeconomic ladder as readily as children of earlier white immigrants did, and many have faced stagnation or downward mobility over the last few generations (Telles and Ortiz, 2008: 131–132; Feagin and Feagin, 2011: 226–228). In addition, even middle-class Asian immigrants and their children—the most stereotyped "model minority"—are not being assimilated into white middle-class society nearly as completely as numerous assimilation analysts have suggested. These immigrants and their children continue to report numerous serious problems with whites' racist views and associated racial barriers (Tuan, 1998; Chou and Feagin, 2008). Certain physical differences, especially those associated with stereotyped cultural differences, remain highly visible and negatively viewed by large numbers of white Americans.

A more fundamental problem with contemporary assimilation theories lies in the very concept and term of "assimilation," especially its underlying unidirectional assumption. As some assimilationists like Milton Gordon have recognized, yet not critically and thoroughly questioned, the conceptual as-sumptions of mainstream assimilation analyses have long embedded a serious white-Anglo "establishment" bias. Historically, both popular and academic analysts of late nineteenth- and early twentieth-century immigration to the United States considered certain new immigrant groups to be quite "unas-similable." For example, during the 1870s–1920s era of significant Asian immigration to the United States, Asian American leaders rejected whites' constant insistence that Asian immigrants were inferior and incapable of being assimilated into the white-dominated culture and society. In this era, dominant ideas about immigrant group assimilation were usually racially framed with a built-in assumption that only certain European immigrants could ever integrate well into the core culture and institutions (Feagin and Feagin, 2011: 286).

Note too that, then as now, assimilation theories have been very problematic because of their constant portrayal of "good" assimilation as a one-way adap-tation process to the white-Anglo core culture and institutions. Over many years whites have often said something like, "If Mexicans [or other Latinos] have left their country because they do not like it there, why do they insist on keeping their culture here?" Such persistent commentaries make clear the ordinary expectation that assimilation should be one-way. However, from the viewpoint of most immigrants of color, much of this Anglo-conformity assimi-lation process is *not* good, for it requires them to abandon cultural preferences and other important home-culture elements (for example, language) that they greatly value and depend on. They often, accurately, feel this Anglo-conformity assimilation as a direct attack on their home cultures. Indeed, one might term some of it an effort at "cultural cleansing."

Yet another serious flaw in most mainstream assimilation analysis is that it *hides* the principal white agents who control major societal processes of adaptation by immigrants of color and others coming into the society. These white agents, who are often agents of substantial discrimination, are not called out and analyzed in the mainstream conceptual tradition. Historically, elite whites, and their white and other acolytes, are the ones who shape and control most of the employment, educational, and political access in society, along with the discriminatory barriers (periodically including violence) that restrict and limit societal access for immigrants and their descendants, most especially for those who are racially subordinated. Indeed, as we noted above, the immigrants who are the main focus of most of these contemporary assimilation analyses are typically among the least powerful in the societal assimilation scenarios.

## The Melting Pot: Challenging Traditional Assimilation Perspectives?

Throughout its history the Anglo-conformity perspective on this country's assimilation process has appeared to be in tension with certain variations of a melting-pot perspective. Indeed, a certain pluralistic diversity of early immigrant groups was welcomed by the country's first president, George Washington. In a letter written in 1790 to members of a Jewish group in Newport, Rhode Island, he expressed this view of US tolerance and inclusion:

> The Citizens of the United States of America have a right to applaud themselves for giving to Mankind examples of an enlarged and liberal policy: a policy worthy of imitation. All possess alike liberty of conscience and immunities of citizenship. It is now no more that toleration is spoken of, as if it was by the indulgence of one class of people that another enjoyed the exercise of their inherent natural rights. For happily the government of the United States, which gives to bigotry no sanction, to persecution no assistance, requires only that they who live under its protection should demean themselves as good citizens, in giving it on all occasions their effectual support. (Freeman, 1992: 565)

Washington exaggerated the lack of state-supported bigotry but did extend his welcome to Jewish immigrants from Europe to the new US mixture because they qualified as substantially white, at least for some in the era's white elite. This is evident too in the fact that the Jewish immigrants being admitted were given access to naturalized citizenship under a 1790 law, one that limited such US citizenship to "whites" (Jacobson, 1998: 177).

In the 1780s, J. Hector St. John de Crèvecœur, a French agriculturalist who immigrated to the United States, penned a panegyric praising his adopted country, one reflective of this supposed open-immigration perspective. His

*Letters from an American Farmer* stated that "Americans" were a "mixture of English, Scotch, Irish, French, Dutch, Germans and Swedes" (De Crèvecœur, [1782] 1997: 42). The result of their interactive and mutual mixing and amalgamation, he averred, would be the emergence of a "new man" in the United States. He was apparently the first to write so publicly of these Americans as "melted" into a "new race," a new people whose "posterity will one day cause great changes in the world." His view was essentially a melting-pot perspective without that exact name, and he envisioned various European immigrants blending together in an apparently reciprocal adaptation process to create this new "American man." However, de Crèvecœur and others in the early white elite viewed this emergent new man as involving only a *limited* melding of US groups. For these analysts only white Europeans were part of the exciting new meld, and they excluded the fifth of the new country that was then African and Native American. This French American adhered to the early white racial axiom that only whites could be truly "American."

This conception of some type of a new American blend seems to have been accepted by some members of the white elite of the nineteenth century. Confronted with the need for white laborers and farmers in newly conquered western areas of the United States, many (but by no means all) of the nineteenth-century white elite manifested an uneasy but receptive attitude toward millions of new European immigrant workers. They further developed a version of this blended-American ideology—a cluster of ideas including the "belief that a new nation, a new national character and a new nationality were forming in the United States, and that the most heterogeneous human materials could be taken in and absorbed into this nationality" (Gleason, 1964: 20). Yet again, the new and diverse "human materials" said by white leaders to be blending together in a new American character were white and European in ancestry.

At the beginning of the twentieth century, Israel Zangwill, a Jewish immigrant from England, wrote an acclaimed play, *The Melting-Pot* (1909), that continued and amplified this ideology. Indeed, this play appears to be the first influential public statement to make explicit use of melting-pot language. Its melting-pot imagery was similar to de Crèvecœur's, and also sanguine, but with a new twist. Not surprisingly, Zangwill's concern was to find a niche for eastern European Jewish immigrants and their children in the ever-growing United States. To facilitate that task he pushed for their being truly "American" and "white." In Act 1 of his influential play, one of the central characters proclaims these famous lines:

> America is God's Crucible, the great Melting-Pot where all the races of Europe are melting and re-forming. . . . Irishmen and Englishmen, Jews and Russians—into the Crucible with you all! God is making the American.

Like de Crèvecœur earlier, Zangwill constructed a roster of the peoples who would idealistically make a mutually melded composite of important immigrant groups, again termed the new "American." Yet Zangwill too envisioned a restricted melting pot of only those with European ancestry. Unlike de Crèvecœur's entries, however, Zangwill's list included European Jews. Still, even as he brought the proclaimed melting pot fully into US discourse and legend, Zangwill and fellow publicists did not include the substantial proportion of the US population that was then Native, African, Latino, and Asian American.

Not surprisingly, many US residents still celebrate a rather idealistic vision of an interactive blending of people from many countries into one US melting pot. We will see this celebration in the commentaries of our Latino respondents in Chapter 6. However, empirically speaking, the melting pot, conceptualized as a mutually blended composite of peoples, has *never* happened. It is one of the enduring fictions of US society, for even the later European immigrant groups adapted in a substantially one-way Anglo-conformity process of assimilation, with mostly only modest reciprocal influences on the core Anglo-American legal, political, economic, educational, and other major institutions. In addition, to the present day, most European Americans have never envisioned the melting pot as a mutual blending of European Americans with Americans of color to make a truly "new American blend." The melting pot that matters to them has been viewed as a white-dominated cauldron. Today, as in the past, most whites reciprocally adapt only to modest aspects of the cultures of immigrants of color, such as certain food and music, that do not endanger continuing white dominance in the core culture and major societal institutions such as those of law, politics, and the capitalistic economy.

## What Would Full Assimilation Mean?

Today, many assimilation analysts envision eventual societal assimilation to a status and position roughly equal to that of whites to be possible for immigrant groups, including for immigrants of color and their descendants over time. However, in US society, being truly "white" in societal status has always been much more than a matter of individual socioeconomic achievements or self-chosen identity. Full integration into the core culture and institutions has required being accepted by those whites in power, and by their well-institutionalized defining processes, as truly white. Full integration into the core society is thus all but impossible for Americans of color. Even more than other racialized statuses on society's dominant racial ladder, the white racial status is *institutionally enabled* (Bracey, 2013). Institutionally enabled means being vetted in many overt and subtle ways through the institutional procedures enacted by the white-Anglo creators and maintainers of the deep underlying structures of this society. Virtually no individual or family has become fully white in societal status just on their own, but only by means of physical appearance, key cultural symbols, and accumulated resources recognized by the dominant group collectively, including endogamic marital linkages and the well-institutionalized definitional and screening processes of the major economic, legal, political, and educational institutions. This is true no matter what the socioeconomic achievements of an individual person may be.

Being fully "white" in societal status, power, and privilege means much more than individual achievements or being considered an "honorary white" by the mostly white controllers of society. It includes an individual or family fitting all key aspects of the white individual or family template created by the centuries-old white-run institutions and core culture. Conforming by means of assimilation to much of the core culture and institutions is only part of this process, for those conforming also have to be actively vetted and fully accepted in dozens of ways by elite and ordinary whites in order to rise significantly in the societal hierarchy, much less to rise to the level of full white status.

Over several centuries the white elite has played the central role in creating and perpetuating our core culture and institutions. As a result, this mostly white elite has long had the ability to shape or determine the exploitative contexts, wealth distributions, and accommodation actions of others in society. Thus, from the first century of this country's development, whites as a group have been, unjustly, the racialized beneficiaries of many government and other societal programs facilitating their prosperity, upward mobility, and wealth creation. For example, the major federal and state homestead acts provided extensive lands that generated over the generations much family wealth and prosperity, almost exclusively for whites. Then, later federal government programs—such as major housing, veterans support, and contracting programs after World War II—assisted a great many white individuals and families to develop assets and prosperity much more substantially than their counterparts in communities of color (Feagin, 2010).

As a result, centuries of *unjust* enrichment for whites has meant centuries of *unjust* impoverishment for most Native, African, Latino, and Asian American groups. Today, unjust enrichment and unjust impoverishment remain central to this racialized society, with huge wealth and other resource differentials across major racial groups. For example, today whites have on average many times the average family wealth of Latino and African Americans (Feagin, 2010). Other major resources remain very unequal as well. For white individuals and families today, these white privileges and advantages include the ability to secure jobs, rent or buy housing, access banking and legal systems, utilize public accommodations, deal with the police and other government agencies, and engage in dozens of other everyday activities *without* facing racial discrimination (McIntosh, 1988; Feagin, 2010). And these are only part of a long list of such advantages available to those who are institutionally enabled as white in our still systemically racist society.

## The Costly Impact of Assimilation Pressures

Being forced to adapt in a unidirectional fashion to white folkways and institutions and a white framing of society—so that even for partial societal success one must regularly walk, talk, and think from some version of a white racial framing (see below) of society—is not the type of societal adaptation that is personally and collectively healthy as seen from a broader human rights perspective. In effect, the heavy assimilation pressures and realities are recurringly unhealthy and damaging. Incontestably, for many immigrants and their descendants, the unidirectional, often discriminatory assimilation pressures have significantly harmed them and their families. For Americans of color, this conforming process usually involves a great many personal, family, and community costs (Feagin and McKinney, 2003). In the chapters that follow, we will frequently observe the serious price that Latinos pay in dealing with these persistent pressures to assimilate to the white-dominated core culture and institutions.

For instance, social science research on immigrants of color and their descendants indicates that their physical or mental health often declines as they face the intense assimilation pressures and conformities of US society (Rumbaut, 1997: 483). In a study of third-generation Japanese Americans, communications researcher Janice Tanaka (1999) found that a significant number endured great personal distress, painful self-blame, mental and physical illnesses, alcoholism, or drug abuse that is connected to the intense pressures to conform and adapt in a one-way fashion to the requirements for success in this white-normed society. Moving from their home-country culture to the white-Anglo culture of the United States often does not bring the broad positive results typically depicted in the official "American dream" rhetoric.

Historically, these one-way assimilation pressures have been so intense that some Latino organizations and organizations of other Americans of color that have developed since the 1930s have at some point in their histories adopted a very strong assimilationist thrust in strategies for dealing with white oppression. For example, as José Gutiérrez (1985: 143) has summarized, Mexican American assimilationists have operated like many in other groups of color and

> believed that Anglicization would lead to acceptance by the dominant group and that subsequent entry into the Anglo middle-class world would inevitably follow. Thus, these early leaders and followers believed that speaking English

without an accent, obtaining an education, being effusively patriotic, and adopting many trappings of Anglo America would solve the social, political, and economic problems of the Chicano people. In other words, they accepted the notion that their culture and heritage was the cause of their problems. Their solution was to change themselves to be mirrors of the dominant society.

Historically, especially in the period before the civil rights era of the 1960s, numerous Latino leaders and organizations emphasized assimilation to the white core culture and institutions. Because of the negative effects of one-way assimilation, their leading of Latinos in that direction has involved a collaboration in their own oppression and that of those they lead—a type of self-hatred or "symbolic violence," to use Pierre Bourdieu's term, that we accent in Chapter 4.

## Racialization and Systemic Racism: The Latino Experience

The major barriers to more substantial Latino incorporation into numerous areas and levels of our historically white institutions clearly involve whites' racial perspectives and associated discrimination. To understand this societal reality better, we now turn to the central issue of the racialization of US Latinos over more than a century and a half. Important to this process of racialization is the concept of "race" that is central to the white folkways and framing of this society. Consider briefly some relevant history. Centuries back, in the 1400s and 1500s, the Spanish government's colonizers and associated entrepreneurs were the first Europeans to colonize and dominate on a large scale the numerous indigenous societies in the Americas in order to seize their material resources by force. This extensive Spanish imperialism was soon countered by the imperial expansion of competing English, Dutch, and French nation-states. Early on, Spanish and English conquerors and enslavers in the Americas rationalized the oppression of indigenous and African peoples in both Christian religious terms (for example, uncivilized and un-Christian) and physical-biological terms (for example, ugly and dark).

By the last decades of the 1600s, European and European American thinkers were laying the groundwork for a rigid hierarchy of biologically distinctive "races," which was developed more fully over the eighteenth century. For example, Sir William Petty, an influential English anatomist, portrayed enslaved "blacks" as physically and culturally inferior to "whites." Petty advocated a ladder-like ranking of unchangeable human "species" (also termed "races") characterized by distinctive physical and cultural differences (see Shore, 2000: 87). His racialized views on this were in concert with views of the European colonial elite in North America. Meanwhile, the famous Western philosopher Immanuel Kant lectured on both philosophy and social science topics in the area that would become Germany. His treatise *On the Distinctiveness of the Races in General* ([1775] 1950) laid out what is apparently the first Western hierarchical model specifying named human "races." Kant's racist theorizing, which he claimed was based on science, viewed "races" as "differences in the human genus" shaped by different environments. Races varied in physical traits such as skin color, physiognomy, and body type, as well as in psychological temperament. Kant paid special attention to negative "Negro" traits. In his racist view, these individuals looked and smelled funny and were "lazy, soft and dawdling" ([1775] 1950: 22). This early white racial framing of African-descent people by Europe's racist thinkers had a shaping impact on most subsequent models of racial hierarchy in Western societies.

The conceptualizations of "race" in North America in the late 1600s and early 1700s were—not surprisingly, given the interactions of elites across the Atlantic—developed more fully over the eighteenth century, always with a firm white belief in the supremacy of the white "Anglo-Saxon" race. Thomas Jefferson, the famous US founder and a major slaveholder, was the first North American intellectual to write extensively on "race" matters in a vein much like that of Petty and Kant. He argued that enslaved African Americans did not have significant group achievements demonstrating any racial equality with whites in almost all areas. His major book, and the first by a secular intellectual in North America, *Notes on the State of Virginia* ([1785] 1999), articulates a very strong racial framing of very "superior" whites and "inferior" blacks. Together with numerous other white founders, Jefferson fostered a white racial framing defending the US racial hierarchy. Within a few decades Jefferson and other founders' broad white framing of the racially "inferior" others would be extended by elite and ordinary whites to the first Latinos brought into the US sphere (Mexican Americans) and to the first Asians (Chinese Americans). Both groups were brought into the US Southwest and West in the mid-nineteenth century (see below).

## Systemic Racism and the White Racial Frame

We can take a moment to explain key elements of our conceptual perspective in this book. Today, as in the distant past, the closely related concepts of "race" groups and racial hierarchy are central to the operation of the systemic racism that is foundational for this North American society. In our thinking about this foundational and systemic oppression, we are heavily influenced by scholarly and activist traditions of African, Chicano, and Native Americans. The oldest and most developed counter-framed theoretical tradition targeting white racism and its racist framing is that of critical black scholars and activists such as W. E. B. Du Bois ([1935] 1992), Kwame Ture (Ture and Hamilton, 1967), Derrick Bell (1993), and Angela Davis (1971). Also important for us is the Chicano (Latino) tradition of critical analysis of US racism (J. Gutiérrez, 1985, 2001; Barrera, 1979; Acuña, 1996; Delgado, 1996) and the Native American activists' sustained critiques of US racism (for example, Means, 1980, 1995).

Especially since the African, Chicano, and Native American uprisings in the 1960s, a revolution in the institutional and systemic analysis of US racism has developed in this counter-framed tradition. This can be seen in the related critical traditions of critical race theory, which arose initially in 1970s scholarship of legal scholars of color, and systemic racism theory, which initially arose among black activists and a few social scientists of various backgrounds (see Ture and Hamilton, 1967; Delgado and Stefancic, 2012; Feagin and Feagin, 1978).

Accented in these conceptual and activist traditions, the centuries-old foundational reality of white racism accounts for why it has long shaped the most important aspects of this racially hierarchical society—most major institutions, much everyday interaction, many societal conflicts, and the dominant racial framing. It also shapes in basic ways how mainstream scholars, media analysts, and politicians have publicly discussed and researched this society's racial realities. As we suggested in our critique of assimilation theories, the *hierarchy of racialized groups* in this country centrally involves a hierarchy of important societal resources. Over time, whites have secured much "racial capital" from this hierarchical system of oppression. Not surprisingly, such racial capital has long included not only the economic capital of substantial income and wealth but also the dominant social status and social networking capital. Those at the top of this societal racial ladder, those with predominant white-European ancestry, on average have much more of these types of social capital than those on lower rungs of the racial ladder.

Significant access to these types of social capital, as we will emphasize in Chapter 3, frequently plays out over much physical space, such that many spaces of the United States are racialized, segregated, and resegregated at the behest and control of whites, most especially those whites with significant political and economic power. Such spatial oppression has a strong historical dimension. Over the course of US history—and especially during the black, Latino, and other liberation movements of the 1960s—numerous activist-scholars have accented the reality of much land and labor stolen from those racially oppressed. Some Latino activists—like Reies Lopez Tijerina, defender of the right of self-defense and recovery of stolen Mexican lands—have strongly accented the central importance of this theft of land as a major way that whites have exploited and oppressed Mexican Americans and other Latinos. Recovery of lands and of political control of predominantly Latino communities is thus viewed by these activists as essential to end impoverishment of these and other communities of color (J. Gutiérrez, 1985: 152; see also Means, 1995).

Systemic racism, to be more specific, encompasses the persisting racial hierarchy, the discriminatory practices, and the racist institutions integral to the long-term white domination of Americans of color. This group domination involves not only racialized institutions, the macro level of oppression, but also the micro-level reality of a great many whites repeatedly discriminating in blatant, subtle, and covert ways against people of color in everyday settings (Feagin, 2006). Sociologist Philomena Essed has accented this interactive reality. Everyday racism involves much more than "an individual problem, a question of 'to be or not to be a racist.'" She adds that everyday racism involves "systematic, recurrent, familiar practices. The fact that it concerns repetitive practices indicates that everyday racism consists of practices that can be generalized" (Essed, 1991: 3). Clearly, all individuals in society, both perpetrators and recipients of racialized oppression, are caught in an ongoing societal web of hierarchical and alienating individual and group relationships.

As we will see throughout the chapters, systemic racism involves an important and extensive *white racial frame*—a racialized worldview that has been created and perpetuated to rationalize and maintain whites' unjustly gained privilege and power in this country's racial hierarchy. This commonplace white framing is a worldview containing the dominant group's racial metaphysics. From the seventeenth century to the present, this powerful racial frame has provided the vantage point from which whites and many others regularly view, interpret, and act or react in society. This broad white racial framing includes at least these important dimensions: (1) racial stereotypes, (2) racial narratives and interpretations, (3) racialized images and language accents, (4) racialized emotions, and (5) recurring inclinations to discriminate (Feagin, 2013). For centuries, whites have utilized this socially embedded set of racial stereotypes, narratives, images, and emotions in the process of maintaining the racial subordination of Americans of color, including Latino Americans. One finds various forms of racial "common sense" among different US racial groups today, but the age-old white racial frame still prevails because whites have long had the power and resources to impose it on all the residents of this country.

Over nearly four centuries this strong white racial frame has had a very positive orientation toward whites and white-generated institutions (the pro-white subframe) and a very negative orientation toward the racialized others who are exploited and oppressed by whites (the anti-others subframes). Whites have long legitimated and rationalized this society's dominant racial hierarchy by defining a "superior" white group that is justifiably dominant and several "inferior" groups that deserve their subordinated places in society. Americans of various backgrounds and classes, white and not white, are indoctrinated in numerous elements of this centuries-old white racial frame, although many have resisted that intense pressure. Embedded deeply in human minds (brains), this white racial frame has long been a concrete and powerful social force in US and global history (Feagin, 2013).

By the eighteenth century, an increasingly elaborate racialized framing that targeted African Americans, and to a lesser but still significant degree Native Americans, was legitimating and shaping the major institutions of this country—including the economy, law, politics, education, the media, and religion. Early on, both of these oppressed groups were highly racialized in negative terms, against very positive images of white American superiority (Feagin, 2013). By the latter part of the nineteenth century, the concepts of race and racial hierarchy in the United States were linked to an ascendant scientific racism trend called "social Darwinism," which further celebrated the individualism and success of white entrepreneurs and workers over all Americans of color. The dominant racial frame was also powerfully presented in, and central to, the momentous 1896 US Supreme Court *Plessy v. Ferguson* decision reinforcing and legitimating the rapidly spreading reality of the near-slavery of Jim Crow segregation that most directly affected the country's African Americans. Moreover, over the course of the nineteenth century, many other people of color were brought into this system of racial oppression and increasingly racialized.

### Early Racialization of Latinos: US Imperialism

In this book we give primary and sustained attention to an array of racial issues affecting contemporary US Latinos—most especially to their experiences with and reactions to this white-imposed system of racial oppression. For more than a century and a half, Latino groups' positioning on this society's racial ladder has been a powerful determinant of their members' racialized treatment, socioeconomic opportunities, and access to various types of social capital. We examine in detail the consequences of their denigrated position on the societal racial ladder, including their many decades of oppression and racialization by whites.

By the *racialization* of Latinos, we are referring to their original and continuing definition as a not-white racial group by Anglo whites, especially those with significant power and influence, and to the commonplace negative white framing of their real or alleged physical and cultural characteristics—including phenotype, language, and family characteristics, among others. Note here a point that will arise in various ways throughout this book: Groups socially constructed as inferior "races" by those with power, in this case Latinos defined by whites, are often defined as such in terms of both *real* and *alleged* physical characteristics, with phenotypical characteristics typically *linked* closely to certain cultural characteristics of the targeted group. Thus, the fact that some Latinos are "white looking" in some ways does not deter whites from defining and denigrating them as racially inferior and as "not white." A possible parallel to the situation in the United States is that involving the treatment of German Jews as not "white Caucasians" (even though most "looked Caucasian") by powerful German Nazi leaders of the 1930s and 1940s. In both situations, the dominant group used often interconnected biological, physical, and/or cultural inferiority arguments to impose racialized oppression on the subordinated group.

As noted previously, in the early centuries of English expansion in North America, the white racialization of subordinated groups initially targeted the indigenous "Indian" Americans, whose land was stolen as most were killed off or driven beyond the boundaries of white communities, and the African Americans, who were enslaved to generate much white prosperity and wealth on those stolen lands. The racial vilification of African Americans increased as their enslaved labor became more important to ever-expanding numbers of white farms and plantations, most of which were in the southern and border areas. Soon after the United States was created in the late 1700s, white elites and their supportive cast of ordinary whites created systems of racial oppression for yet other Americans of color similar to that for African and Native Americans.

As the US empire continued to expand westward and outward, a series of Mexican, Puerto Rican, and Asian groups were actively brought into the white-dominated society, usually for purposes of exploiting their labor to further increase the prosperity of many whites. Since the US-Mexican War of the 1840s, those targeted for labor and other exploitation by whites have often included Spanish-speaking people from former Spanish colonies in the Americas. Early on, both white leaders and rank-and-file whites assertively racialized these newly exploited peoples—frequently highlighting, denigrating, and racially framing their physical appearance, intelligence, Spanish language, Catholic traditions, and community or family values.

Prior to the English and British dominance in North America, the colonizing Spanish invaders had set up their own North and South American colonies. The indigenous peoples therein suffered greatly from this often brutal imperialistic domination and racialization by Spanish colonizers. Significantly, Spain's mostly male invaders had mixed, often by force, with the women in the Indian- and African-descended populations in Spain's American colonies, and this resulted in a racially heterogeneous (later often called "mestizo") population. With the English and British invasion of North America, the Spanish were shoved aside by territorial expansion that eventually became the United States. Most readers may recall something about the 1830s–1840s expansion of Anglo-American whites into the part of the former Spanish empire, northern Mexico, that came to be called Texas. After a period of a white-controlled independent Texas Republic, US officials, especially the slaveholding president James K. Polk, intentionally engineered the US-Mexican War. Endeavoring to secure "all Mexico," Polk ordered military units into an area of southern Texas borderlands that he and his political associates knew had long been treated as sovereign Mexican territory by the Mexican government, thereby starting a border war (Anonymous, 2013). Motivated to a substantial degree by the desires of US slaveholders to secure territory for the expansion of the slavery system, the annexation of Texas and other areas of northern Mexico was sharply criticized at the time by the young US representative Abraham Lincoln and later by Ulysses Grant. Grant was blunt about this imperialistic war: "I was bitterly opposed to the [Texas annexation], and to this day regard the war, which resulted, as one of the most unjust ever waged by a stronger against a weaker nation. It was an instance of a republic following the bad example of European monarchies, in not considering justice in their desire to acquire additional territory" (Anonymous, 2013).

White slaveholders provided very strong support for the annexation of the Texas Republic and other lands of northern Mexico. Indeed, at the time, northern critics cited much evidence that the war and the annexations were caused by southern whites seeking to protect the slavery system. Many southern leaders and members of Congress spoke of these annexations as providing "security" and "prosperity" for the slavery system. One major South Carolina newspaper argued that the battles fought with Mexico would "widen the field of Southern enterprise [slavery] and power in the future" (Livermore, [1850] 2009: 15–30). Reviewing extensive commentaries by US officials in the South and North, the New England theologian and scholar Abiel Livermore concluded that the annexation of Texas and war with Mexico "without a doubt or controversy" were a matter of "territorial aggrandizement, under the dominion of domestic slavery and the internal slave-trade." The goal was to convert lands that were formerly free of slavery into "the area of slavery, and of spreading over new parallels of latitude the blight of national injustice and eternal wretchedness" (Livermore, [1850] 2009: 31–32). Not surprisingly, attempts to abolish slavery in all of the newly acquired territory were unsuccessful.

The US victory in the war with Mexico resulted in the annexation of huge areas (over half of pre-1836 Mexico) into the United States and thereby incorporated more than 100,000 Mexican residents. The first major group of US Latinos was *not* composed of immigrants but of people who were forced by imperialistic military conquest into the United States (Feagin, 2002). There is thus much irony in the contemporary white fears about and attacks on Mexican Americans and Latinos in the US Southwest, as they are currently living in lands that were once part of their home country but were unjustly taken by the US government in large part to please the many thousands of white slaveholders in the South. In fact, one could argue that the "illegals" have actually been the whites in the Southwest.

During and after the 1840s the vituperation directed against these and other Mexicans could be heard across the United States, including among top white leaders in Washington, DC. In the late 1840s, for example, Senator John C. Calhoun, a former vice president and secretary of state, vociferously opposed the US annexation of northern Mexico. He injected much overtly racist language from the dominant white frame into a political jeremiad against incorporating racially "inferior" Mexicans into the United States:

> We have never dreamt of incorporating into our Union any but the Caucasian race—the free white race. . . . I protest against such a union [the US annexation of Mexico]. . . . Ours, sir, is the Government of a white race. . . . Sir, I should consider such a thing as fatal to our institutions. (Calhoun, [1848] 2007)

Unmistakably, the influential Senator Calhoun put Mexicans in their fully racialized social "place" by insisting that they were *not white* but were well down the racial hierarchy among the uncivilized "colored races" and thus in his view very threatening to white-controlled institutions.

Calhoun was unable to stop this forcible incorporation of former Mexican citizens into the imperialistic United States, but his openly racist jeremiad helped reinforce the anti-Mexican subframe of the racial frame central to the minds of elite white leaders and rank-and-file whites. These whites already had a centuries-old negative framing of African and Native Americans. The white frame accenting the racialized others' inferiority has long been quite adaptive to new settings of subordinate group exploitation, and its central racist doctrines, stereotypes, images, and narratives have regularly been imposed on each new group of color that has been added to the US mixture.

In the 1840s the influential US journalist John L. O'Sullivan ([1845] 1980: 522) made up the term "manifest destiny" in a white narrative insisting that the obvious destiny of the United States was "to overspread the continent allotted by Providence for the free development of our yearly multiplying millions." Not surprisingly, O'Sullivan saw this expansionist mandate as bringing civilization to "backward" peoples, which meant Mexicans and Native Americans. This manifest destiny narrative was linked to a commonplace narrative of the superiority of the "white Anglo-Saxon race." The right of this dominant white group to rule the Americas was hailed enthusiastically even as the "inferior Mexican race" and the country of Mexico were increasingly denigrated.

This influential white framing with its imperialistic narrative was applied not only to Mexico but to numerous other Latin American countries. In the 1850s the same President Polk who annexed northern Mexico, together with other white leaders, feared that the British might try to buy Cuba from Spain, and US slaveholders envisioned expanding their powerful slavery system to that Caribbean island. However, like Calhoun, the northern free-soil journalist James Pike wrote that the United States should not try to annex the more densely populated Cuba—a territory filled "with black, mixed, degraded, and ignorant, or inferior races" (Horsman, 1981: 282). Such hyper-racist views were commonplace in both the North and the South. Various presidents—from Polk to Ulysses S. Grant in the 1870s—also considered acquiring parts of the Dominican Republic in the Caribbean, but yet again a major impediment was the concern of many white leaders that most Dominicans also had substantial African ancestry. Significantly, the US government annexed neither the Dominican Republic nor Cuba, but Puerto Rico—a Caribbean island perceived by these European American leaders to have a population with somewhat "better" racial ancestry (see Horsman, 1981).

Notice again the significance of how most Latinos' ancestors ended up in the United States. Most of these ancestors came into this country because of US government imperialism and/or military intervention in places like Mexico, Cuba, Puerto Rico, and Central America. As a result of this imperialism, many Latin American and Caribbean immigrants, in terms of ancestry and entrance conditions, are unlike most European immigrants who came to the United States in the nineteenth and early twentieth centuries. Typically, these millions of European immigrants have not been so directly linked to the United States by recurring US imperialism. Juan Gonzalez (2000: xiv) succinctly describes this "harvest of empire":

> The Latino migrant flows were directly connected to the growth of a U.S. empire, and they responded closely to that empire's needs, whether it was a political need to stabilize a neighboring country or to accept its refugees as a means of accomplishing a broader foreign policy objective (Cubans, Dominicans, Salvadorans, Nicaraguans), or whether it was an economic need, such as satisfying the labor demands of particular U.S. industries (Mexicans, Puerto Ricans, Panamanians).

Moreover, numerous Mexican American leaders and scholars have pointed out for decades now that the very first Mexican Americans were *not* immigrants who crossed the US border but rather that the border actually "crossed them" as a result of the empire-expanding war on Mexico in the 1840s. Given such an imperialistic origin, Mexican American analysts like Mario Barrera (1979) have accented the numerous ways in which the Mexicans brought in by that war and their descendants have lived under conditions that took the form of a type of "internal colonialism."

Note too that in our historical and contemporary discussions, the situations and experiences of Mexican Americans frequently loom large because they are essential to an accurate understanding of the racialized background and white racist framing that affects all Latinos, past and present. Indeed, for the long 1850–1950 era of blatant and overt white racist oppression, the overwhelming majority of Latinos were Mexican Americans, and their demographic and racialized presence was primarily the one against which whites historically generated the anti-Latino subframe of the white racial frame that has persisted in white thought and practice to the present day.

## More Racist Framing of Latinos

Today, as in the past, the societal positions of different racial groups and their members are substantially determined by white Americans, most especially by more powerful whites. Each new immigrant group is socially placed, initially by dominant whites, somewhere on the centuries-old white-to-black status ladder, an imposed position that signals a group's racial status and degree of social acceptability. Historically, and to the present day, whites have been centrally obsessed with oppressing black Americans within this society, and thus have regularly placed blacks at the most oppressed end of the societal hierarchy. Whites as a group are generally positioned at the top as "superior" and "civilized," with "inferior" and "uncivilized" blacks as a group at the bottom. This centuries-old racial hierarchy utilizes selected physical and cultural characteristics to place a particular group in what is considered by whites to be a group's appropriate racialized position. Certain prized European physical characteristics and cultural norms (including the English language) have been central in the white placement at the top of this persisting US racial hierarchy (Feagin, 2013).

For immigrant groups of color and their descendants, the dominant white group, and especially its powerful elite, has substantially determined the conditions and positioning of their incorporation, their racial framing, and their racialized treatment in society. In the United States, as elsewhere, group and individual racial identities can involve (1) externally imposed identities and (2) sometimes conflicting self-chosen, internal identities. In spite of their own desires, for example, Latinos and certain other people of color entering the United States in significant numbers since the 1840s have frequently been defined by Anglo whites as "constructive blacks"—that is, as being at or near the inferior black rung of the racialized ladder (Wu, 1995). Not surprisingly, being considered black or near black has often been viewed as quite negative by Latino and Asian Americans and probably helps explain some of their often stereotyped reactions to African Americans.

In the past and present, moreover, where and how immigrants of color and their descendants get placed by powerful whites in this racial hierarchy vary in terms of their time of entry into the United States, as well as by the size, culture, physical characteristics, and/or economic resources of their group. For example, during the nineteenth-century era of US expansion into the western area called California, the Mexican, Asian, and Native American groups there came under white control at different points in time and under varying conditions. They did not get oppressed or racialized by the white colonists coming into the area in exactly the same way, but all these groups of color did face racial subordination by whites at or near the negative end of the dominant racial ladder. They also faced a well-developed white frame rationalizing this oppression and accenting white supremacy, as well as a great concern for firm white dominance. In the 1840s, thus, the California area's first English-language newspaper insisted: "We desire only a white population in California" (Almaguer, 1994: 7, 210).

Since that era, whites have long imposed on Mexicans and other Latinos brought into the US political and economic sphere, including a series of immigrant groups, an "uncivilized" and "implicit deficit" imagery and racial framing. Whites have also been fearful of the mixed Indian, Spanish, and African ancestry of Mexican and other Latin American immigrants coming into the United States and have periodically spoken of the supposed "race mongrelization" that results from such migration. During the 1920s one white member of Congress framed Mexicans as a "mongrelized" mixture of Spanish and "low-grade Indians" and African slave "blood." In that same decade a white "expert" on immigration, speaking before an important House of Representatives' committee, asserted what the committee wanted to hear—that the "Mexican race" was a serious threat to the "white race" (Cárdenas, 1975: 70–71). White academics regularly chimed in with analyses insisting that people of Mexican origin were an inferior race threatening whites. One Ivy League professor feared the elimination of Anglo-Saxons because of future interbreeding in "favor of the progeny of Mexican peons who will continue to afflict us with an embarrassing race problem" (Guzmán, 1974: 22).

The mass media of the late nineteenth and early twentieth centuries were very important in crystallizing and spreading this racist framing. Over decades the widespread racialization of Mexican Americans and other

Latinos could be seen in many of the paperback novels read by ordinary white Americans, novels in which Mexican Americans were frequently portrayed as lazy or villainous. That these Latino groups were firmly racialized in the white mind can be seen in some court decisions made by white state and federal judges discussing the racial inferiority of Mexicans. This racialization can also be seen in the decisions of other officials, such as those at the US Census Bureau, who created the wording of the 1930 census to list "Mexican" as a category under "race" on that particular census form (I. López, 1996; C. Rodríguez, 2009). Moreover, in the 1970s, a white California Superior Court judge sentencing a Mexican American teenager targeted this US citizen with blatantly racialized rhetoric in a state court: "We ought to send you . . . back to Mexico. . . . You ought to commit suicide. That's what I think of people of this kind. You are lower than animals and haven't the right to live in organized society—just miserable, lousy, rotten people" (Anonymous, 2008).

## Contemporary Racial Framing: Some Examples

For Mexican American and other Latino immigrants and their descendants, including those in the working class and the middle class, this white pattern of racial categorization and everyday discrimination persists today in many areas of society. Latinos have frequently been framed by whites in sharply racialized terms—with substantially negative evaluations on the societal dimensions of racially superior/inferior and insider/foreigner. The dominant white framing has often insisted that these Americans of color are inferior in intelligence and are, among other things, uncivilized, criminal, unhygienic, and/or threatening to the "American way of life."

"Undesirable immigrant" and "foreigner" narratives among whites have continued to be important in the denigrating of Mexican, Puerto Rican, Cuban, and other Latin American immigrants and their descendants. The perceptive linguist Otto Santa Ana examined certain language references and metaphorical imagery in the mostly white reporters' and editors' reporting on undocumented immigrants at a leading California newspaper. These newspaper reporters and editors often used, consciously and unconsciously, negative language images and metaphors suggesting that Mexican and other Latin American immigrants were some type of animal or were invaders or disreputable persons (Santa Ana, 1994: 194–219; see also Santa Ana, 2002, 2013).

In numerous cities, especially in the Southwest, Latinos of various class and nationality backgrounds who display what law enforcement authorities perceive as "illegal" clues—for example, an older car with "Mexican trappings" or playing Latin music—are often racially profiled and stopped under the pretext of a traffic violation, yet with the main purpose of checking immigration status. In addition, much hostile imagery targeting "illegals" can be seen in various aspects of the mainstream mass media and in violent video games created by and for the mostly white video gamers. One video game, for instance, even encourages players to play at killing undocumented Latino immigrants crossing the US border (Navarrette, 2006). Not surprisingly, the salience of a certain anti-Mexican or anti-Latino framing has resulted in numerous bodily injuries and deaths of Mexican immigrants and others of Mexican descent. In 2012 several US border patrol agents shot and injured or killed Mexicans on the border who were throwing rocks at them to protest their border enforcement actions (Stellar, 2012). Such shootings seem to signal a negative view of Mexicans as not fully human, a view that also leads to violent attacks like the one in a suburban area that we opened this chapter with. In the present day, racialized framing and associated hostile treatment are facts of life for Mexicans and other Latinos coming into and living in the United States. Unlike millions of European immigrants in the nineteenth and early twentieth centuries, Latino immigrants and their descendants have faced several generations of significant racial exploitation and other racial discrimination.

Today, as in the past, the anti-Latino subframe of the dominant white frame contains common racist images, stereotypes, and narratives about US Latinos. One recurring racialized portrayal emphasizes their alleged criminality, much as the dominant frame does for African Americans. Research on the US mass media has shown that over the decades the white-controlled mainstream media has historically presented Latinos as criminals such as pimps, prostitutes, drug dealers, and gang members. Only recently have some of these images begun to change. Yet many stereotypes persist. This can also be seen in opinion surveys. One 1990s survey offered white college students a list of numerous personal and social characteristics. When asked to compare whites and Latinos, these whites viewed Latinos as more likely than whites to be violent, dirty, and criminally inclined (Jackson, 1995; see also Varela, 2013). The criminalizing of Latinos can be observed in numerous recent media reports. Not long ago, some US Forest Service officers gave a media briefing in which they warned hunters and others going into Colorado national forests that those there who "eat tortillas, drink Tecate beer and play Spanish music" might well be "armed marijuana growers." Latino organizations protested this hostile stereotyping, and Forest Service administrators apologized for what was lamely termed their "regrettable references" but did not specifically address the racialized stereotyping and other negative framing that was clearly involved (Associated Press, 2013).

## Imposing Racial Stereotypes and Choosing Identities

Most Latinos regularly face social environments where whites have the power to racially characterize who they are, including their racial identities. A few research studies have suggested how this works out in everyday life for both working-class and middle-class Latinos. For example, in recent research on Latino professionals, political scientist Maria Chavez has provided numerous examples of whites imposing a stereotyped racial identity on her well-educated respondents. In many years of dealing with whites, one Latino lawyer in a western state commented on how he regularly gets racially stereotyped and profiled in a distinctive way:

> I'm always aware of it. . . . It's subtle because, for example when I bought my home on [names area] and it overlooks the water. I was outside and I don't know what I was doing and my neighbor says: "Oh, are you the gardener?" . . . And that's what I have experienced for 55 years. . . . As a Latino or Native American or any kind of minority, you're just another wetback or you're just another migrant farm worker or whatever. (Chavez, 2011: 1–2)

For decades this experienced Latino lawyer has been seen by Anglo whites repeatedly as what he is not, as a poor Mexican American worker or Mexican "illegal." This recurring and stereotyped framing of people who look to whites to be a "typical Mexican" signals how powerful such ingrained racial stereotyping and other racial framing are, even in regional areas where there are not many Latinos. Several researchers (for example, Millard and Chapa, 2004) have discovered this type of stereotyped framing of Latinos to be commonplace in yet other US areas. In this research, as in the quote, we also observe the negative impact of the imposition of racially stereotyped identities.

From the research available, it seems likely that most Anglo whites do not view any group of color as "white" in spite of numerous media analysts' and some scholars' insistence that certain groups of color are actually becoming "white." Thus, one research study by Feagin and Dirks (2004) found that most younger, well-educated whites do not view any major Latino group as "white." They gave a questionnaire to 151 white college students and asked them to place a long list of US racial and ethnic groups into "white" or "not white" categories. Not surprisingly, large majorities (86–100 percent) classified groups such as Irish Americans, English Americans, and Italian Americans as clearly white. Not one student listed African Americans as white, and large majorities classified all Latino groups—including Mexican Americans, Puerto Ricans, and Cuban Americans—as not white. These relatively well-educated white students made use of centuries-old white racial framing, thereby signaling that it remains central to the everyday conceptions and interpretations of white Americans. These student perspectives are shared by many mainstream television and radio news commentators who regularly report on issues regarding Mexican and other Latino immigrants in which they are described in an array of racialized terms, such as by regularly alluding to them as a "race" (see DMIer, 2006). While much more research is needed on how whites actually develop and construct the identities of Latinos, such data as we have indicate problems with the aforementioned arguments that a blending-into-whiteness process for these Americans of color is speedily moving along in this society.

Interestingly, some surveys of Latinos have also revealed that a majority do not identify themselves as white when given an array of reasonable options or an open-ended question to which they can provide any answer they desire. For instance, Americans with ancestral ties to Mexico mostly use identity designations such as Mexican, Mexican American, Chicano, Hispanic, Latino, or a combination—an array of terms signaling a considerable diversity of opinion about how to indicate their ancestral origin or group identity. A mid-1990s Houston-area survey found that a majority of the Latino respondents, including a majority of the US-born, did not think of Hispanics as members of the "white race" (Mindiola, Rodriguez, and Flores-Niemann, 1996). Moreover, a more recent Pew Hispanic Center and Kaiser Foundation report (2002) in which several thousand Latinos were interviewed found that, with just one exception, modest percentages of various Latino groups identified their own group as white. Majorities of the Mexican American and Puerto Rican respondents, from the two largest Latino groups, mostly named themselves in terms of their national origin (Mexican or Puerto Rican) or umbrella identity terms (including Latino/Hispanic) rather than as white.

Moreover, using a fixed-choice item to assess whether Latino respondents would choose national origin, Hispanic/Latino, or American most often, a 2011 Pew survey (Taylor, Lopez, Martínez, and Velasco, 2012) found a pattern of a bare majority of Latino adults most often identifying by country of origin, with another quarter most often identifying with the umbrella identities of Hispanic or Latino. This survey also asked the respondents a separate question about which of the following terms described their race—white, black, Asian, some other race, mixed race, or Hispanic/Latino. About 64 percent of the sample chose something other than the white option, which was the first term listed in the survey item. For the modest number of third-generation Latinos in the sample, however, that percentage dropped to 56 percent (see also Tafoya, 2004).

As we will demonstrate from our interviews in later chapters, if you are an American of color, white-imposed constructions of your personal identity often crash in as you maneuver through everyday worlds, especially outside your home and community. In the US setting, when you are at home or at other settings in your local community, you are more likely to be able to identify racially or ethnically as you wish and to be accepted as such—that is, without direct interference from US-born whites. Indeed, in the home community you can more easily identify as white if you wish, as some Latino immigrants with known European ancestry often do, and without any capricious intent. Although it is typically an unacceptable choice from most Anglo whites' perspectives for Latinos, even those with European ancestry, to identify as white, this identification would likely seem reasonable to Latin Americans and Europeans. Indeed, this insistent nonwhite definition of such Latinos reveals a display of arrogance on the part of Anglo whites who view themselves as the possessors of the "true" criteria of whiteness even for Latino immigrants and other Latinos who have had that white (blanco) identity for generations, especially in their home countries.

In addition, the possibly greater ease of asserting self-chosen identities at home does not mean that there is no tension about such choices in many Latino families. Because of the often differential pressures to hang onto the home country's culture between the first and later generations of Latinos, there are frequently serious tensions within Latino families over individual racial-ethnic identity choices.

We should note too that over recent decades some whites, frequently elite whites, have singled out individual members of a particular Latino group for a type of "model minority" or "honorary white" social status. Not surprisingly, certain political trends, such as the increasingly obvious one moving in the direction of a much larger Latino voting population over the coming decades, indicate that white political leaders will increasingly need the votes of these Latino voters in order to be elected their party's candidate. As a result, there is more courting of Latino voters and more discussion of how, in some ways, they supposedly "share the interests" of a particular political party (Feagin, 2012). Still, as we previously suggested in regard to assimilation theories, being racially flattered and categorized by whites as moving away from the "black end" and moving nearer to the "white end" of the US racial ladder does not result in these white-chosen Latinos actually securing the full societal resources and privileges of whites—or even being viewed as truly "white Americans" by most Anglo whites. Nonetheless, such white courting and flattery have encouraged some Latinos to try to much more vigorously assimilate to the local white racial framing and folkways, a strategy we will periodically see in the responses of some of our interviewees in later chapters. We will return to this issue of assimilation into whiteness in Chapter 6.

## Resistance and Counter-framing

Let us emphasize one final but very important point about our conceptual approach and analysis of the interview data we present in later chapters. While systemic racism and its rationalizing white frame have long been very powerful and pervasive in this society, for centuries people of color have *actively resisted* this racial oppression in a great variety of ways. Their strategies have ranged from quietly passive resistance to assertive antiracist organizing and counter-framing. Numerous Mexican American and other Latino movements since the early 1900s have resisted racial oppression in various ways, including the assimilationist tactics we discuss in Chapter 4. And we will discuss even more critical and radical Latino approaches to resisting racial oppression in several chapters as well.

As Feagin (2013) has demonstrated, there are at least two perspectival frames that are important in understanding resistance by Americans of color to racial oppression today, as in the past: (1) the assertive anti-oppression counter-frames of Americans of color and (2) the home-culture frames that Americans of color utilize in everyday life and elements of which are drawn on, passively or actively, to develop anti-oppression counter-frames. Over the course of North American history, the dominant white racial frame has never operated long without significant and open resistance to it from people of color, for nearly four centuries. Latinos, as well as other Americans of color, have regularly resisted out of the home-culture frame and periodically have developed an even more openly defiant antiracist counter-frame that has helped them to better understand and more actively and openly resist US racial oppression. We will observe numerous examples of these two types of resistance frames in our interviews in the chapters that follow.

## Our Research Method and Respondents

In this book we employ new data from seventy-two in-depth interviews of mostly middle-class Latinos carried out in the early twenty-first century in states with substantial Latino populations—mainly Arizona, California, Florida, Illinois, New Jersey, New York, and Texas. In this research we have intentionally focused on those Latinos generally considered to be successful in US society, including teachers, small business owners, managers, government administrators, and other white-collar workers. (Only a few hold manual jobs.) More than 90 percent of these Latino respondents have had at least some college course work; over half have completed at least a college degree. Our roughly representative sample consists mostly of respondents from the three largest groups in the US Latino population. Sixty percent are Mexican American, 18 percent are Cuban American, and 13 percent are Puerto Rican. The rest are from other Latin American countries. Sixty-four percent of our sample are women, and 36 percent are men. Most interviews were done in person, and all but two were carried out by bilingual Latino interviewers. We used a snowball sampling design with many different starting points in cities across the United States to ensure significant sample diversity. Initial respondents were referred by our colleagues and friends across the country. As we proceeded, our participants suggested yet others for possible personal interviews.

We focus here on middle-class Latinos because when we started this project they had never been studied nationally and in depth in regard to the white racial framing and discriminatory practices they face. Even today, we know of only one other study that meets this goal (M. Chavez, 2011), but only for Latino lawyers in the Northwest. While middle-class Latinos are often considered economically and socially successful, and while they do not have to endure the more violent types of discrimination as often as working-class Latinos, they do suffer much racialized mistreatment that takes a variety of damaging forms—in spite of their usually significant attempts to assimilate to aspects of the white-dominated society. Additionally, the fact that they typically have more economic and other resources than working-class Latinos to use in reducing and resisting white discrimination does not mean that they still do not suffer substantially from it. Indeed, because they frequently spend more time in the middle and upper reaches of certain white-controlled institutions, they encounter certain distinctive types of racialized mistreatment that are characteristic of those particular white spaces.

In addition, the various classes within Latino communities are interconnected in myriad ways. Many middle-class Latinos have working-class roots, and most have many working-class people in their kinship and friendship networks. As we will see in our interviews, this interconnectedness comes up periodically as they discuss not only their own lives but those of other Latinos in their networks and in the world beyond. Additionally, considering the larger societal context of their everyday lives, all US Latinos, whatever their class level, share one thing in common: They all face the anti-Latino subframe and the pro-white subframe that are part of the dominant racial frame in the minds of most Anglo whites. This has been true since the mid-nineteenth century, and for Latinos at all class levels. Today, as in the past, they face commonplace anti-Latino stereotyping and other racist framing of white discriminators and assailants who, like the white youth in the opening example of this chapter, see only racially framed "spics" no matter who they are or what their achievements may be. Another clear example of this cross-class racial reality can be seen in the recurring white attacks on the Spanish language or Spanish accents faced by a great many Latinos in many settings. The cross-class anti-Latino framing by whites is one important reason that we periodically discuss in this book the racialized oppression of working-class Latinos, in the historical past and in the present, as intimately connected to the racialized oppression of middle-class Latinos over many decades. In effect, our data reveal as much about that racial oppression and its rationalizing racial frame in the minds of whites as they do about the lives, pain, and resistance of those Latinos targeted by that white oppression.

## Conclusion

In this book we demonstrate how extensive racialization of contemporary Latinos by US whites is based on an old white racial frame, a white-generated worldview in which Latinos and Latin Americans regularly appear as an inferior "race" and whites appear as the superior "race." This overarching white racist perspective on Latinos has echoed constantly in the halls of the US Congress, underscored myriad articles in major newspapers, and exploded loudly from prestigious pulpits since the mid-nineteenth century. As we have seen, this racist perspective extends well into assimilationist thinking inside and outside academia. The white expectation is that immigrant groups and their descendants will accept their white-imposed place on the US racial ladder of inegalitarian status, privilege, and resources and assimilate to the white core culture and institutions without complaint.

The persisting and dominant white racial frame is regularly employed to cast a wide net into which Latinos and Latin Americans are dumped for recurring economic exploitation, political control, and other institutional control by white employers, white government officials, and rank-and-file whites in many societal settings. This is true for Latinos of various class backgrounds, including middle-class Latinos like our respondents, who are often considered to be successful according to a commonplace societal standard. For instance, the omnipresent white framing has given much recurring impetus to white groups seeking to establish English as the official US language and to habitually attack and denigrate the Spanish language. Such attacks on Spanish, as we show later, are about more than whites' linguistic concerns and language competition. Latinos, whether Spanish speaking or not, are denigrated by a great many whites because they are considered to be dangerous, threatening, "foreign," or "un-American." The dominant racial framing is pervasive across this society and has often placed older racialized US groups of color in the alienating position of periodically enforcing the white frame for yet newer racialized immigrant groups. In addition, this framing has long provided a white-oriented vocabulary that the racialized Latinos and Latin American immigrants can use on occasion to vilify each other or even other Americans of color.

Sometimes old-fashioned social ideologies in old interpretive frames can have unintended or even beneficial consequences. But the racial hierarchy, the racialization process, and the rationalizing white racial framing have demonstrated an inability to generate a substantial reality of human rights and great socioeconomic progress for any but a majority of the dominant white group. The white racial framing has been powerful and evil throughout its operations since the seventeenth century. Why does it persist against substantial resistance by those targeted by it? The answer is sadly obvious: The white frame and its associated racial hierarchy serve the interests of US elites and rank-and-file whites splendidly, and whites have the socioeconomic and political resources to support and propagate it widely and relentlessly. Indeed, as part of that white racial frame, its racial "common sense" habitually makes racial injustice almost inevitable.

In the following chapters, we examine an array of everyday barriers that whites create for Latinos across the country, barriers that give the lie to commonplace optimistic assumptions and projections about the speedy integration and rapid assimilation of Latinos into the core culture and institutions of this still-white-dominated society.

# 2

# Spanish Language:
# Denigration and Racialization

Not long ago, a white anti-immigration group in Arizona burned a Mexican flag near a Mexican Consulate. Periodically, other such groups do vigilante patrols of the US-Mexican border. The steady rise in the US Latino population and the supposedly "massive waves" of undocumented and other Spanish-speaking immigrants from Mexico and Central America in recent decades are societal developments that many whites view with great and continuing alarm. As a result, frequent acts of aggression or exclusion have been aimed at these Spanish-speaking immigrants and their numerous descendants.

Since 2000, the US Congress has passed several laws expanding security fencing and border patrol agents and operations over large expanses of the US-Mexico border. Such actions have been pressured by the anti-immigrant hostility of many white voters, much of which is backed up by an intensive racialized framing of Latino immigrants and their children as inferior to whites in terms of race, language, values, and civilization. Indeed, in a great many white (and other) minds, much of the US Latino population is thought to be made up of "illegal immigrants." A spring 2012 Hill and Knowlton survey of 1,500 non-Latino voters found that a majority exaggerated the proportion of undocumented Latinos. Remarkably, one-third of those interviewed thought *over half* of all Latinos were undocumented (Varela, 2013). The actual figure is much lower—about 17 percent of US Latinos. Why this collective ignorance? Evidently, the mainstream media's constant stereotyping of, and harping on, undocumented Mexican immigrants constantly reinforces this very distorted framing of the US Latino population (see Santa Ana, 2013).

Much anti-Spanish and other anti-Latino framing can be observed not only among ordinary whites but also in the writings and speeches of prominent white politicians, media pundits, and academics. It is especially strong among many white nativists and white supremacists, and some of the latter have periodically made violent threats against Latino leaders and others supporting Mexican or other Latino immigrants (Navarrette, 2006).

One of the reasons whites give for their often great alarm is that Latino immigrants and the Latino population generally represent some type of "alien" threat to "American values" and the dominant white-Anglo core culture and institutions (Cornelius, 2002: 178). They are often viewed as a burden for these institutions. For example, in the aforementioned Hill and Knowlton survey of non-Latino voters, nearly 80 percent thought Latinos were a particular burden on the US health care system, while 70 percent felt they were a burden on the country's educational system (Varela, 2013). Evidently, too, a central issue for fearful whites seems to be the threat of being displaced in cultural and institutional terms by this growing non-European immigrant population and its descendants. The habitual attack rhetoric of this fear, of Spanish-speaking "foreigners" and "aliens" of color threatening "American values," is usually racialized and taken out of the old white racial frame examined in the first chapter.

## White Fears of Spanish and Spanish-Speaking Americans

Today, the United States has one of the largest Spanish-speaking populations among all countries across the globe. This reality has many important dimensions, some often noted and others almost never discussed. The English language lies at the heart of our still-white-dominated core culture, and for that reason the dramatic growth of the immigrant and US-born Latino populations is viewed by many whites, including white elites, as a direct threat to the survivability of English, what is frequently termed the "official language" of the United States. This sense of language threat from Spanish is relatively new. As recently as 1987, most people questioned in a national survey thought that the US Constitution already had made English the official US language (Crawford, 1992), and thus they saw no real threat. In addition, as Lippi-Green (2012: Kindle loc. 8066) has pointed out, before the heavy immigration from Cuba to Florida after 1980 the Miami area was comfortably bilingual with the local newspaper in Spanish and English and numerous bilingual facilities such as ATMs. Significantly, this benign perception changed in a large part of the white Florida population. After the immigration of thousands of Cubans, the county in which Miami is located developed English-only laws and regulations covering official business, and there was growing protest against Spanish and Spanish speakers in the private sector as well.

Since the 1990s numerous major white public officials and intellectuals have increasingly expressed nativistic fears for the Anglo core culture and English language. The late Harvard professor Samuel Huntington (2004), who served as a political adviser to top government officials, regularly articulated strong anti-Latino sentiments in his stereotyped framing of contemporary immigration. Like other prominent white officials and corporate executives (Feagin and O' Brien, 2003), Huntington assertively worried about Latino immigrants and their descendants and was concerned that the United States might become yet more divided by language—with English-speaking and Spanish-speaking sectors supposedly incapable of comprehending each other's languages, cultural practices, and values. Even prominent immigrants to the United States from northern Europe, such as the former editor of *Forbes* magazine and British immigrant Peter Brimelow, have worried openly about issues of continuing white Eurocentric dominance. Brimelow has argued that Mexican and other Latino immigrants are indeed "alien," which for him means "not white European." In his writings he has suggested that continuing immigration of Spanish speakers from Mexico may even lead to a restoration of the US Southwest to Mexico (Brimelow, 1995).

White analysts across the political spectrum have commonly echoed these fears of Spanish-speaking immigrants of color harming the dominant culture and language. For instance, the liberal historian and top presidential adviser Arthur Schlesinger Jr. has expressed fears that substantial immigration, especially from Latin America and Asia, will threaten the US fabric if the immigrants of color do not wholly assimilate to the "language, the institutions, and the political ideals that hold the nation together" (Schlesinger, 1991: 120–124).

Nonetheless, in spite of numerous white efforts to reduce or eliminate its use, Spanish remains the second most important language of the United States. Indeed, although it is rare to see it said in the mainstream English media, it is a *critical* language for the continuing functioning of the United States, most especially for its everyday economic, political, and other bureaucratic operations. One sees evidence of this in the reality of many major corporate retailers and small businesses voluntarily putting up bilingual English/ Spanish signs in stores and other places across the country. However, unlike other non-English languages spoken in this country, Spanish has been constantly conceptualized negatively and linked by whites to one significantly racialized group, US Latinos. This enduring and widespread language attack signals not only that English is viewed by whites as the central language of the United States but also a white insistence on significant home-cultural abandonment on the part of Latinos. It reveals much white fear that the Spanish language and other home-cultural features of Latino communities might eventually displace the dominant Anglo-white culture. This repeated and widespread attack on Spanish and Spanish speakers is so distinctive that we give it special attention in this chapter.

## Historical Background: Fearing Non-English Cultures

This white nativism and fear of the phenotypically and culturally "foreign" others has a long history in the Anglo-American world. Accordingly, in 1611, not long before the English colonists imported enslaved Africans into the new Jamestown colony in what is now the state of Virginia, the play *The Tempest,* by English playwright William Shakespeare—set apparently on an island near North America—centrally portrayed the sinister figure of Caliban as a dark "savage" and "deformed slave" and a threat to the play's "civilized" European character of Prospero. At this early stage, the English already had fearful images of overseas "others" who were being encountered by various European imperialists in their explorations.

When English colonists arrived on what came to be called the North American continent in the 1600s, they imagined themselves as bringing real "civilization" to it. To most white colonizers this civilization meant, among other things, the English language and Anglocentric culture. North American Indians, whom the colonizers often viewed as Caliban-like "savages," constituted a serious barrier to their land-theft plans (Fischer, 1989). They were killed off, driven beyond colonial borders, or pressured to assimilate to English folkways. Later on in the 1700s, the numerous culturally distinctive German immigrants to North America represented for some English Americans another possible societal obstacle. The learned founder Benjamin Franklin feared the culture and character of German immigrants, at one point in the 1750s describing them as the "most ignorant Stupid Sort of their own Nation" and fearing that their increasing presence would mean that "even our government will become precarious" (Franklin, 1753). Consequently, Franklin established a school in Pennsylvania to reeducate the Germans because he was concerned that they could become so numerous "as to Germanize us instead of us Anglifying them" (Conklin and Lourie, 1983: 69).

By the early eighteenth century, the civilized-savage polarity was added to a dominant racist worldview privileging whites and denigrating both African and Native Americans—one held to vigorously by major US founders like Thomas Jefferson, James Madison, and George Washington. This dominant racist worldview became ever more developed over time, and in the nineteenth century it frequently played up the achievements of a superior white "Anglo-Saxon race" against the shortcomings of the racially inferior "others"; by the 1840s and 1850s it included many people from Latin America and Asia.

We noted in Chapter 1 prominent officials of this era, such as former vice president and senator John Calhoun, who held an extraordinarily and blatantly racist perspective on the superiority of whites and the inferiority of the Mexican people about to be brought by force into the United States. The evolution in the British American vocabulary to accent a putative "Anglo-Saxon race" was due in part to the advent of social Darwinism and its increasingly widespread ideas on societal evolution favoring the dominant British American group in US society. In the late eighteenth and early nineteenth centuries, social Darwinists like England's Herbert Spencer and North America's Josiah Strong, together with numerous other white US intellectuals and political writers, sold many thousands of books and magazines in which they insistently defended the notion of "survival of the fittest," a doctrine with the clear implication that white Anglo-Saxon institutions and peoples occupied the apex of the human evolutionary and racial ladder. As nineteenth- and early twentieth-century immigration increased, many British Americans envisioned this powerful position as significantly threatened by growing numbers of non-British Americans (Hofstadter, 1955).

For centuries, the continued and forceful ranking of the white racial group as superior has provided ideological support for white political-economic hegemony over incoming immigrants of color in most societal arenas, including the area of culture. A common element in white conceptions of the racialized others has involved the dominant group viewing the home language and other cultural aspects of the latter's home culture with great suspiciousness and frequently seeking to reduce or eliminate them. Linguistic ethnocentrism was evident among whites in the first two centuries of this country's development. We have noted the efforts of founders like Franklin to root out the German language. In addition, since the late 1800s many Native Americans have faced similar white efforts at forced assimilation. Native American children were long pressured or forced by white officials to attend white-run boarding schools where they were frequently forbidden to speak their mother languages and were taught English instead (Noriega, 1992).

Another example of whites' linguistic ethnocentrism can be found in the aftermath of the 1840s US-Mexican War, discussed in Chapter 1. The eradication of Spanish became an important goal of US leaders in regard to the newly conquered Mexican territory. Over time, this Anglo-American objective was pursued with great diligence in areas such as the public schools of the Southwest (G. Gonzalez, 1990). The necessity of English linguistic dominance was firmly placed in the dominant white racial frame early on.

Note too that the first major incorporation of Spanish-speaking people into US society involved these early Mexican residents coercively incorporated into the United States by the US-Mexican War. From the 1840s to about 1950—the first century or so of US Latino growth—Mexican Americans made up an estimated 90 percent or more of the US Latino population. Only in the 1940s–1960s era did that Latino population begin to include sizeable and significantly increasing groups of Puerto Rican, Cuban, and other Latin American and Caribbean immigrants and their descendants.

## English and Spanish:
## Linguistic Capital in Linguistic Markets

Today, major language critiques and pressures persist for all US Latino groups. As in the past, many Spanish speakers at various class levels still feel in their daily lives much white pressure to give up their Spanish mother tongue in favor of English. Margaret Montoya (1998: 574) has described her own life experiences poignantly:

> We learn from our teachers to speak the over-corrected speech of the over-achiever. We learn to value the syntax, the cadence, and the accent of the monolingual English speaker. . . . Over time Spanish, our mother tongue, becomes an "outlaw" language. Spanish joins other languages, dialects, and patois that have been devalued and prohibited. . . . Being obliged to surrender a language is akin to losing parts of your senses.

Unmistakably, the Anglo-American hostility to the presence and use of the Spanish language signals far more than just modest or technical linguistic issues. For centuries now, white Anglos have had the power to decide what is the appropriate language for Americans to speak, although that cultural power is now increasingly being challenged in various ways by growing numbers of US Latinos.

The French sociologist Pierre Bourdieu developed some theoretical ideas that shed light on the vital language issues in this quote from Margaret Montoya and in the quotes of the Spanish speakers in our sample examined below. Considering various forms of important "social capital" garnered and used by people in a society like the United States, Bourdieu (1991) accented not only the normally discussed economic capital but also the much less discussed linguistic capital. The very important linguistic capital held by some people includes the command of a prestigious "educated" language or dialect instead of a lower-status language or language dialect. For example, in France the linguistic capital of Parisian French is much more important than that of the

French of the rural countryside. There have long been international varia-tions in the value of certain linguistic capital, as in the case of the French and English languages over recent decades. Indeed, the once-dominant linguistic capital of the former has been decreasing in recent decades in relation to that of the latter. French has been replaced in many areas by English—the latter, ironically, now the "lingua franca" of much of the world (Bourdieu, 1977: 651).

Various public and private linguistic "markets" are the sites where the value of the different language competencies—for example, the ability to speak white-middle-class English—is established. According to Bourdieu (1977: 653), when individuals are operating in such a linguistic market, the value of their speech typically depends on the social status of the speaker:

> The dominant class can make deliberately or accidentally lax use of language without their discourse ever being invested with the same social value as that of the dominated. What speaks is not the utterance, the language, but the whole social person.

Bourdieu (1991: 67) further suggests that the outcome of a linguistic exchange is often contingent on the speaker's choice of language, such as in situations of bilingualism, when one of the languages has a lower social status:

> What happens between two persons . . . in a colonial situation, between a French speaker and an Arabic speaker . . . derives in particular form from the objective relation between the corresponding languages or usages, that is, between the groups who speak the languages.

Thus, one societal group can strive for advantage in the linguistic market in order to bring about political and material gains, and vice versa. One way to achieve this end is by promoting the language it commands. Bourdieu (1991: 47) provides the example of postrevolutionary France in the late eighteenth and early nineteenth centuries, where members of the bourgeoisie and profes-sional classes pushed for the elevation of the Parisian dialect of French to the status of the national language because it was highly advantageous socially and politically for them to do so.

A societal group's efforts to achieve linguistic dominance are periodi-cally met with significant resistance. Although some social classes, such as members of the bourgeoisie in postrevolutionary France, operate from an advantageous economic position, the linguistic ascendancy of a social group is the result of a struggle in the language market that is often not permanently resolved. Achievement of language dominance does not necessarily mean that other languages simply disappear or that the subordinated languages' speakers fully acquiesce in this dominance. Even so, the dominant language thus becomes the "norm against which the [linguistic] prices of the other modes of expression . . . are defined" (Bourdieu, 1977: 652).

These insights are helpful in our interpretation of certain white-Latino relations in regard to the attempts to denigrate the Spanish language and related linguistic accents. We view white efforts to delimit or suppress Spanish as thrusts to enhance the reach of English and its value and prestige vis-à-vis Spanish in the US language market, and thus in the larger society. Consider, for example, the efforts to limit the Spanish-speaking of Latino employees by many white employers, which we demonstrate in more detail in a later section. Such actions represent an attempt on the part of employers of Latinos to strengthen their position against these workers. By speaking a supposedly "second rate" language or accent, the voices of Latino workers will likely not carry much weight (linguistic capital) in struggles with their employers.

In addition, note that English is the dominant language of US courts, public schools, and voting booths. By the commonplace suppressing of the speaking of Spanish in white-controlled institutions and by increasingly limiting its use to Latinos' private worlds, whites thereby encourage many Latino immigrants to become yet more ensconced in their communities, and as a result often socially and politically weaker. As Montoya (1998: 574) put it above, surrendering your home language is "akin to losing parts of your senses." Furthermore, since English competence has become a commonplace and rigid standard for measuring the skills of most Latino children in schools, and since successful bilingual education has generally been rolled back or eliminated, the number of adequately educated Latino competitors for better-paying jobs in many US areas may be decreasing (Shannon, 1999). At the same time, the number of poorly educated Latinos available for low-wage work may well increase in some employment arenas, thereby resulting in advantages for numerous white employers.

## Contemporary Hostility to Spanish and Spanish Speakers

We can illustrate the position of English as the most valuable linguistic capital in the United States with a few examples of powerful white politicians. The sociopolitical mechanisms they and other whites use to assert and establish the value of English linguistic capital over Spanish linguistic capital vary, but there are some common discriminatory themes that can affect Latinos at all class levels.

For example, attempts at linguistic subordination of US Latinos include the widespread notion, especially among many whites, that English capital is always superior to Spanish capital. Whites periodically proclaim this idea in rather blatant ways, as when former presidential candidate Bob Dole ignorantly equated bilingualism with a lack of US patriotism:

> Last week, Senate Majority Leader Bob Dole called for an end to most bilingual education programs in an attack to those he referred to as the "embarrassed-to-be-American" crowd. . . . The leading candidate for the GOP presidential nomination told the 77th national convention of the American Legion that "if we are to return this country to greatness, we must do more than restore America's defenses." (Santa Ana, 2002: 235)

Other white political figures, such as former Speaker of the House and Republican presidential candidate Newt Gingrich, have made similar ethnocentric statements. Speaking against bilingual education, Gingrich advocated English immersion programs. At a meeting of the National Federation of Republican Women, Gingrich formulated his Anglocentric argument as follows:

> The American people believe English should be the official language of the government. . . . We should replace bilingual education with immersion in English so people learn the common language of the country and they learn the language of prosperity, not the language of living in a ghetto. (Hunt, 2007)

Note the language of unreflective white framing here. English immersion programs are necessary so that those people can speak the language of "the country," which is also "the language of prosperity." His terminology here, including the phrase "American people," undoubtedly references whites and white-Anglo culture as the standard and as quite superior. Indeed, there are many Latinos and other Americans who would not agree with his assertion about the "official language" of the United States.

In addition, G. Gordon Liddy (2008), a white "dirty tricks" political operative in the 1970s Richard Nixon administration and recently a conservative radio talk show host, took his turn at the damnation of Spanish in singularly offensive language:

> You've just heard Barack Obama insisting that we all teach our children Spanish. Well, not mine, no way. Round here, let's see, I speak some French, some German as well as English. Franklin [the show's producer] speaks fluent French, fluent Italian, as well as English. But none of us here, so far as I know, speak illegal alien.

In one fell swoop the ever-ethnocentric Liddy fiercely castigated President Obama for allegedly "insisting" that all children be taught Spanish and characterized it as the language of an immigrant canaille. (Obama did not make such a suggestion.) English is again and again signaled by a great many white Americans as the only valued linguistic capital.

Local white officials with substantial power over Latinos also operate out of an anti-Spanish and anti-Latino subframe of the white racial frame. For example, not long ago, a top white official at the Texas Election Division, in a state with a large Latino population, joked that election officials there should "speak slowly and loudly, in broken English" to Latino voters requiring some language assistance—a response required under US law (MALDEF, 2009). Such negative language mocking often reveals a racially stereotyped view of those whose linguistic capital in English is regarded as deficient. Note too his apparent assumption, again from a white-framed perspective, that election officials are not Latino, even though many in areas of Texas are both Latino and bilingual. Not surprisingly, such official negative reactions to Spanish and Spanish speakers have resulted in some anti-Spanish ballot propositions, state and national legislation targeting Spanish and bilingualism, and new nativistic organizations insisting on English as the only official US language. Indeed, during the 1990s many white and other Californians voted for major ballot propositions designed to abolish government services for Spanish-speaking immigrants and to reduce bilingual government programs.

As we noted previously, hostility to Spanish arose early in the history of white contact with Mexican inhabitants of what is now the southwestern United States. In recent years, however, one finds throughout the country an "English only" movement among both elite and ordinary whites. For example, in 1996 the US House passed an English-Language Empowerment Bill, mostly with Republican members' votes. While the Senate did not pass this bill, which would have made English the only official language, the House vote and support of leading Republicans made clear the strength of this view in the white population. Two years later and spearheaded by nativistic whites, a California initiative passed that effectively banned bilingual Spanish-English programs and imposed an English immersion alternative instead (Schmidt, 2000: 3). More recently, some white legislators, together with a few conservative Latinos, again proposed federal legislation in the form of H.R. 997, the "English Language Unity Act of 2011." If enacted, it would make English the official language of the United States. One obvious goal is the elimination of government documents (for example, ballots for voters in numerous areas) written in immigrants' languages, such as Spanish or Creole, the language of Haitian immigrants. This would interfere with these immigrants' and their older children's ability to vote, and especially vote against such conservative white legislators.

One notable figure among supporters of the English-only movement is Mauro Mujica, a Chilean American immigrant who has adopted a strong white framing of other immigrants of color. He is board chair of U.S. English, a very influential organization in the official language cause ("About U.S. English," 2013). Testifying in 2012 at a US House of Representatives hearing on the H.R. 997 legislation, Mujica (2012: 65) made the following tendentious statement:

> We immigrants do not come to this country because of the weather or the quality of the drinking water. We come here to make money. You can only make more money if you know English. . . . We cannot send the message to the new immigrants that English is optional. They can come here, live in Miami all their lives, speak Spanish and not bother to learn English. I have seen it firsthand with members of my family that live in Miami. . . . They think English is optional.

Shaped by anti-immigrant notions in the white racial frame, Mujica's statement defies not only logic but also much empirical evidence. First, knowledge of English in itself is not conducive to material success in this society. Despite their native proficiency in English, African Americans and Mexican Americans who have been in the United States for generations have long been denied access to many well-paying jobs and other mobility opportunities. Second, although this might not be the case for Mujica's relatives in Miami, more than half of English-language programs for immigrants, including those from Spanish-speaking countries, have long waiting lists or have been reduced or eliminated by government budget cuts in recent years (NALEO, 2006). Thus, Mujica's immigrant who supposedly sees English as optional is a straw man because most immigrants do seek to learn English if they can find a local program. Most also know they have to learn English to become US citizens— fluency in English has been a citizenship requirement for more than a century. Third, when one looks at the inflammatory rhetoric employed by groups promoting the establishment of English as the only official language, such as the U.S. English organization, it is evident that it is not as much pro-English as it is anti-immigrant, especially against Spanish-speaking immigrants from Latin America.

## Devaluing and Mocking Spanish: Racialized Joking

One common way that many whites in all classes belittle and devalue Spanish as linguistic capital involves commonplace mocking and joking using so-called broken English. Whites also engage in this devaluing by making up their own mock Spanish. Renowned anthropologist Jane Hill has done much research on the white-generated mock Spanish one encounters across the United States. Whites often make up many sardonic phrases like "no problemo," "el cheapo," and "hasta la vista, baby," and they use such made-up phrases and actual Spanish words like "adios" and "mañana" in extremely nonstandard and ungrammatical Spanish ways (Hill, 2008). This derisive use of Spanish is observable in many white-controlled places, such as in advertising, in movies, and in upscale gift shops, and it is often part of white discourse from the café to the boardroom. Such ridiculing and devaluing of the Spanish language also reveals an underlying negative and racist framing of Mexican Americans or other Latinos.

Revealingly, mock Spanish is the only acceptable form of Spanish for many whites because it typically is anglicized, does not sound like real Spanish, and is said in a sardonic, insulting, or joking manner. This is true for an array of whites at all class levels, including many who might reject more blatantly racist anti-Latino commentaries. Jane Hill has successfully defended her linguistic argument about why such white mocking and derisiveness typically involve a racialized framing: Much Spanish mocking regularly "indexes" (the linguist's term for "points to") racist stereotypes of Latinos and cannot be fully understood without an understanding of the underlying anti-Latino racial stereotypes. In addition, much of the language contempt and mocking is accompanied by offensive racist images of, or narratives about, Mexicans or other Latinos. The language mocking and disrespect are routinely connected to yet other racist commentary and to openly hostile actions (Hill, 2008: 147–148). Indeed, one study of white servers and Latino kitchen staff in a white-owned Mexican restaurant found that the white servers used mock Spanish in condescending ways, thereby accenting their superior racial status, in interactions with the Latino kitchen workers. Most strikingly, these whites seemed to consider their use of mock Spanish as a concession and signal of their tolerant attitude toward the Latinos (Barrett, 2006: 165–170). Once again, the accent on white virtuousness at the center of the white racial frame is conspicuous.

Latinos are not the only Americans of color who endure significant language mocking at the hands of scornful whites. Such mocking of the speech of other Americans of color is commonplace among whites, many of whom apparently do not think of it as harmful. There are many websites that have extensive mocking of what their white originators consider to be "black English" (Daniels, 2009). In addition, the mocking of Asians and Asian Americans can be found in various areas of white America. For example, a white disc jockey at an Ohio radio station phoned nearby Asian restaurants using an array of mock-Asian speech such as "ching, chong chung" and "me speakee no English" (Chin, 1994). Such hostile mocking of Asian speech is commonplace among white comedians and in anti-Asian jokes in numerous white conversations. Notice in these cases how this language mocking often involves negatively characterizing language *sounds*, which whites take to be characteristic of the speech of the derided people of color. Rather obviously, certain language sounds are negatively rated and racialized as part of the dominant racial frame.

## Resisting Linguistic and Related Oppression

Derogatory mocking of the language of Americans of color may appear harmless to unreflective people; however, it not only causes pain for people of color who must endure it but also assists whites in sustaining hierarchies of racial power and privilege without seeming to be "racist" in the most blatant sense of the term. Given this harsh reality, oppressed groups often resist and defend to the best of their ability against efforts to defame their home-country languages or erect significant barriers against their use. Some examples are the Basque, Catalan, and Bosnian peoples (Shafir, 1995; Wood, 2005) in various areas of Europe. These and other culturally different, nondominant groups struggle to keep their languages because they are fundamental to their social life and express the understandings of their associated cultures in an essential array of overt and subtle ways (Fishman, 1989: 470).

For most people, the language they grew up with at home is the one with which they are most comfortable. Not surprisingly, many Latinos prefer to use Spanish because it affords them a richer and more comfortable form of everyday communication, one contextualized and nuanced by their home cultures. In the United States numerous groups have struggled to protect their communications in their ancestral languages. For example, for more than a century, Native Americans have struggled to preserve their languages against recurring and belligerent white attempts to replace them entirely with English. This linguistic struggle continues to the present day (Feagin and Feagin, 2011: 150–164). Asian Americans have also struggled to preserve their languages against white attempts to restrict them. For example, in Monterey, California, many Chinese Americans have worked against language barriers proposed by the Official English movement, including the elimination of signs in Chinese and other Asian languages (Horton, 1995: 211).

White nativists' attempts at language discrimination have stimulated Latinos in some states to organize protest demonstrations or file antidiscrimination lawsuits. In La Puente, a Los Angeles suburb, Mexican Americans organized with some Mexican immigrants to fight a school board trying to get rid of bilingual Spanish/English educational programs in favor of an English-only curriculum. In addition, several lawsuits have been filed by Mexican Americans and other Latinos in attempts to knock down English-only requirements in employment settings. In a 2006 case, *Maldonado v. City of Altus*, a federal court overturned a Texas city's English-only policy for work-related interactions. Nonetheless, a majority of federal court decisions on such English-only workplace requirements have so far ruled in favor of language discrimination (Feagin and Feagin, 2011: 224–225).

Consider for a moment the various sources from which Americans of color have drawn to resist white oppression that includes not only language and other cultural suppression but also numerous other types of discrimination. As we noted in Chapter 1, Americans of color oftentimes resist quietly and at other times resist with more aggressive antiracist organizing and counter-framing. In addition to the dominant white racial frame, there are at least two other perspectival frames important to understanding such resistance to oppression: (1) the anti-oppression counter-frames of Americans of color and (2) the home-culture frames that Americans of color utilize in everyday life, elements of which are often used in developing the anti-oppression counter-frames. Indeed, as we have previously noted, the dominant white frame has never gone long without significant resistance. The resistance movements of Latinos, African Americans, and other Americans of color have frequently developed significant counter-frames that help them to better understand and actively resist white oppression. Typically, these assertively antiracist counter-frames have drawn on resistance elements in the home cultures of those thus oppressed (Feagin, 2013: 163–198).

For many generations, very large segments of the black and Native American communities have passed along a spirited antiracist counter-framing of US society. Given that the majority of Latinos have been in the United States only a few generations, it is unsurprising that social science data indicate that a strong antiracist counter-frame is less extensively developed or utilized in most Latino communities (M. Chavez, 2011; Cobas and Feagin, 2008; Feagin, 2013).

There is, nonetheless, an antiracist Latino counter-frame with elements critical of US racism in its variations, but this counter-frame runs across a continuum in the degree of its overt criticism of that racism. At one end of this continuum there is a well-developed view aggressively critical of white racism in the United States—a perspective found, for example, among Puerto Rican independence and Mexican American activists. During and after the 1960s–1970s Mexican American civil rights movements, such as in the La Raza Unida Party and other Chicano resistance groups, an antiracist counter-frame developed in Latino communities in Texas, California, and some other states. For a time Chicano and Puerto Rican activists, like those in black protest movements of that era, formulated and published a strongly counter-framed analysis assessing just how a white racist society has regularly oppressed US Latinos (J. Gutiérrez, 2001; Feagin and Feagin, 2011: 220–221). This more assertive anti-racist counter-framing can still be found in most Latino communities.

In contrast, at the other end of this framing continuum there are numerous Latino groups or organizations that openly hold to, at best, a weak critique of contemporary white racism. As we discuss more fully in Chapter 6, certain Latino organizations have historically insisted that Latinos fully adapt to white folkways, including accepting uncritically significant elements of the dominant white frame and not openly critiquing anti-Latino racism. Variability in the degree of antiracist counter-framing is true for people in all communities of color, but those in the United States for many generations typically have larger numbers of community members and organizations actively making use of this more assertive antiracist counter-framing (Feagin, 2013).

Home-culture frames accenting the Spanish language and family values, as well as other important elements, do offer some everyday resistance resources for Latinos. They are indeed strong among all Latino groups represented in our sample, as we will see later. Indeed, recent research has demonstrated that, even as they endure continuing inequality and discrimination, Latino communities still maintain strong family support structures, community organizations, and traditional cultural elements (Telles and Ortiz, 2008). Often having significant ties to their home countries, many Latinos make much use of elements of their home-culture frame in everyday life. This includes choosing traditional Latino cultural preferences over those pressed on them by the dominant Anglo culture. These values and preferences typically involve language, music, and religion. As we have already seen, the Spanish language is well regarded and often emphasized in these home cultures. One survey of Latinos found that, when questioned about what in "Hispanic culture and tradition" was important to preserve, over half stressed the Spanish language and strong family values (Cheskin Company, 2002). Elements of the home cultures provide an important basis not only for everyday living but also for resistance, albeit often more subtle or restrained, against white cultural and institutional dominance. On occasion, moreover, these home-culture elements provide protest movements with the foundation from which to mount a more aggressive antiracist counter-framing against white oppression.

Although Latinos are regularly disadvantaged and discriminated against in the US language "market" due to the greater power of whites, they as individuals often resist attempts to squelch their languages to the best of their ability. For instance, when told by whites to stop speaking Spanish because

Spanish is out of place in the United States, as our interviewees discuss below, they often respond, briefly or insistently, by asserting the legitimacy of their mother tongue. At a deeper level, this recurring language interaction can be seen as an ongoing dialectical disagreement in which the white side is regularly trying to disparage Latinos' language, and the Latinos are individually or collectively working hard to counter such repeated white efforts. Sometimes the counterargument is expressed forcefully, as in the following example from a Puerto Rican interviewed by researcher Bonnie Urciuoli (1996: 169):

> There is a little phrase that goes around, "Speak English, you're in America." . . . You see when I was growing up, people would really try to put you down because you spoke Spanish. It was like [imitating snide tone of voice] "Don't speak Spanish, speak English," very nasty. Now very few people tell you that. . . . I think that if anybody today would tell me that, I'd tell them go fuck yourself. I'll speak whatever I want to.

In this instance, a Latino persists against insistence that he or she speak Spanish through different means. In a celebrated court case, Héctor García was employed as a salesperson by Gloor Lumber and Supply in Texas. Gloor Lumber allowed its employees to communicate in Spanish on the job *only* if there were Spanish-speaking customers who wanted to be helped in their language. García broke company policy by openly speaking Spanish with Latino coworkers. He was fired. He sued but lost his court battle (see J. Gonzalez, 2000). García drew on his home culture's values and insisted on his right to speak Spanish even though it cost him his job. In numerous other federal court cases, Latino plaintiffs protesting English-only and other language discrimination in the workplace have also lost. For the most part, protesting anti-Spanish and other language discrimination successfully in US courts has historically been hard.

## Language Control and Resistance: Our Respondents' Experiences

The anti-Latino framing in the dominant white racial frame regularly generates a great array of what we might term *racial-linguistic aggression* by whites. Our Latino respondents delineate a number of different white techniques that they view as attempts to undermine the status of Spanish and of Spanish speakers and to discourage the everyday use and spread of the language. Unquestionably, a common goal of the language control methods of whites is to disparage and devalue the language capital of Latinos. White hostility to Spanish is regularly demonstrated in the white arrogance, central to much white racial framing, that insists on the abolition of Spanish even from the white presence. Such attacks are transparent statements about the illegitimacy of Spanish, Spanish speakers, and Latino home cultures in an assumed white-centered America. Our data show that whites use a variety of anti-Spanish strategies, and these attempts to control or disparage Latinos' language often provoke resistance responses from the Latinos involved in the interaction or witnessing it.

## Silencing Spanish Speakers

One language control strategy is what we call "silencing." It is the stratagem most frequently mentioned by our Latino respondents. The silencing technique is typically straightforward: It consists of a command from members of the white group to Latinos to *stop* speaking Spanish. It carries the supposition, central to the dominant white framing of society, that whites have the legitimate authority to interfere in any Spanish conversations of Latinos to stop them from speaking any Spanish. The command is usually based on the explicit or implied assumption by the interlocutor that "*we* speak English in America."

For instance, a Cuban American attorney in her thirties remembers this story from her childhood a few decades back. It shows a classic case of white silencing:

> We were in [a supermarket]. . . . It was during the Mariel Boatlift situation . . . there was a whole bunch of negative media out towards Cubans 'cause . . . many of the people that were coming over were ex-cons or what-not. . . . And so my mother was speaking to us in Spanish . . . and this [white] woman passed by my mother and said . . . "Speak English, you stupid Cuban!" . . . And then my mother turned around, and purposefully, in broken English, because she speaks pretty good English . . . said, "I beg your pardon?" . . . [The woman] repeated the statement.

The Cuban interlocutor's resisting response to this white attack on her and her language is insightful and thoroughly assertive:

> And my mother . . . asked her if she was a Native American Indian. And when the lady responded "No . . . I'm Polish," . . . my mother responded . . . "Well, you're a stupid fuckin' refugee just like me." . . . And, the lady, I don't know what she said, but my mother said, "Do you know why I'm here, in this

country? . . . I'm here because I just came in the . . . Mariel Boatlift [which was not true] and the reason . . . was because I killed two in Cuba, [and] one more here will make no difference!" . . . And so then [the woman] thought my mom was being serious and left there really quickly.

By forcefully asking the white interlocutor about her own national ancestry, the mother of the respondent ripostes cleverly to the racist intrusion by saying in essence that she and her language are as American as that of the white woman, whose Polish ancestry is also not indigenous to North America.

In the account that follows, the attempt at silencing is more indirect. A white employee complains to the postmaster, a Latino, that fellow workers are speaking Spanish and asks his boss to make them stop that type of communication. The postmaster refuses to comply:

> I had that situation when I was working for the post office. I had two Chicanos that were talking in Spanish. There was an Anglo carrier right in the middle, and she approached me and told me that I should keep them from speaking Spanish. I said, "You know both of them are Vietnam [Marine] veterans, and I think that they fought for the right to talk any language they want to."

The postmaster's response attributes legitimacy to the men's speaking any language they choose in the United States because they are veterans who fought in the Vietnam War in the 1960s. In other words, these US Latinos are full-fledged Americans whose patriotism entitles them to speak any language they please in their everyday communications in the workplace.

The following interview excerpt involves a white man's attempts to silence Latinas as he insists that English is the official US language. The respondent who provided this account witnessed the event:

> There were two women in the grocery store behind me and they were talking about the lottery [in Spanish]. . . . And the [white] man in front of me turned around and looked at them and he said, "Why don't you speak English?" to them. And I was right behind him. And I said, "Well they have a right to speak their language." [He replied] "No they don't. They're in the United States. They should speak English." And the two women . . . ignored him. They just kept talking. But I'm the one who spoke up.

The witness did not elaborate on the reason for her statement to the insistent white intervener that the two women had the right to speak their Spanish language in public communications. Regardless of her intention, however, her individual response to the white man's arrogance was somewhat restrained but still countered his assertion and strongly affirmed that speaking Spanish is indeed quite permissible and legitimate in the United States.

Another Latino respondent in a southwestern city was politely trying to help a Mexican immigrant at a convenience store. Their conversation was also in Spanish. As they talked, a white interlocutor interrupts and voices his displeasure of their use of Spanish:

> [This] farm worker . . . is Mexican. I was speaking to him [in Spanish] . . . and this [white] individual asked us if I had to speak so loud. "Can you guys lower your voice?" . . . *Were you guys talking out in the street?* No, there is a Circle K right by [work]. We were standing right by [the counter]. . . . *Did you respond to this man?* I very politely explained to him and he was shocked [at the quality of my English] when I looked at him and I said, "Pardon me, sir, I am speaking to him in Spanish . . . because he doesn't speak English." His response then was, "Maybe he should move out." I said to him . . . "If he moves out, then why don't you go pick the stuff out in the field?" *What did he say to that?* He just turned around and walked away.

White stereotypes and hostility are demonstrated first by the indirect means of complaining about the supposed loudness and then more directly by suggesting the immigrant worker should leave the country. The countering Latino response says, in essence, that the Mexican immigrant is performing an important agricultural function in the United States, doing necessary work that the white interlocutor and other whites apparently are unwilling to do. At the least, the respondent appears to say that the immigrant has a right to communicate in his mother tongue.

In the next episode, a successful Latino executive relates an incident that happened when he was on vacation with his family and visiting a famous amusement park. He and his wife came to the United States at an early age, and they have an advanced proficiency in English. Yet they decided to often speak to their children in Spanish while they were young so that they would learn the Spanish language. He provides this revealing account:

> I had a really bad experience at Disneyworld. . . . My son at the time was . . . three. . . . He jumped the line and went straight to where there was Pluto or Mickey Mouse or something and I said, "[Son's name], come back" in Spanish and . . . ran after him. And I heard behind me somebody say, "It would be a fucking spic that would cut the line." Now my wife saw who said it, and I said, "Who said that?" in English and nobody said a word. And I said [to my wife], "Point him out, I want to know who said that," and she refused. I was like, "Who was the motherfucker who said that?" I said, "Be brave enough to say it to my face because I'm going to kill you." You can see me, I'm 6'3", 275

[pounds]. Nobody volunteered. . . . *So nobody stepped up?* No, no and there was a bunch of guys there, and I would have thrown down two or three of them; I wouldn't have had a problem.

The executive's resisting response to overt white racism was clear and to the point, and came from the heart. His child was insulted, and he was deeply offended. Clearly, his strong reaction suggests elements of an antiracist counter-frame, and it could have led to further serious consequences for the respondent. Yet, he was willing to take this personal risk and provide a model of Latino resistance to racism for all who were present, by responding very assertively to the ultimate racist slur used by whites for Latinos.

These practices of silencing Spanish speakers are very revealing of the asymmetric values of English and Spanish language capital in the United States. It would be *inconceivable* for a Latino to ask a white Anglo to stop speaking English in any Latino (or other) neighborhood across the United States. Such reciprocity in action would suggest a language equality that does not now exist, and Latinos are well aware of this commonplace societal situation. Indeed, one of us said to a South American respondent, "Sometimes . . . I ask people I interview . . . have you ever seen a Mexican at a grocery store turn to [a white person] and say, 'Please do not speak English'? Have you seen this happen?" She laughed, "No, no!"

Despite attempts at the imposition of barriers, however, Spanish-speaking respondents frequently answer back, sometimes with restraint and sometimes more aggressively, thereby often insisting on their right to use their native language and, thus, to *be* in the United States. We will return in more detail to such strategies of everyday resistance in our last chapter.

## Voicing Suspicion: Fear of Spanish-Speaking Americans

In the everyday worlds of Latinos, whites' language-suspicion actions differ from the aforementioned silencing acts in that the latter emanate from a conviction that English is the only acceptable language in the United States. Silencing draws from a type of nationalistic and ethnocentric discourse, one that goes back at least to the eighteenth-century British American fears of the German immigrants and their language (Perea, 1997). In contrast, language-suspicion actions are usually less confrontational white objections to Spanish linguistic capital. Whereas silencing actions derive from a strongly held notion about what should be the dominant US language, suspicion actions likely reveal a notion that Spanish speakers need to be watched and that they are often perfidious or sneaky (Urciuoli, 1996). The suspicion response is undoubtedly rooted in emotion-laden stereotypes and narratives common to the white framing of Latinos. Both white silencing and suspicion actions share a common substratum of racialized thinking: When Latinos speak Spanish, they are not playing by the "right" societal rules as envisioned and asserted by whites. Yet again, Anglo interlocutors assume a white right to interfere in a Spanish language interaction and end or alter it.

A major difference between silencing and voicing suspicion is that some of the white interlocutors who object to Spanish on the grounds that they are excluded express, at least on the surface, a desire to be included in the conversational interaction. This inclusion is, however, one that is consistently seen and defined in rather white terms, for the conversation must be in the white person's language and socially comfortable for that particular white person.

The following account is taken from the interview of a university professional who was speaking Spanish on an elevator with friends in the presence of a white woman who strongly registered her personal displeasure:

> A [white] woman was on the elevator with me and some friends, and when she got off the elevator she commented, "Well, you people have been here a long time in the United States. I don't know why you're still speaking Spanish." And we just looked at each other and laughed. . . . And I believe she said that simply because she resented the fact that she didn't know what we were saying and she assumed that we were talking about her because we were laughing and it was just conversation.

The Latinos on the elevator laughed off the white woman's racialized "you people" language and attempt at didactic comments because the woman failed to understand that their choice to speak Spanish had nothing to do with their English proficiency. They were all American-born, university-educated Mexican Americans who spoke their mother tongue because they *preferred* to use it among themselves. As this savvy respondent underscores, their decision had nothing to do with the white woman's presence or exclusion in this setting.

Another confident respondent provides an example of suspiciousness on the part of a white supervisor who did not want her Latino workers speaking Spanish in their workplace:

> Most of the coworkers and the supervisors or managers are bilinguals . . . but . . . my manager was only unilingual. . . . She does not understand . . . that we were not talking about her. . . . We were talking about our business . . . and personal stuff, but she doesn't have to know what we were talking because we don't need for her to give us her . . . point of view. If we need for her to talk we are going

to ask her in English, not in Spanish. . . . [She said] "I don't want you speaking Spanish," and I told her, "I do not agree with you because this is not right." *And what did she say?* She said, "Well, it's not right; it doesn't matter." And I said, "Yes, it does matter and you're not going to stop me from speaking my first language."

The interviewee's response is an unequivocal statement about her right to speak her first language where she sees fit. It resonates with the theme so frequently seen in the ripostes given by numerous other respondents: "I'm entitled to speak my language." Her sharp, on-target analysis is clear in underscoring one reason for such frequent white reactions—the white *fear* that Latinos are talking about the white person behind her back.

A male respondent reports on a similar suspicion situation. He was speaking in Spanish with another Latino in a bank when a white stranger broke into their private conversation:

On one occasion we were at a bank. . . branch. . . . We were talking [in Spanish], and all of a sudden this [white] lady comes and asks us [in English] what we were talking about. *What did you reply?* We told her we were talking about our business.

Although we do not know what the white woman had in mind when she interfered in the Spanish conversation, her action suggests the recurring concern of many whites that those not speaking in English may be plotting something seriously contrary to white interests. There is no doubt that she was operating out of the center of the white racial frame: She took it for granted that she as a white person was *entitled* to interrupt and that this bank area was some type of white space. This Latino's response is polite and matter-of-fact and seems to convey the notion that in his mind what he and his friend were doing was quite legitimate and of no concern to the white interloper.

Another respondent, a female manager in a public agency, was asked, "[Do] Anglo whites ever object to your speaking Spanish at work?" She replies in this candid manner:

Yes. They are like, "Could you please speak English because we don't understand what you are saying." . . . Even the supervisor tells us sometimes that we should talk in English because there are some people that don't know Spanish. But you know what, I feel better speaking Spanish . . . because that's my primary language. There is a [white] lady that actually, that's always complaining. . . . There are times that . . . she just feels like left out of the conversation. She's like, "I want to know what's going on." But there are times that she's kind of rude, so . . . *How do you usually respond to her?* I'm like, "Well, you need to learn Spanish."

The respondent asserted the legitimacy of her Spanish use in a different form by suggesting the obvious action—that those who want to partake in her Spanish-language conversations should just learn Spanish. Such a request will seem ludicrous only if one believes that English is the only language worth speaking in the United States. From the respondent's reflective perspective, even when a language like English has been granted a dominant or semiofficial status, individuals should not be forbidden to use other tongues in settings like the workplace.

Active suspicion of Latinos speaking Spanish constitutes yet another strategy by whites to regulate Latino speech and speakers. In several instances like this last account, the reason given is that whites feel that Latinos are talking about them or are leaving them out of an important discussion. Our respondents are not unique in this regard. Other social science research has reported a chronic suspicion on the part of many whites that Spanish-speaking Latinos are talking about them behind their backs (Barrett, 2006). The justification for such white suspiciousness reveals or implies the white-framed view of Spanish speakers as sneaky or untrustworthy—and frequently too the arrogant view that whites should be included in interactions among Latinos, and on white-framed terms. Despite whites' objections, however, many Latinos respond by asserting their individual and collective right to use their Spanish mother tongue, a central linchpin of their home culture and a type of everyday resistance against recurring discrimination.

## Questioning and Doubting English Proficiency

Since whites' anti-Latino rhetoric and framing place such a heavy emphasis on Latinos' abandoning their home-culture language, one would expect that when Latinos venture into the world of increasing English proficiency they would receive much encouragement from whites. Oddly enough, this is usually not the case. There is frequently white framing and white-centered obstinacy involved: Latinos speak Spanish, an inferior language, and hence they are presumed to be tainted by their heritage language when they speak or write English even when there is significant evidence to the contrary.

In some cases, their English is assumed to be *too perfect*, a white reaction also faced by other Americans of color (Essed, 1991). One example comes from the college experience of a southwestern professional. She was born in a mining town, and her English does not have the particular Spanish accent that many whites consider undesirable. In her self-assured interview she reports on a white instructor who questioned her integrity:

> [A professor] in college refused to believe that I had written an essay . . . because she assumed that Mexicans don't write very well and so therefore I couldn't

have written this paper. *Did she tell you that?* Yes she did. . . . And so she asked that I write it over again. . . . *So what did you do?* I rewrote the assignment, and she still didn't believe that it was my own. . . . She still refused to believe that it was my handwriting or my writing because she still felt that Mexicans could not express themselves well in English. . . . *Did she use those words?* Yes she did.

In her provocative and revealing interview, this well-educated woman explained that she came from a mining town where labor unions had helped Mexicans gain access to good schools, so she had very good English skills. The white instructor was remarkably persistent in her discrimination and candid in her racially stereotyped and emotionally loaded framing: Mexicans cannot express themselves well in English. We see here too an active countering response to rejection. The courageous student stood up to the white instructor but was unable to change her mind.

Another respondent, a woman with graduate training, relates a similar educational account. Also speaking English without the white-stereotyped Latino accent, she was an excellent student and performed well on the usual standardized tests. One white teacher still felt the student had cheated somehow:

I was . . . accused of plagiarism because I wrote better than the white kids did. *What grade was this?* . . . In eighth grade. . . . I scored higher on all of the standardized testing that we were given to place us into classes in high school than most of my Anglo-American peers, and there was a question as to how I could have possibly cheated and how I could have cheated on the essay. When if the teacher had simply thought about it, my writing was always better than theirs. I've always been a strong writer. *So she never perceived that?* She didn't until . . . I indicated that I happened to be a really good writer and why was she questioning; why wasn't she questioning anybody else? Why was she questioning me? *So what was the teacher's reaction?* It was so strong, she didn't think I could possibly have written it, and I know what that was about. She didn't come right out and say it—"Because you're Spanish speaking." I know what that was about. It had to do with my being Latino. As opposed to one of the Anglo kids had done that. I think she would have just thought they were smart.

Unlike the instructor in the previous example, this respondent's teacher did not come out and say, "Latinos don't write well." But the respondent had significant evidence that her teacher's suspicions were likely based on her home language and racial characteristics. As the respondent pointed out to the white instructor, she was the only one among the successful students who was suspected of such cheating.

The process of whites' linguistic questioning of Latinos often includes the expression of skepticism or surprise when they evidence excellent command of white-middle-class English—the racialized linguistic "standard." It is as if the linguistic abilities of Latinos and other Americans of color are so culturally contaminated that, when they show their abilities in writing or speaking the white-middle-class dialect of English, some whites are unprepared to believe what they actually see or hear.

Such white questioning can create serious educational barriers and much pain for Latino students and other students of color. Other studies regularly confirm our findings in this regard. One major study at a midwestern university delineated numerous similar barriers faced by its Latino and black students. A Latino student made this comment about the questioning of his abilities: "I have to show that I'm smart enough to be here. . . . I feel I have to justify. . . . People are impressed if I do extra work because of the fact that they don't expect that [amount and quality of work] from somebody who's Hispanic" (Allen and Solórzano, 2001: 277). Additionally, such recurring challenges to student abilities can often affect academic performance. Much research by social psychologist Claude Steele (Steele and Aronson, 1995) has shown that when racist stereotypes about students of color are intentionally recalled to them before a test, their test performance is frequently affected. In many educational settings, racial stereotypes are intentionally or unintentionally pushed to the front of such students' minds ("stereotype threat"), create significant anxiety, and thereby affect student test performance in many cases.

Another Latino respondent reports on a different kind of everyday experience, this time with language accents. Asked whether white store clerks ever act rudely after they hear her Spanish accent, she answers in the negative. She then discusses some left-handed compliments she receives on her supposedly unaccented English:

> [White] people go out of their way to tell me that I don't have an accent. *Is that a compliment?* I think so. . . . *Tell me in more detail.* Well, you know, they begin to ask me, "Well, where are you from? Am I from Arizona?" "No, I am not from Arizona. . . . I'm from Texas." And then their comment is that "you don't have an accent." And I'm like, "What kind of accent are you talking about?" I don't have a Texas accent, the twang. And then I'll say, "No, and I don't have a Spanish accent." I speak both languages. And they are like, "Well, wow, you don't have an accent." Never fails.

According to her nuanced account, various white interlocutors express surprise at her particular English proficiency. In other words, her English is "too perfect." When she mentions that she is from Texas as additional information, this only creates more confusion for the unthinking white commenters. The astonishment expressed by these intrusive whites is reflective of white framing concerning another form of Latinos' English proficiency—in this case, expected Spanish accents of a certain stereotyped type in speaking English.

The Latino interviewee in the next excerpt recounts a similar experience. When he is called by credit card companies or other phone solicitors, the individual on the other end of the line frequently expresses surprise at the respondent's supposedly unaccented English:

> I think that, many times when people call here for me, such as courtesy calls or calls from the credit card company . . . either trying to sell me a credit card or, you know, I owe money or something like that . . . they ask for [Latino name], and I say who this is. They're like, "Is this [Latino name]?" And I say "Yes." I guess because I don't speak with so much of a Spanish accent. They're kind of held back or, you know, just like, had to stop and think there for a second.

These repeated examples of white reactions to Latinos' language proficiency illustrate not only how extensive the stereotyped white framing is but also the quotidian and recurring impact on the Latinos who are called out or targeted in this irritating fashion. From the Latino targets' perspective, these are obviously not trivial events, for they signal constantly that they are somehow different, foreign, or suspected.

In the next interview excerpt, a respondent from Latin America relates her persisting negative experiences with a white college instructor in regard to a paper she wrote for a class:

> I wrote a paper and I used some contractions, and most of the time I have some problems with contractions. . . . I took my paper to the English writing center, and nobody corrected anything. And so when I got my paper back [from the instructor] and all the contractions were corrected, and so I didn't say anything. But I took the paper back [to the writing center] and they explained to me that there was not any specific reason to have changed them. . . . *Did you get a bad grade on the paper?* No, but the teacher made a comment in class about "foreign" students and that we were in graduate school, and we should write free of mistakes. . . . I said to myself that if I had been an American student using these words he would not have changed it. . . . It was because there was nothing else to correct on the paper. *He just was looking for something to correct; that's what you are saying?* Yes, or maybe if there was a choice or you could use something else. I felt that if this person had not known that I have an accent he would not have noticed that you could use other contractions.

This savvy respondent had previously had problems with contractions and thus had her paper checked by a campus writing facility. The experienced staff found no mistakes. Nonetheless, the white instructor did not approve of how she used contractions. Even though he did not take off points, he made comments to the class about problems with "foreign" students. This respondent did not confront her instructor, but in going back to the writing center, she refused to accept the "alien" definition he attempted to impose on her, and expressed anger at how he had treated her. Such discriminatory experiences in regard to writing and other educational proficiencies have been documented for many other students of color (Essed, 1991; Feagin, Vera, and Imani 1996).

Whether intended or not, this commonplace white skepticism toward Latinos' demonstrated proficiency in English is part of the linguistic denigration of Latinos. Although it is usually not a direct attack on the Spanish language, it reflects notions of deficiency in linguistic capital among the mass of US Latinos—this time often based, ironically, on the deviation of Latino interlocutors from negative and stereotypically framed expectations about their English proficiency.

Unmistakably, there is much ignorance in the US population, especially among whites, about this issue of Latinos' ability to speak English, or to speak English well as viewed from a white perspective. For example, in a 2012 Hill and Knowlton survey of US voters, more than 80 percent of non-Latinos associated Latinos with not learning English (Varela, 2013). Yet, according to a recent Pew Center survey, fully 61 percent of all Latino adults report that they can speak English "very" or "pretty" well. In the first generation, some 38 percent of immigrants reported speaking English well, as compared to *92 percent* of those born in the United States. That huge percentage appears to be unknown to most whites, and it is all the more remarkable given that most US-born Latinos have ancestry going back only a generation or two. Indeed, the overwhelming majority of US-born Latinos speak only English or are very good English speakers and also bilingual. In addition, fully 87 percent of the Latino adults in this national survey believed that Latino immigrants *should* learn English if they want to be successful in this country (Taylor, Lopez, Martínez, and Velasco, 2012).

The contradiction between the reality of US-born Latinos knowing and speaking English well and the negative and racialized white framing of Latinos' language proficiencies suggests how critical to such a framing are fictional notions about these racialized "others" that constantly reinforce the society's centuries-old racial hierarchy.

## Denigrating Spanish-Accented English

Putting down the language of Latinos frequently involves the white denigration or deriding of Spanish accents, and the target is often some type of Mexican accent. This Latino accent frequently appears in writings by white authors as an unsophisticated, over-accented pidgin English. In a biography of the outlaw Billy the Kid, one of the passages renders a Mexican woman's admiring statement about Billy in what linguists call "eye dialect"—that is, in a white conception of how a Mexican American accent should look and sound:

> Billee the Keed. Ah, you have heard of heem? He was one gran' boy, senor. All Mexican pepul his friend. You nevair hear a Mexican say one word against Bellee the Keed . . . Nombre de Dios. Every leetle senorita was crazy about him. (Burns, 1999: 65)

Such white attempts at eye dialect are revealing of bias, not only because they often do not capture the actual language sounds correctly, but also because few such writers of autobiographies about white Americans put the speech of whites, especially important figures (for example, the famous Texan-accented English of former President George W. Bush and some of his advisers), into this flamboyant type of eye dialect.

Indeed, various other foreign accents among immigrant speakers of English are usually not judged in the same harsh terms as the Spanish accents, as language analyst Lippi-Green (1997: 238–239) has underscored well:

> It is crucial to remember that it is *not* all foreign accents, but only accent linked to skin that isn't white, or which signals a third-world homeland, that evokes . . . negative reactions. There are no documented cases of native speakers of Swedish or Dutch or Gaelic being turned away from jobs because of communicative difficulties, although these adult speakers face the same challenge as native speakers of Spanish.

As we have already observed, when they speak English, many Latinos periodically experience a monitoring and policing of their language by whites, and if some sign of a denigrated Spanish accent is detected, they run the risk of white interruption or ridicule.

The second author, a Cuban exile, recorded in his notes his teenage experiences of this phenomenon of certain accents (in this case a Spanish accent) being much more likely to be called out and socially punished than other language accents:

> In an effort to reduce the concentration of Cuban exiles in Miami, the US government and charities, such as churches, sponsored exiles' relocation to other cities. I was 17 years old at the time and was given the opportunity to live with a family in Ithaca, New York, while I finished my last year of high school. I learned English very quickly and did A-work in my classes, which pleasantly surprised my sponsors and my teachers who thought it was an extraordinary achievement for a kid who had arrived just two months before. One teacher,

however, was not impressed. I was in a French class and had all A's on the tests. When I got my first marking period grades, the French teacher gave me a C. I spoke with her and expressed my puzzlement at my grade. She said that I spoke French with a very strong Spanish accent. I told her that the Anglo-American students in the class spoke French with a strong Anglo-American accent. She mumbled something and changed my grade to a B, but said that I should go to the language lab to work on *my* accent.

Clearly, the classroom performance situations here for the author and the white Anglo students were similar, with numerous non-French accents being heard, yet the teacher showed her biased framing not only by calling out the Spanish accent but also by punishing the young scholar. Once again, we observe the white framing that stigmatizes Spanophones to such an extent that even their speech in a foreign language other than English evokes discriminatory reactions by many whites. It is as if these arrogant white Anglophones view Spanish as creating a *permanent* language deficiency or character flaw in its native speakers.

Consider this account from a highly educated Latino who went to a computer store to buy an item. In response to our interview question asking if a white clerk had ever acted abruptly after hearing his accent, he replies:

Oh, that has happened several times. I have had owners of a store imitate my accent. *To your face?* In my face, yeah. I went to buy a printer. . . . I said, "I'm here to buy a printer." And the owner imitated my accent back. . . . *Did you buy the printer?* No, I did not. . . . I felt that I was growing red in the face. . . . And I said, "You know what, just forget it. I'll buy it somewhere else." And I turned around and left.

In refusing to purchase the printer, the respondent strongly registered his displeasure at the way he was treated. Note too that having the painful experience of someone mocking his English accent was not just an isolated event. In numerous respondents' commentaries we observe this cumulative reality. Many forms of discrimination take place on a recurring basis in their lives. Here something as simple as buying a printer turned into a humiliating occurrence, and the emotional costs are clear. Over time, some Latinos feel so self-conscious in such white-dominated settings that even speaking English becomes more difficult for them (see Hill, 1999, 2008).

One of our respondents, a case worker in a social services agency, was trying to talk to a client by telephone. The client's reaction to the respondent's accent was very harsh:

On my first case I needed to talk to this mom [by telephone] about her son and she got very frustrated and she told me, "Anyway, I cannot understand you because you have a very big accent. You don't speak English well; you should go back to school." . . . It was my first case. . . . I had wanted to resign. I had not wanted to keep working as a case worker. I was very frustrated; I don't want to work with [white] Americans. . . . But my boss talked to me and gave me support.

Significantly and ironically, this Latina case worker was actually trying to help the woman who verbally attacked her. When things were not working out in the phone conversation, the woman decided to put the case worker in her *place*. The Latina's initial reaction was not to resist but to withdraw from this hostile environment. Such a response signals well the damage that such white discrimination creates for those who are thus singled out. Again, the emotional and other costs for the targeted Latina in this setting are evident. Discriminatory white actions, as we see throughout this book, have many negative emotional, social, and material costs for those targeted.

In an array of business and government settings, white clients or customers sometimes refuse to deal with Latino personnel because their English is Spanish-accented, or as whites often say, "not American." A Latina respondent who works at the customer service department of a retail store provides this very revealing everyday example:

> There was one time that I answered [the telephone] at my work currently. I had this [white] lady, . . . and she goes, "I don't want to talk to you. You have an accent!" I was like, "You don't want to talk to me?" She goes, "Yeah, I want to talk to an *American*." I was like . . . "Well, I'm sorry you're gonna have to redial to speak to someone that you want." She goes, "Well, go ahead and transfer me over." I was like, "I'm sorry, I'm not going to be able to transfer you over. I have to take the call. I'm here to help you if you need anything." She goes, "Well I don't understand you." And I just kept going, "Well, if there's anything I can do for you, I'm here." So she finally gave me her number, and we went over the account. And at the end she goes, "I'm really sorry that I was too rude to you at the beginning."

The white caller condescendingly assumed that the individual answering the telephone could not be a *real* American because she had a certain type of Spanish accent, and went on to say that she wanted to deal with "an American." The suggestion was that the Latina could not offer the same level of service. The respondent politely and firmly resisted the hostile framing, and the caller finally gave the service representative a chance to help. We observe here much more than white anger over Spanish-accented English, for the caller viewed the respondent out of a white framing that views "Americans" as only those speaking a type of white-middle-class-accented English.

The common view that white-accented English is acceptable while a Latino's Spanish-accented English is unacceptable illustrates a racial framing whether whites who articulate this view realize it or not. This is because such stereotyped discourse arises out of the pro-white center of this omnipresent white framing. Significantly, it often operates in an atmosphere of assumed tolerance among members of the dominant group who vigorously deny being racist, yet at the same time act as if their white norms and values are far superior to those of Americans of color (see Essed, 1991).

Note too that in numerous settings like this one, our respondents encounter whites who exhibit a certain racialized arrogance from the center of the white racial frame. Another of our Latina respondents described in her interview how she has suffered much discrimination from whites when they hear her Spanish accent. In one instance, she was on the street in a city in California speaking to her spouse in French (the language they spoke with each other) when a white woman stopped them and remarked how "refreshing" it was to hear people in the city speak a foreign language other than Spanish!

We should note too that, from time to time, some Latinos show intolerance toward other Latinos who speak Spanish in certain settings or who have strong Spanish accents. Such critical responses directed at other Latinos indicate that those acting in such a fashion are doing so because they too have accepted elements of the negative white framing of Spanish speakers, at least for selected social settings. Moreover, in the rare cases when one Latino asks another to stop speaking Spanish, the request is unlikely to be as persuasive as that of a demanding white person—because of the comparatively greater power of the white requester in most interactive settings of this sort.

Latinos of all class backgrounds and education levels face this questioning or denigrating of Spanish or their particular Spanish accents. A South American doctor who is working as a medical assistant while she attempts to validate her medical credentials in the United States told us about problems she has experienced when dealing with white patients. One in particular was very discourteous to her:

> There is a white female patient who has not come out and said it but lets me know that my accent bothers her. . . . I called another patient, an elderly woman who was a little ways from me, and she did not hear me. The first patient, in a rather aggressive way, said to me, "Who is going to understand you with that accent of yours?" *What did you say?* I called the elderly patient again. . . . *Do you prefer to remain quiet?* I don't like to get in trouble over things that don't matter that much.

This white patient took it upon herself to intervene where it did not concern her, using the opportunity to make a scornful comment that served no purpose other than to demean the doctor's accent. Note again the repertoire of countering responses. Here the Latina quietly ignored the white behavior and kept her professional demeanor. Quiet and restrained countering strategies are common, and often necessary, in the quotidian lives of most Americans of color. The array of these everyday strategies has been recounted by numerous people of color in a few other research studies (see Feagin and McKinney, 2003).

Another woman's Spanish accent has caused her personal discomfort in dealing with some white clerks. She responds to the question about a white clerk ever acting abruptly after hearing an accent this way:

> All the time. . . . They tend to say, "What?" And in a rude way. . . . Always it is this "What?" . . . Yes, it is never, "Oh, I am sorry I couldn't hear you." . . . They are gesticulating . . . this nonverbal behavior that is telling you . . . "Who are you?" or "I can't understand you" or "Why are you even here?" . . . you get all these messages. . . . [They are all] very negative.

This respondent's language accent has frequently evoked unwelcoming and alienating white behavior. She understands well that her identity and the legitimacy of her status in the country are being questioned by verbal and nonverbal means. We observe again the way in which repeated language attacks by whites can crash into a person's everyday life when he or she least expects it. The accumulation of discriminatory incidents causes much emotional pain and unwanted cognitive efforts to make sense of what is happening. Shopping should be a pleasant experience, but for this respondent it commonly becomes an unpleasant chore.

Language questioning and mocking can influence a person's deepest emotions and personal relationships, as the next Latino respondent's account illustrates well. The perpetrator of the attack was a dear friend who evidently thought she was just joking when she mocked the respondent's accent. Asked in our interview if anyone had approached her about her accent, she answers:

> Yeah, all the time, all the time. . . . I had a very . . . bad experience with somebody I love very much. I was in . . . nursing school and I had this friend, and we're very, very close. I mean, we went through the nursing school together and we were great friends and I adored my friend, but she would always make fun of my accent. Because there's still a lot of words, I still can't say some words, a few words. She would always make fun of either the way the word sounded or whatever and I would never say anything because that's the type of person I am. I just take everything in and I don't verbalize my feelings most of the time. But that's me. So when we were graduating from the program I wrote her a letter, and I told her that I loved her very much and I wanted to continue to be her friend, but that if my accent bothered her that much that it was OK with

me not to be friends anymore. And that I felt very uncomfortable with the way she criticized me with my accent. *She was a non-Latino?* . . . She was Italian.

The white friend evidently did not realize the very substantial pain that such regular language mocking was inflicting. White racial framing often generates this significant insensitivity, a type of social alexithymia, toward the slandered racial others (Feagin, 2013). Note how the emotional and other personal damage persisted over some years. In this case, our respondent took it as long as she could but eventually decided that if taking the derision was the price of the friendship, she could dispense with it and stood up for herself. Ironically, too, her friend apparently was not aware that for a generation or so in the early 1900s her own Italian immigrant ancestors had their Italian-accented English regularly mocked by US-born whites. Moreover, in cases like this we observe that whites, who apparently have let lessons about politeness go out the window in favor of stereotyped racial framing, can pay a price too, as here in apparently losing a good friend.

In another interview, a Mexican American with a master's degree sounded apologetic about being US-born and maybe having "an accent." She notes in her commentary that some white coworkers have been supportive, but others have made fun of her apparent accent:

> English is my first language, so I really don't know if I have an accent, but there are some times where some words come out different and that does get recognized by some people that I work with. And I don't think it's an intentional making fun of [it], but it's noticeable and you know they kind of make a slight joke off of it. But I'd have to say I work around both types of people, [some] that have been really supportive despite some other people which, you know, they really look at you as not knowing as much [as whites].

Self-consciousness about a disapproved language accent is common among Latinos, including those who are US-born (Urciuoli, 1996). In a related vein, Bourdieu (1991) once discussed the self-censorship experienced by speakers who anticipate a low value for their speech in a country's linguistic market. This often causes a certain personal demeanor—for example, tense or embarrassed—that in turn can reinforce the white-controlled language market's negative verdict about a particular accent.

The white belittling of Spanish and Spanish-accented English, whether in joking or serious commentaries, is generally insidious and commonly part of the social woodwork in many communities across the United States. Incidents similar to those our respondents have described periodically appear in the newspapers and in lawsuits filed by those Latinos who suffer such language discrimination. These cases often entail serious dangers and inflict harm on the Latinos involved. For example, in one recent case, a middle-class Colombian American who earned a college degree in the United States was turned down several times by the Roanoke, Virginia, school system when she applied to teach courses *in Spanish*, her native language—mainly because some high school students evaluated her Spanish-accented English as being "hard to understand." In another example, a Honduran American who was appointed as postmaster in an Oregon city got numerous hostile comments from a variety of whites, including the city's mayor, and even physical threats because of her Spanish-accented English, racial characteristics, and national origin (Lippi-Green, 2012: Kindle loc. 5050–5053). In both examples it appears that Spanish accents were closely connected to whites' negative framing of these Latina professionals' national origin and/ or racial characteristics.

Many white critics of Latinos' accents, as well as the accents of other people of color, seem quite uninformed in regard to the empirical reality that *all people* speak English with an accent of some type. It is just that the most privileged accents in the United States are generally white middle-class accents, such as those of most white network newscasters. Not surprisingly, whites rarely belittle the distinctive accents of their fellow white English speakers in the routine and often caustic ways they regularly do for Latinos and numerous other people of color.

These excerpts illustrate the range of linguistic persecution and consequent emotional and other personal pain that Latinos speaking Spanish or English with a Spanish accent frequently experience. They regularly run the risk of not only having their accents derided but also having their writing or English proficiency called into serious question. As we have seen, too, most resist through an array of restrained or more active strategies. At work, for example, they sometimes refuse to go along with demands that they not speak Spanish. However, there are instances, such as when they work in jobs involving clients or customers, when they are in no position to resist passively or actively. In most cases, Latinos come back with passive or more active resistance responses that do say in some fashion that we *are* Americans too and we belong in this country.

## Ignoring Spanish Speakers

Another form of language devaluing entails whites ignoring speakers of Spanish even when they have a good command of the white-middle-class version of English. In various social settings Latinos are oftentimes ignored by whites as people not worth listening to, as if their Spanish mother tongue renders their message meaningless and undeserving of white attention. Many, including our respondents, report that whites regularly dismiss them as not being worthy of attention after hearing them speak Spanish. Unlike silencing, deriding accents, or voicing suspicion, such ignoring of Spanish speakers is a more passive form of expressing white disapproval of Spanish and Spanish speakers.

The social situation reported by the following interviewee occurred in Arizona. Asked if she had been mistreated recently by whites because of her racial characteristics or for speaking Spanish, she offers this example of events at a high-end resort:

> Yeah, we went to [resort restaurant] and we tried to order some drinks, but the lady kept passing and passing and said that she would come, but never came to ask what we want to drink. I think because she heard us speaking Spanish. . . . *And was the server, the person white?* She was white and we told her, we called her and told her if she wasn't going to take our order or what, because why that discrimination? We asked her a few times to come nicely and she kept saying, "I will be back, I will be back," and so she apologized and excused herself of course because if not we were going to make a problem. *Then you told her that you felt discriminated?* Yeah. *And you say "we." With whom were you at the hotel?* My mom and her husband and other friends. *And you were speaking Spanish?* Yeah. And so the lady then came and . . . she kind of apologized. And we said, "If not, we want to talk to your managers." *Did she change her attitude?* Yeah.

The Latina and her family went for drinks, and, as they understood the situation, the waitperson overheard them speaking Spanish and ignored repeated requests for service. They felt they had been discriminated against, and their assertive response caused the server to change her attitude. Such neglect and other mistreatment in white-run restaurants is commonly reported in research studies of the experiences of other Americans of color (see Feagin, 2010). We observe here the dialectical and interactive reality of everyday racism highlighted throughout this book—the reality that Latinos who suffer discrimination, like other people of color, must develop significant countering perspectives on, and strategies for, handling the discrimination they regularly face. Note again the emotional and other personal costs of this experience for the Latinos involved.

Another woman reported her negative experiences at stores in cities in New Jersey with white sales personnel. Asked if white clerks ever acted rudely after hearing her accent, she answers:

> A few times. . . . In Jersey. . . . *What kind of comments?* Nothing, it's almost like their attitude changed. . . . If you ask them a question about whatever it is that you interested in buying, you get ignored. You're ignored. *Are you able to complete a purchase? Do you walk away?* It depends on how much I want to

buy. If I don't really need it, I'll walk away. If I need it, I ignore them. I mean, I'm not just gonna walk away from something that I need. I'll have to go back to another store.

The white sales personnel, as the respondent experiences it, are reacting to her Spanish-accented English. As a result, they have periodically ignored her. Faced with the alternatives of leaving and looking for merchandise elsewhere or going ahead and buying the merchandise, she has to waste time and mental energy in deciding whether to even make the purchase she intended.

In the following excerpt, translated from an interview in Spanish, the respondent, a recent Latino immigrant, relates how she and her Spanish-speaking adolescent son were treated by whites when they visited a particular department store:

My son likes nice clothes, brand-name clothes. He likes to buy at [names store]. . . . At first they didn't have an attitude that said, here is a customer who can buy merchandise . . . but rather here is a customer who is going to waste my time. [Before they got to know us] they wouldn't pay attention to us. . . . Once we were looking for a certain brand of pants and we could not find my son's size. We asked [the sales clerks] for help and they would not listen to us.

Whether the respondent's supposition for reasons behind the store's personnel ignoring her and her son is accurate, she and her son did speak Spanish to each other in the store. This was probably one of the reasons for their mistreatment, their repeatedly being ignored. Intentional or not, ignoring Spanish speakers in public places such as retail establishments again reflects a low evaluation of their utterances and of their linguistic capital and can create significant personal and material costs for those thus targeted.

## Conclusion

In this chapter we observed a substantial array of anti-Latino racial-linguistic aggressions. Ironically, many whites do not recognize Spanish, the *oldest* European language widely spoken in North America, as a "truly American" language. This is obvious in white reactions to Spanish and Spanish speakers. Our respondents delineate a number of different white techniques against Americans who speak Spanish or Spanish-accented English. Some whites ask Latino participants in conversations to stop speaking Spanish because English is viewed as the "appropriate" language of the land or because the white interlocutors want to know "what's going on." Others intentionally ignore those Latinos who speak Spanish in particular white-populated settings. Other forms of language control include deriding Latinos' accents, raising questions about their proficiency in English, and expressing disbelief when Latinos demonstrate great skill in English. Whites seem to view Latino speech as highly tainted in several senses. When Latinos speak Spanish, they are viewed as using language that does not belong in the United States or as saying something critical of whites behind their backs. Alternatively, when Latinos speak English, their accent is viewed as inferior and thus does not belong. Indeed, whites everywhere seem to see themselves as the authorities to adjudicate language use and character.

Some analysts might question whether these chronic white attempts to restrict Latinos in regard to language matters involve real racist framing directed toward them, rather than just discomfort with not knowing what they are saying. However, this is an impossible position to sustain in light of the many white racist stereotypes and other racist framing of Latinos that are regularly invoked in recurring white actions mocking the Spanish language, deriding Spanish accents, or trying to shut down Spanish speakers. In the racially framed accounts studied by several researchers, including in our research, the speech of Latinos is frequently thought by the white perpetrators to also reveal low intelligence, untrustworthiness, and other negative traits long associated with Americans of color (Santa Ana, 2002; Feagin and Feagin, 2011). In linguistic research terms, Spanish speaking and Spanish accents are cues that *index* a broad array of racialized stereotypes, images, and narratives about Latinos in a great many white minds.

Some might dismiss such arguments about this white racism by saying that interference with Spanish speakers is only occasional and just the product of a few uneducated white individuals. Certainly, cross-cultural ignorance does link to whites' racial framing and hostility. However, white-arrogated interference with Latino speech, according to much testimony from our respondents, occurs *regularly* and the interlocutors and challengers are often well-educated whites. In addition, regular white language interference commonly takes place together with other strong white signals of white superiority and Latino inferiority. Chronic and insistent white interferences with Latinos in settings such as those described here derive from strong white stereotypes, narratives, images, and emotions out of the dominant racial framing of this still-white-controlled country—one that Silverstein (1996: 284) characterizes as having a "culture of monoglot standardization."

Demographic changes (see Chapter 6) involving a major increase in the Latino percentage of the US population over this decade and coming decades probably factor into the discriminatory treatment of Spanish and

Spanish-speaking people by many whites. As underscored in Chapter 1, the United States already has a very large Latino population of more than 51 million. In just a few years this population is projected to be more than a fifth of the US population. By about 2045, a majority of Americans will no longer be white. This so-called browning of America has raised much fear among whites about non-English-speaking immigrants and their descendants. As we have noted, one reason offered by whites is that a metaphorical "flood" or "wave" of Latinos represents a threat to the "American way of life," with the English language as a major symbol of that supposed way of life.

Many whites have responded to these demographic changes by further denigrating Spanish and its speakers and attempting to reduce that language's cultural and societal importance. As we have documented, many white efforts occur at an interpersonal level, while others occur at institutional and societal levels. In their turn, Latinos often resist these incursions into their home language and other aspects of their home cultures, sometimes actively but more often indirectly or with significant restraint. Many resist mistreatment to the best of their ability. Not surprisingly, their social capital and other societal resources are usually limited when compared with those at the disposal of many of their white antagonists. Today, the Spanish language and accents are ridiculed by ordinary and powerful whites, and we often hear local, state, and federal legislators call for much stricter government control over Latin American immigrants or all Spanish speakers. Such language attacks emanating from the dominant group may mask for some Latinos the structural basis of their everyday victimization and interfere with their ability to see the underlying and systemic structure of their racial oppression. Nonetheless, there is very strong evidence of the willingness of many Latinos to resist whites' anti-Spanish and other anti-Latino discrimination, with some understanding of the ultimate implications of this discrimination for their cultural and group survival.

The often xenophobic discourse aimed at US Latinos commonly relies heavily on the notion that they and their culture are sounding the death knell for English and its associated societal buttresses. This white Anglo discourse is usually heavy in rhetoric and short on evidence. Indeed, as we mentioned before, many English-language programs for those Spanish speakers and others eagerly seeking to speak English typically have long waiting lists or have been eliminated or reduced in scope by white legislators and other white officials (NALEO, 2006). Unmistakably, facility in multiple languages is a very valuable cultural resource for many individuals and for society generally. Indeed, there is a widespread belief among our study's respondents that there should be much more tolerance of languages other than English in the United

States. Asked about attempts to ban Spanish in many US institutional areas, one savvy respondent gave a pointed and typical answer:

> I think the more languages you speak, the more culture you have, the more educated you are. We're in a global society; I mean Spanish is the number two spoken language of the Americas. *Is it OK with you to use Spanish in ballots or other official documents?* You know this is the United States and English should be the number one language, but if they are US citizens and they are paying US taxes, then they should have Spanish ballots.

Significantly, too, *not one* of our seventy-two respondents argued that language tolerance should be limited only to Spanish. Additionally, not one advocated that Spanish should replace English as the language inside or outside Latino communities in the United States. Substantial tolerance of language and other cultural diversity is a strong and healthy position in US Latino communities. Indeed, there is a recognition in at least the better-educated segment of the white population that knowing more than one language is desirable and a significant cultural asset. Bilingual and multilingual whites who have learned other European languages such as French and German are not viewed as culturally deficient but as "very cultured." Such conspicuous and contrasting examples indicate again that there is much more than just language involved in the omnipresent white attacks on Spanish, Spanish accents, and Spanish speakers.

Nativistic white analysts such as Samuel Huntington (2004) and Patrick Buchanan (2002, 2008) accuse Spanish-speaking immigrants and their descendants of being a serious threat to the supposed US democracy and to the "American way of life," which for them means white-Anglo ways of framing and folkways. On close examination, this is a peculiar accusation because most Latinos in our research and others' research (M. Chavez, 2011; Telles and Ortiz, 2008) accent the virtues of language diversity, other cultural diversity, and some cultural blending into the English-based US system that the public rhetoric of the United States has long accented in its recurring America-as-a-melting-pot imagery (see Chapter 6).

Contrary to mainstream perspectives on racial issues in the United States, the past and present struggles between Latinos and whites as groups have almost never taken place on a level playing field. Since the 1840s, group interactions between whites and Latinos, indeed between whites and all subordinated racial groups, have mostly been played out on a highly tilted playing field that whites invented and still firmly control in terms of normative framing, societal position, group power, and racial privilege. Given their position in the persisting US racial hierarchy, whites as a group have tremendous socioeconomic and framing resources at their disposal in major institutional worlds, including those of politics, business, finance, mass media, and education. Powerful white elites substantially control the country's linguistic and other normative structures (Gramsci, 1988), as well as much of the dominant framing about what is right and proper in society, including what is racially "correct." In this white-dominated milieu, Latinos struggle to preserve their Spanish language and other elements of their home cultures as best they can, but that remains a very difficult task in this highly racialized society.

# 3

# The Racialization of Place and Space: Latinos in Public Spaces

In 2008 white high school students in the northern town of Shenandoah, Pennsylvania, violently attacked and beat a Mexican American to death in a park while yelling racist epithets and other racist commentary. The attackers were sentenced to only nine years in prison, and just for a federal hate crime. According to the judge, "The jury found that Mr. Ramirez died as a result of his ethnicity or race." The white attackers reportedly yelled out, "This is Shenandoah. This is America. Go back to Mexico" (Hing, 2011). In their hostile view, and in the racially framed views of other whites interviewed after the attack, the growing Latino population in the area was *intruding* on what was considered to be white space.

Much racial patterning in the United States has historically involved white control and protection of many public and private spaces. The European sociologist Georg Simmel was probably the first Western social analyst to emphasize *space* as a very important analytical dimension of human relationships. For him, social space depicts contrapuntal relationships between physical and social distances in interpersonal relations. His 1908 essay "The Stranger" is a powerful exploration of this topic: A societal stranger is physically in the midst of an unfamiliar society, yet is often socially distanced therein. "In the relationship to [the stranger], distance means that he, who is close by, is far, and strangeness means that he, who is also far, is actually near" (Simmel, [1908] 1964: 402).

## Racializing Individual and Collective Space

More recently, social scientists Pierre Bourdieu (1991) and Nicholas De Genova and Ana Ramos-Zayas (2003) have developed a broader concept of social space and applied it to the racialization of Western societies, including to urban spatial zones in the United States. Bourdieu mapped the contours of social space by tracing the commonalities and dissimilarities among individuals on collective dimensions such as class and ethnic characteristics. As people's affinity and attraction in regard to these social dimensions increase, their distance in social space typically diminishes. The reverse also happens:

> To speak of a social space means that one cannot group together just anyone with anyone else while ignoring the fundamental differences, particularly economic and cultural differences, between them. But this never completely excludes a possible organization of agents in accordance with other principles of division—ethnic, national, etc.—though it should be remembered that these are generally linked to the fundamental principles. (Bourdieu, 1991: 233)

He adds that one of these fundamental principles in Western societies is that ethnic and racial groups are "hierarchized in the social space."

Research studies have shown that important spaces within major US institutions are often white controlled and racialized for Americans of color. For example, researchers at one major historically white university showed from focus groups with black students and parents that the campus had numerous white-controlled spaces. In such racialized social spaces, whites of various statuses frequently behaved protectively or defensively when encountering people of color, such as students or staff who were black (Feagin, Vera, and Imani, 1996). Moreover, specific areas within US rural and urban settings are commonly associated with specific racial groups and their ascribed characteristics. Many of our public schools are either heavily white or predominantly children of color. Recurring research on this school segregation by Harvard's Civil Rights Project has found that for many Latino and black children school segregation is greater now than in the 1960s civil rights era (Orfield and Lee, 2006: 11–12). Much school segregation is in urban areas that also have extensive housing segregation along racial lines.

Once certain urban spaces are racialized by the dominant group, such as in the mainstream media, the connection is made not only by them but by people of color as well. Here, two leading scholars note this reality for the city of Chicago:

> A simple reference to "26th Street" could automatically trigger discourses about Mexican "illegal aliens" or "gangs." The racialized connotations about space in Chicago certainly are projected by hegemonic institutions of white power, but also are simultaneously generated, debated, and contested within these Latino communities. (De Genova and Ramos-Zayas, 2003: 32)

In some cities, attempts at territorial control have motivated white violence and other discrimination against urbanites of color. In spring 2010 a white man in the city of Phoenix shot and killed his Mexican American neighbor in a residential neighborhood while reportedly yelling racist insults like "wetback" and "You . . . go back to Mexico!" In this case, as in numerous other violent attacks on Latinos in recent years, the white man's target was actually a native-born US citizen whose family had been in the United States for several generations. The trial report indicated that the white attacker had approached his Mexican American neighbor to talk about Arizona's controversial new Senate Bill 1070 allowing police officers to take action to stop anyone who looked like an undocumented immigrant in order "to make attrition through enforcement the public policy of all state and local government entities in Arizona" (Lemons, 2010). Indeed, some critics of such legislated policies designed to reduce the Mexican population in historically white places have suggestively called them "ethnic cleansing." Notice, too, that official legitimating of racial profiling helps reinforce anti-Latino thinking and action on the part of ordinary whites.

Our conception of white social space rests on the reasonable assumption, supported by the data in this book, that racial oppression and racialization of physical space are inextricably intertwined in a great many areas of US towns and cities. Social space obtains its "color" when whites appropriate it and racialize themselves as superior and each group of color as inferior, as they have done now with every indigenous or immigrant group of color since the seventeenth century. Much of the relatively public space in this society is normatively white-determined, if not white-dominated. This is true of numerous spaces in historically white institutions such as the economy, education, politics, law, health care, and religion.

Today, as in the past, much white-on-Latino oppression occurs in racialized spaces that proclaim the latter's inferiority. The raison d'être for white social space is racial exclusion or subjugation. Whites pursue this hegemony through a variety of means. When Latinos are in white spaces, the whites who are present often attempt to make them feel out of place, even when the Latinos perform important tasks and services for whites. The message of deprecation may be communicated by verbal comments or nonverbal cues, such as looking at Latinos askance or refusing to be physically close to them. In some instances Latinos are physically harassed or attacked. They are frequently victims of a double standard. For instance, Latinos are often overlooked in places of business or profiled by the police in settings where whites usually proceed unimpeded. Many Latinos do not take this white domination of social space meekly. Although their resources are frequently no match for whites' means, Latinos often resist this and other racial profiling to the best of their ability and as limited by the character of a particular social setting.

In this chapter we provide some of the first empirical evidence from in-depth interviews of the racialized mistreatment faced by Latinos in important spaces of this still-white-dominant society. We hope to move a few steps forward in the social science conceptualizing of the racialization of this ordinary social space.

## Latinos in Important White Spaces

When Latinos enter the omnipresent white-controlled spaces, they generally run the risk of being regarded with significant suspiciousness. Whites in these spaces frequently hold to a racial framing with its negative stereotypes and images depicting people of color, including Latinos, as threats, delinquents, or criminals (Russell-Brown, 1998). For decades, Hollywood films and television dramas have regularly criminalized Latinos and spread or reinforced this white racial framing. Numerous films, such as *Dirty Harry* (1971) and *Gran Torino* (2008), and many television crime shows have presented Latino characters disproportionately as drug users, pimps, prostitutes, other criminals, or problematic welfare recipients (Feagin and Feagin, 2011: 212–215). Not surprisingly, Latinos who encounter whites on the highway or on city streets, in places of business, or on the frontier with Mexico often are treated with some type of suspicion, disdain, or fear.

### Encounters with Police Officers

Streets and highways frequently become places of discrimination for Latinos. Research studies in Texas and Connecticut have revealed that local police officers have illegally issued tickets to Latinos for the nonexistent crime of "non-English-speaking driver" or have given tickets very disproportionately to Latino drivers in a process of obvious racial profiling (Lippi-Green, 2012: Kindle loc. 8479). One of our Latino respondents related an experience he had while driving in Louisiana. He encountered a white officer who, upon seeing the respondent's Spanish surname on his driver's license, became suspicious and began to ask questions about the background of the respondent's family:

> [Once] I got pulled over [for speeding]; this was in Louisiana. The police officer . . . when I gave him my driver's license, he looked at it and he said, "Boy, where are you from?" I said, "Miami." He goes, "No boy, I didn't mean where are you from; I wanna know where your people are from." And that was a very hair-raising experience. *So what did you say?* I said my people are from

Miami too, and I was praying to God that . . . *He didn't push it?* No, he didn't push it; he let it go and gave me my ticket. But I was definitely concerned.

The officer addressed this young man with the inaccurate and pejorative "boy" and then proceeded to insistently ask him questions about his ancestral background that were irrelevant to the traffic violation. Since the incident took place in the Deep South, where black Americans have long reported recurring police harassment (Russell-Brown, 1998; Feagin, 2010), this young Latino driver was understandably worried about what might happen as he tried to honestly counter the officer's apparently negative framing of him.

The following story resembles the previous one, except that several Latinos are involved. In this account the Latinos are riding in their car looking for a local mall:

A few years ago, I was with a couple of friends and we were in like our mid-twenties and so we were just shopping on a Sunday afternoon. . . . I don't know if it [our car] fit a profile, but, you know, it was a . . . small little gray car with dark tinted windows and a very loud stereo. And so we did get stopped by the police; and he didn't have a really good cause for stopping us. We weren't speeding, you know; we were not running red lights or anything. . . . He didn't have a real reason; he just had a lot of questions about what we were doing, where we were going, you know, why we were so far away from home? . . . You know, we wanted to go to the mall, and there is no mall there. And so it [their current location] was about an hour away from where we live. And so he wanted to know what we were doing so far away.

The young men unwittingly penetrated a white territory, which caused a white police officer to stop them. However, the officer did not bother to offer an explanation. Apparently, the young men's car fit a certain racialized framing for some drivers of color. Numerous respondents recalled similar instances of this type of racial profiling in connection with a police stop that had no obvious cause beyond their racial characteristics.

Recently, a middle-class Latino graduate student who likely "looks Mexican" to white police officers was racially profiled and terribly harassed by two carloads of police officers as he was driving into a major Texas city from his university town. Talking to one of us on his cell phone about his doctoral dissertation, which, ironically, was on undocumented workers, he pulled briefly onto the side of the road. Several white police officers pulled up behind him and pressured him to open his car's trunk so that they could look for drugs. They had no search warrant. When he protested their demand to open his car's trunk, they said they were going to make him wait a long time while they got drug-sniffing dogs and checked his car out. Quite probably, they had profiled him as an undocumented Mexican or drug dealer. Even though he is a US military veteran, similar racial profiling has happened to him several times in Texas at the hands of the US border patrol, including once at gunpoint. Having graduate degrees and middle-class status does not protect Mexican American and other Latino drivers from the commonplace racial profiling and the great stress that it causes.

Driving a car in a white space is just one of the ways that Latinos can arouse substantial white suspicion and increased surveillance. The following detailed vignette comes from an interview with a Latino who was just quietly and harmlessly walking through a white neighborhood. Suddenly, two police patrol cars came out of nowhere:

> I went to visit a friend and it's kind of beautiful. There are lots of trees and green areas, and so I wanted to [go to] my friend's apartment. And I was going to [go first to] the library to do some work, and so I was walking in the street and walking towards the library. And two cop cars stopped in the middle of the street and they came down to check me. . . . There were two cops. There was a guy and a lady, and the guy came down and the lady was waiting in the car. And so he came down and he asked me for my identification, and then they took it to check it out just to see if I had any felonies or something. *Why do you think that they stopped you?* They were saying that somebody from the neighborhood called them because I was walking in the neighborhood and I looked weird. *Why do you think they would say you looked weird?* Well, St. Louis is in the Midwest, and there are not as many Hispanics in the crowd as in the [Southwest].

A resident of this area called the police because a Latino was walking along the "white streets." This man's intention simply was to walk through a beautiful area on his way to the library. On the face of it, the likely white resident and white officers overreacted, although we do not know what information was provided by the person's phone call. Sending *two* patrol cars to investigate one Latino who gave no indication of criminal intentions signals the high level of suspiciousness and surveillance that whites often maintain over many such residential spaces.

## Other Discrimination when Traveling

As the passages from our respondents throughout this chapter illustrate, whites often claim historically white public spaces as their own. When they cannot have full control of these historically white spaces, they are uncomfortable or hostile and regularly take some kind of discriminatory action against people of color who venture there. We see this in numerous social settings in our interviews, ranging from a seat on an airplane to a time-share apartment. For instance, the following illustrative incident was obtained from an interview with an astute college professor:

> I got the last seat at the very back of the plane. . . . There was . . . an older couple [next to] me, and I noticed that the lady switched seats with her husband. . . . She called the flight attendant and complained she wanted another seat. . . . And she was very upset, this white lady, maybe in her mid-sixties. But then, I got up to go to the bathroom and she did too. And there are two bathrooms. . . . Both bathrooms are being used, and we're both waiting in line . . . the lady is standing right behind me. . . . I go to the bathroom, and then I come back out and then the other bathroom is busy. And I notice that the lady doesn't go into the bathroom where I came out. . . . She's standing in line waiting for the other bathroom, and I tell her, "It's OK; it's vacant now!" And she said, "I know," and right there I understood what was going on. She wasn't going to use it because I used it. And then I understood at that moment why she was complaining about the seats. It wasn't that she didn't like the back seats. It was that she didn't want to be sitting next to me.

The older white woman's extended array of on-plane actions signal her negative framing of Latinos: She does not want to be near them and does not want to touch what they have touched. For whites with heads full of racial framing, Latinos are thus racially tainted. Note too that the target of the ongoing discrimination was cautious and took a while to conclude what was going on, perhaps because, like many Americans of color, he tries not to see white-imposed discrimination as much as he can. We observe in this case not only the reflection forced on the target of the racial framing, but also some of his dismay and pain over the prolonged incident. Repeatedly throughout our interviews, one observes the numerous personal and social costs of everyday racism.

In another interviewee's account of spatial discrimination, a white manager invited his employees, among them our Latino respondent, to join him at his private club for a pleasant evening. As soon as the Latino arrived, however, he encountered some difficulties:

> My boss had invited all the guys. . . . I asked the individual [employee he spoke with upon arrival]. . . . I said I'm here for . . . the Smith party. So he goes, "Let me check on that," and he walks away. . . . As I was standing there, this other person [employee] walks up to me. . . . He asked me, "Are you a member?" And I said, "No, I'm not a member," and he said, "Members only." And I looked at him and I said, "You don't understand." And he said, "No, you don't understand. Only members are allowed in this club." I said, "You don't understand. I am checking on the name of an individual who is a member, who has invited us

as a group." And he goes, "Let me check on that." . . . [My boss] happens to be walking by and he said, "What are you doing here?" [The club employee said] "Oh, Mr. Smith, how are you doing?" And he shook his hand and said, "This gentleman is waiting for you." And he . . . changed his song and dance. . . . I [went later] to the bathroom, and the guy was standing there. And I go, "Is it OK for nonmembers to use the bathroom?" He gave me a dirty look. It was pretty obvious he meant what he meant.

The employees at this elite club attempted to dissuade an invited Latino from entering this eminently white space. From the time he arrived, he received transparent hints that he did not belong where apparently few, if any, people of color had ever been. Only when an important white man vouched for his presence in this white space was he made temporarily "acceptable." We also observe a considered countering response that is sometimes available to those who face such everyday discrimination. The respondent did not accept the treatment meekly and in a clever riposte asked a sarcastic rhetorical question of a white employee.

Another respondent describes in detail an incident that she and her husband had experienced while on vacation in what was a rather white place:

On our vacation, we went to [a time share apartment]. . . . And when we signed up we were treated differently, [because of] our names. We got the good rooms because we paid for those rooms, but it's the services. They make us wait, or they ignore us, or something like that. *They don't make you feel welcome?* No. . . . [A white man] didn't want his children using the swimming pool because my husband and I were in it. . . . And then, when we wanted to go to the Jacuzzi, he was in there. He took his kids out, and himself and his wife, and then we could use it. He made it in a way that [communicated that] we were not welcome. . . . My husband was so pissed. . . . [The father] was acting inappropriately, and he was making it obvious. . . . My husband . . . wanted to go over there and beat the shit out of him.

A vacation is supposed to be a time of rest and relaxation, but that was not the case for this middle-class couple. They had entered historically white space, and their presence set off a series of discriminatory reactions by white employees and a white family. In spite of their being paying customers, and contrary to common business practice, they got rather poor service in several instances. Their unpleasant experiences with that service paled in comparison to the blatantly racist behavior of a white family. This latter action strongly signals the racial framing of Latinos as dirty or dangerous. Note too the consideration of countering actions: The husband was so incensed that he wanted to fight the white man. While he did not do so, one can understand such feelings in regard to this recurring white discrimination.

## Mistreatment in Retail Store Settings

Ignoring the widely asserted business practice of "the customer is always right" (as we have seen previously), an array of white employees and managers regularly let their racial framing get in the way of US businesses' raison d'être, which is usually profit. A common theme in our respondents' experiences involves being a Latino customer who a white salesperson assumes cannot afford the desired merchandise he or she is seeking. In such cases the salesperson's assumption is based merely on the customer being a negatively framed Latino. One well-off Latino relates the following typical incident:

> It was at [an expensive car] dealership. The [salesman] didn't want to show my husband and [me] the car. He didn't want to open the doors to the car to even let us sit in it, because I think he said that we couldn't afford it. Or something like that. . . . He was Anglo, white Anglo. *Obviously he knew that you were Hispanic, right?* Obviously, yes. We asked him to open the door to the car or to give us a test drive. We were interested in one of the cars, and he . . . didn't want to do it. *He simply said you guys couldn't afford it?* Yes. . . . [He] said we could see the car from the outside; there was no need to open the doors. . . . On our way out my husband saw some business cards on a table and picked one of his. He held it up and said to the guy, "Is this one of yours?" The guy said yes. So he tore it up in small pieces, right in front of him, threw them down and we left. We bought [another car] . . . someplace else.

Given the conventional business practice of seeking profitability, the salesperson's reaction is surprising yet surprisingly common for people of color. The Latino couple could certainly afford the car at issue, for they owned a prosperous business. But the white salesperson had negatively framed them as Latinos who were unable to pay, and perhaps also as tainting the car's expensive interior. The dealership and its cars were clearly white space, with several white stereotypes and other negative framing doubtless underlying the treatment of racialized intruders. The would-be buyer did not take the discrimination lightly; instead, he resisted and expressed his anger at the discriminatory way he and his wife were treated in a fashion that the salesperson would understand. We observe again the substantial pain caused by such cavalier discrimination.

According to our respondents, this questioning reaction to Latinos is commonplace in a variety of retail stores, which again reveal themselves to be spaces accenting white privilege and dominance. When Latinos attempt to purchase various goods, they are periodically ignored, with a number of negative stereotypes, images, and emotions likely lying behind such discriminatory white actions. One omnipresent white-imposed stereotype is the one we just saw—that Latino customers are poor and unable to afford certain merchandise. Another racial framing is that Latinos are likely criminals or otherwise socially deviant. It does not matter what the social-class level of a Latino is, as this account of a recent experience by the second author reveals:

> I was at a gas station in Phoenix, and since I didn't have my credit card with me to pay at the pump, I gave the man at the cash register $20 in cash so that he would turn the pump on. I didn't use the entire $20 and went inside again to get my change. This time a white woman was at the counter. When I told her that I had left $20 with her fellow worker and needed my change, she furrowed her brow and a strong look of suspicion showed on her face. The man I had given the money to was helping another customer a few feet away, and she walked next to him and whispered, "This man said he gave you $20." Her coworker acted surprised and said emphatically, "Yes, he did!" It was then that she gave me my change. Still, her brow remained furrowed the entire time, and she wouldn't look me in the eye. She was acting like I was robbing a bank and was pointing a gun at her. I couldn't believe it.

A key feature of the white frame's commonplace view of Latinos is that they cannot be trusted. This means that, as here, they frequently get more surveillance and interrogation during interactions that should be routine. Here we also observe the ways in which the white framing gets communicated in numerous nonverbal ways. In addition, as in our accounts below, the key elements of the racial framing are usually loaded with certain emotions, as here indicated by the furrowed brow and whispering.

The next account of everyday discrimination is from an interview with a very successful entrepreneur. She and her husband own a boutique at an airport and another successful retail store. She made a purchase and produced an American Express Platinum card:

> One time I was in [a department store] and I gave my card, and it was an older sales associate. And she said to me, "Did someone lend you this card?" And I said, "Why would I be borrowing somebody's card?" And she said, "Well, where did you get this card?" . . . *Why do you think this happened?* [When I go] shopping someplace and . . . I show them [an American Express] Platinum card, there is . . . [the] perception . . . how can this fat Mexican lady have a Platinum card?

Accenting white privilege, the sales associate asked a middle-class Latina the type of question one would ask a small child. She did not believe that a Latina could hold such an exclusive card, likely reflecting the old racial framing about Latino poverty or criminality. Significantly, the respondent stood up for herself and expressed shock at a line of questioning that would never be insistently imposed on an upper-middle-class white person.

An Argentinean American respondent went to a department store looking for clothes. She immediately aroused suspicion from some white store personnel:

> One time I was at [the department store]. And I was in the area of overweight women because I usually go there to buy gifts for my mom, and she lives in Argentina. . . . And they don't sell [her size] in Argentina. . . . [A security guard] was tailing me. . . . [A white cashier had been] talking to the [guard]. *About you?* Yes. . . . [I overheard the cashier say] . . . "They look so innocent," and I felt that the comment was . . . [about] me because I turned around, and I couldn't see anybody else. So, I pretended that nothing was happening, and I kept looking. . . . I refused to go away.

This middle-class respondent was followed around by a security guard reacting to a white salesperson's stereotyped warning that "they" look innocent. The implication was that surveillance was justified for Latinos in this white-controlled space. Interestingly, like others previously noted, this aggrieved respondent reviewed the situation carefully, refused to give in, and in an act of quiet resistance extended her stay at the store.

Another respondent, a Mexican immigrant who is a legal resident, went to a local furniture store to purchase couches and applied for credit. She recounts her discriminatory experience as follows:

> The other day we went to [store's name] to buy couches. And I only had my old driver's license with my old [Spanish] last name, and I didn't have [one] with my new last name. So [when] the lady [the clerk who took her credit application] . . . saw that my . . . last name was Mexican or Hispanic, she automatically wanted more proof that [I] was a legal resident. . . . I just showed her what [document] I had. . . . *Did she take it?* She took it after she saw my husband, because he is Anglo.

The salesperson voiced a common framing of people of Mexican descent as likely being in the United States illegally. The clerk's attitude changed completely after the respondent's husband showed up. This white man, by his mere presence, vouched for his Latina wife. A recurring experience reported by our respondents is that they have to be vetted by whites before they can be fully accepted, especially when they are traversing historically white settings. Such constant vetting reveals yet another aspect of the emotional and social costs of the everyday discrimination that Latinos face.

In the next interview excerpt, a male respondent narrates the experience of being bypassed while waiting in line at a restaurant:

> It happened at the mall, at [a fast-food restaurant]. And I let that person know . . . what I thought. . . . *What did you tell him?* I said I know why you bypassed me and went to that [white] person . . . and I pointed to my skin. *How did they react?* They said that [it] wasn't true. I said the hell it ain't . . . and I walked out.

Again we see the discretionary and racialized power even of white clerks in fast-food restaurants—and the painful decision as to whether to respond to such discrimination. Being bypassed while whites are being served is a common experience for people of color in white-controlled service settings (Feagin and Sikes, 1995; Feagin, 2010). Racism is so pervasive and pernicious in these public settings that it can turn a simple act of going to a fast-food restaurant into a painful affront and likely cause emotional pain.

## Problems Crossing the Border

A national border is the most visible symbol of separation between two existing nation-states. As such, the US-Mexico border is one of the most closely guarded spaces in this white-controlled nation. Individuals who come from the Mexican side are extensively and sometimes antagonistically monitored by US border officials, but the inspections are not carried out evenhandedly. While white Americans usually receive a cursory examination at the US-Mexico border, those perceived to be Latino are frequently scrutinized closely, irrespective of their US citizenship.

Our respondents view numerous actions of the US border authorities as discriminatory. One of our respondents, a Mexican national who has legal resident status in the United States, summarizes her experience at the Mexican border:

> You are in line. Then people who look [white] American come, and they are saying "American citizen" . . . [and] all of them are going across. It always happens that I go to the end of the line because I don't have blond hair and blue eyes, and maybe my accent is not perfect.

While white citizens generally cross the US-Mexico border with ease, this Latina is routinely delayed even though she has the right and proper documentation to enter US territory. Her apparent lack of "American" physiognomy, which again means a white look, and of a white-middle-class English accent make her inferior in the eyes of many US border officials.

These various border officials' discriminations are strong signals that the border is indeed white-controlled space where people of color are constantly under suspicion and surveillance. As discussed earlier, this association of "American" with white is commonplace. Indeed, recent social psychological studies using the implicit association test have shown that whites associate white faces more strongly with the concept of "American" than they do for faces of Americans of color, including the faces of Native Americans (see Devos, Nosek, and Banaji, 2007).

Not surprisingly, Latinos of various class and nationality backgrounds face such recurring Anglo questioning and surveillance. Note this testimony of two Cuban American brothers, both US citizens and reared in the United States, on their experience while crossing the US-Mexico border:

> When we pull in, the guy [a Latino border guard] says, "What were you doing in Mexico?" "No, we were just tourists." The . . . border guard . . . he goes, "How long were you there for?" And we said, "Just two or three hours." And he goes, "And where are you from?" "Miami." The minute we said Miami he said, "What is your nationality?" We said, "USA." "No, no, no, where were you born?" . . . I mean, these were questions that are, you know, didn't have to go along. . . . We said we were born in Cuba, and they said "Pull over" and they tore our van apart. We were Cubans from Miami crossing the border, so immediately we were drug dealers. . . . We were profiled. Now the van they went through thoroughly, and the guy in charge said, "Let 'em go." But the [guard] . . . said, "No, no these guys are crooked." He was the one that really wanted to [go] further. . . . The dog searched the van. There was nothing wrong with the van.

Once again, we see the explicit racial profiling often faced by Latinos—indeed, as here, sometimes from another Latino. The guard apparently had absorbed certain white-framed stereotypes about Cubans. This illustrates the fact that important elements of the dominant white framing of Latinos and other people of color are enforced not just by whites but by some people of color as well. Such are the ways of systemic racism in the United States. Providing testimony or evidence of one's US origin is insufficient, for this border guard frames and suspects these Cuban Americans to be criminals. Their Cuban ancestry alone was enough for their van to be torn apart by the border authorities.

Two other Cuban American men had a similar experience when crossing the northern border of the United States with Canada—ordinarily white space that is not as closely guarded as that with Mexico. One of the men reports the events as follows:

> My friend and I, when we were traveling in Canada and coming back through the border, we did experience, based on our names on our driver's license, we

were treated different. *How were you treated different?* You would see the cars in front just show their license and go, show their license and go. When they saw our names [on our driver's licenses, they knew that] we were Hispanic . . . especially from Miami . . . they pulled us out of the car, made us open the trunk, and searched everything. The other [white] people were just flying through.

The two preceding vignettes show Cuban Americans being profiled as likely drug traffickers at both the northern and southern US borders. While the cars carrying whites were generally moving through without a second glance, in these cases the Latinos were held up, again as likely victims of the racial framing of Latinos as criminals or otherwise socially deviant.

Mexican Americans face similar problems when traversing the white-controlled border space, especially at the US-Mexico border. One Mexican American woman painfully describes this traumatic occurrence:

Once they stopped me to search my car. . . . A [white] lady checked my car. . . . She wanted to force my trunk open. . . . I said, "Ma'am, I can open it." She yelled at me and said, "Step aside, this is none of your business." . . . And finally, when she felt like it, she closed the trunk. I got back in the car and began to cry.

Here is a situation of government authority where the action is abusive and likely discriminatory. White privilege means that one can *harshly* command those who are not white to obey, especially when in white-controlled spaces that are supervised by those who are armed. Her response is crying, a clear signal of the emotional pain generated by such callous actions against those who are likely racially framed as somehow criminal or deviant.

Another Mexican American respondent provides a similar vignette about human degradation while crossing the US-Mexico border:

On one occasion when I was crossing the border with my sister-in-law, they placed her in a room to search her thoroughly. *Why did they place her in the room?* Sometimes they do it because they just thought of it, or because they do not like the person, or who knows why. *What is your sister-in-law's race?* Mexican. . . . My sister-in-law was sick. She was menstruating. . . . They put her in a room . . . and said, "Take off your clothes." They opened her Kotex to make sure she wasn't carrying drugs.

The last two excerpts illustrate the kind of painful experiences that many Latinos encounter when they cross the US border with Mexico. In the first narrative, the subject was needlessly mistreated and humiliated. In the second narrative, the Latina's treatment was even more heinous and humiliating. To make a Latina remove her clothes and sanitary napkin when there is no

apparent evidence of drug contraband signals the often significant callous-
ness of those who operate too authoritatively in this white-controlled space.
Substantial material, time, and emotional costs are clear in all of these recurring border incidents.

## Conclusion

We have noted the commonplace white fears about Latinos "taking over"
white spaces, as articulated by Samuel Huntington and as found in the commentaries of former *Forbes* editor Peter Brimelow. The nativistic writings of
Brimelow (1995: xix, 193–194) have vigorously argued not only that Mexican and other Latino immigrant groups are "alien" but also that there is a
"glaring possibility" that the persisting Mexican immigration could mean a
restoration to Mexico of the US territory taken by the US government in the
nineteenth century. Like other white analysts, Brimelow is concerned that
this large white-controlled space will be taken, and he asserts, wildly and
without evidence, that some Mexican American organizations are "openly
working for Aztlan, a Hispanic-dominated 'political' unit to be carved out of
the Southwest and (presumably) reunited with Mexico." For Brimelow and
many other white anti-immigrant activists, and for ordinary white citizens,
US territory has always had a "specific core" that is, and must continue to be,
firmly white (Feagin, 2002: 962).

   The sense of alarm about immigrants and their children that is disseminated
by ideologues like Huntington and Brimelow is periodically reflected in the
anti-Latino-immigrant actions of white policymakers and ordinary whites.
Thus, many ordinary whites have reacted to areas of the country becoming less
white in population, especially on the coasts, by moving away from the coasts
and creating some new or more white-controlled territorial spaces. Over recent
decades many whites have chosen gated communities and predominantly white
private schools, and some have even joined armed militias with orientations to
protecting white spaces. Millions in California and other states have moved
from large cities with growing populations of Latinos and other Americans
of color to whiter suburbs—and often into rural or exurban areas away from
our increasingly multiracial cities (Frey, 1997).

   Numerous contemporary white actions and reactions can be viewed as
trying to keep historically white social spaces as white as possible in an
increasingly multiracial society. As documented over the last two chapters,
some of that white effort takes place during face-to-face, everyday interactions between whites and Latinos. A variety of white agents and interveners
regularly give Latinos of all backgrounds the clear message that they are

foreign trespassers, criminals, unintelligent, untrustworthy, or lower class or belong to a lower echelon on the racial ladder that is still central to this country.

Increasingly, as we saw in the opening account of this chapter, this framing of Latinos in the mainstream media, including on the Internet, can at times be deadly. In the mass media we reviewed for this book, we ran across many accounts of violence against Latinos of various classes that were evidently motivated by a hostile racial framing. Consider just one recent example of these very troubling and openly racist attacks, in this case in a "liberal" northern state. In November 2008, seven teenagers violently attacked two Latinos near a train station in suburban Patchogue on New York's Long Island. One of the Latinos, who worked at a local store, was stabbed and killed by one of the teenagers. According to the officials who prosecuted the case, this attack was just one of several criminal attacks on local Latinos, violent attacks this group called "Mexican hopping" or "beaner hopping," in a clear indication of racialized anti-Latino framing. In addition, one of the white leaders, who was convicted of this hate-crime killing and assaults on other Latinos, had a Nazi swastika tattoo on his body (Lewis, 2011). Over the past two decades, residents of this New York area, like residents of other suburban and urban areas, have heard numerous discussions by media commentators and public officials that are critical of the Latino immigrants who have moved to these areas to do some of the working-class or middle-class jobs that are available. Some of these public officials have passed laws to try to restrict such Latino migration to their areas (Feagin and Feagin, 2011: 227).

Clearly, *racialized social space* is an apt heuristic concept to analyze this extraordinarily important manifestation of racial domination. As we conceptualize it, the idea of racialized space captures the sense of proprietorship claimed by whites over a myriad of places, together with the discriminatory treatment that Latinos frequently receive when they enter an array of white-controlled places. One of our social science colleagues, on reading a draft of this book, gave us this account on white control of space from a few years back:

> Another example of hostility towards Spanish is when I was still an uneducated Latina at a park in our California community with my daughter and husband at the time and his family. They were all undocumented Mexicans except for me. We were having a picnic and listening to Mexican music, Spanish music. Some white man walked all the way across the lawn and told us to turn the music off. And we did. I remember watching him strutting back to his picnic area, which was quite a distance away, and we just all sat there in silence. It was so shameful. I felt so powerless.

Accounts like this not only demonstrate both the fear and the great pain frequently caused by white controllers of spaces but also show that this white-controlled racialized space is as large as US society.

There is no part of this society where people of color are fully in their own territory, not even in areas where they constitute almost all the population or where they hold some local political power. Communities of color are also in white space because whites ultimately control a great many important facets of life therein, from garbage collection to public school curricula and law enforcement. While the head of the garbage collection department may not be white, this usually has no effect on the convenience of the collection schedule for Latino residents, or how careful the garbage truck drivers are when they collect garbage in Latino areas. The principal of a high school in a Latino community may be a Latino or other person of color, but the important educational curricula, rules, and tactics even in that substantially Latino demographic space mostly come from white-crafted regulations and laws, as well as from white administrators higher up the decision-making chain. Thus, people of color may come to the dance, but whites own the dance hall.

# 4

# Operating Out of the White Frame: Latino Adaptation and Conformity

The white racial framing dominant in this society is important because it is an age-old *worldview* containing powerful pro-white and anti-others subframes. Over several centuries now, this very powerful white racial frame has provided the vantage point from which white Americans have understood and acted in shaping the development of this society. Because this framing is central in almost all white minds, it has become the most dominant racial framing over the centuries in the United States and across numerous other parts of the globe.

In this society all those who are not white are pressured by whites and white-dominated institutions to accept much of this white racial framing of society. One finds various forms of racial "common sense" among different US groups, but the age-old white racial frame has prevailed because whites have had the power and resources across major institutions to impose it on all US residents. To put it another way, this white racial frame is part of the general *hegemonic* common sense of this society. A hegemonic situation occurs when people of color consent in various ways to this white framing and associated racial common sense (Gramsci, 1971). This pressured acceptance varies considerably in degree. Some Latinos and other Americans of color enthusiastically accept and perpetuate significant elements of the dominant racial framing. Thus, we observed in Chapter 2 the anti-Spanish, anti-immigrant framing of Mauro Mujica, a Chilean American official who has asserted his version of the dominant white frame and heads a nativistic organization seeking to suppress Spanish and make English the official US language. Others among those racially subordinated are more reluctant and do not substantially succumb to at least some of this pressure to operate out of the white racial frame. Nonetheless, most are forced to more or less accept the general white hegemony in numerous areas as a matter of accommodation and adjustment to societal conditions much beyond their control.

The systemic character of white racism also stimulates those who are racially oppressed, whether or not they openly rebel, to develop an array of defensive and offensive reactions to racial barriers established by the dominant group. Thus, like other Americans, most Americans of color are "multiframers." That is to say, not only are they familiar with the white racial framing of society and periodically draw on understandings from that framing, but they also to varying degrees draw on their own home-culture framing or antiracist counter-framing in making sense out of their everyday racialized worlds.

## Latinos and the Dominant White Racial Frame

In this chapter we examine four forms of consent to the white racial framing that appear in our in-depth interviews with middle-class Latinos. Three of these mainly reference Latinos: acceptance of elements of the racial frame, active enactment of the racial frame, and symbolic or internalized violence. In these cases, the Latino interlocutors refer to members of their own racial group. The fourth use of elements of the dominant white framing differs in that it is directed by Latinos at African Americans.

Our interviews suggest that many Latinos, consciously or unwittingly, formulate their views on certain societal issues and events substantially from some version of the dominant white frame. Attempting to position themselves or their group closer to that white framing and associated folkways, some express anti-immigrant or antiblack attitudes. For example, they may openly empathize with a white person who flings a racist epithet at another Latino, attributing the white action to the frustration experienced by whites with a Latino whose command of English seems limited. Some echo the white frame by putting its tenets into action. For instance, one respondent actively chides another for acting "like a Mexican." Other researchers (Acuña, 1996; M. Chavez, 2011) have documented and discussed white-framed commentaries and actions among numerous Latinos and other people of color. For instance, adults in several Latino groups periodically make negative comments about a newborn's too-dark skin or downplay his or her obvious Indian or African ancestry. The Chicano historian Rodolfo Acuña has argued that such "internalization of the dominant society's racism by Mexicans and Latinos is irrational and produces a false consciousness." He has offered this collegiate example: "It is not uncommon for first-year Chicano university students to talk about reverse racism toward whites or express anti-immigrant sentiments" (Acuña, 1996: 8).

Significantly, this pattern of internalizing some or much of the dominant group framing and acquiescing in one's own oppression has been explored by neo-Marxist and feminist scholars (Gramsci, [1932] 1975; MacKinnon,

1989). They have probed how those oppressed often assist in reproducing op-pression by internalizing negative racial, class, or gender views of their own group, an internalizing that often leads to such problems as lower self-esteem and self-hatred. "Symbolic violence" is a useful term introduced by sociologist Pierre Bourdieu (1991: 167) that names the social violence that is "exercised upon a social agent with his or her complicity." Symbolic violence is another way to denote *internalized* oppression on the part of people of color. Examples include Americans of color who are racially profiled by a white police officer yet assert that if they had been in the officer's shoes they would have done the same thing. Indeed, they sometimes join the white establishment in victimizing people like themselves by dubbing themselves as evidently suspicious people.

Researchers studying the adaptive patterns of racialized Asian American groups have likewise found these patterns of internalized oppression (Pyke and Dang, 2003). Among Korean and Vietnamese immigrants, significant intra-ethnic stereotyping takes place between recent immigrants and earlier established immigrants and their children. The established subgroups periodi-cally use negative terms for recent immigrants like "FOB" ("fresh off boat") because of their more traditional ways of dressing, speaking, and socializing linked to their home-country cultures. These intragroup relationships, of course, take place substantially because the white-dominated culture and racial framing put constant pressure on immigrants of color to "assimilate" to that dominant culture and framing.

White oppressors benefit greatly from this intragroup reality in several ways. The individuals and their groups who are pressured to, and do substantially, adapt to white framing and folkways are less likely to resist more openly, such as in overt collective resistance like the 1960s black and Chicano civil rights movements. In addition, these adaptive responses by oppressed individuals are part of the everyday reality of US school, workplace, and political settings. Those who most forthrightly and extensively collude with powerful whites and the dominant white framing, especially some leaders in these subordinated groups, do much to buttress and perpetuate the oppressive societal settings. They are dangerous for yet other people of color because they are too enthusiastic about enforcing white control—often so they can improve their own position in the white-controlled system. Of course, many whites in power know how this process works and greatly encourage such actions, especially by leaders of these groups, to yet again strengthen and sustain the society's racial hierarchy.

## Latinos Defending Certain White Framing

Now we can look at some of these issues as they appear in our respondents' commentaries. In the following vignette from our interviews, a Cuban

American respondent is given a hypothetical account and asked to interpret what transpired. His response shows a classic example of agreement with the white frame. The Latino interviewer provided this vignette: "Two Hispanics are having a normal conversation speaking in Spanish in the local bank. One of the Anglo white customers as he walks by asks them if they have to talk so loud." In our vignette the white man then uses a racist epithet for Latinos. Asked what he thought had happened, our respondent replies in this manner:

> Right off the bat, I would have to say that the Anglo who was coming by the Hispanics—because Hispanics are pretty loud to begin with—I would say was just annoyed with the loudness, not necessarily with the language.

The respondent does not demur but goes along with the white customer's characterization of Latinos as very loud and, more importantly, ignores the racist epithet hurled at the Latinos in the story. Moreover, this respondent seems insensitive to the fact that the white man self-importantly breaks into a normal conversation between two other adults and treats them as if they were children. There were two instances of discrimination in this account, but the respondent did not note either of them, probably because his perception is affected by the white frame's conventional view of such a situation.

In another interview, a Latina respondent is presented with a hypothetical restaurant interaction:

> A white Anglo patron is ordering at a fast-food restaurant. The woman taking the order speaks English with a strong accent and the two have a little difficulty in communicating. When she is given her food, the white patron grabs it out of the restaurant worker's hand and stalks out muttering something about how "Spics should speak English."

Asked her reaction to this situation, she comments:

> I . . . work as [a] customer service person and I can appreciate how difficult it is to speak to somebody who has a strong accent, so . . . I can see why she would be impatient . . . [and] see how somebody would say that.

Again a respondent skips over the "spic" racist insult and exempts the white interlocutor from responsibility for her savage outburst. This respondent identifies with the white woman completely, asserting additionally that she has been in the white woman's position and experienced such frustration at her own group's accents. In absolving the white protagonist here, she is avoiding a critique of white agents of discrimination and blaming the only other person in the vignette interaction, the abused Latina worker.

In his interview, a Mexican American respondent relates the story of what happened to his sister while she was looking for an apartment:

> My sister graduated from [college and] . . . moved up to Colorado to work for a newspaper. . . . We went up there with her . . . and we tried to find her an apartment. And we called . . . an apartment [and] they said come on over, there's a vacancy here. But when we got there . . . they said no, there were no vacancies. . . . And my wife [who is white] went and talked to the landlord, and all of sudden there were vacancies there. . . . I just saw it . . . [as] a mistake. . . . They said there were vacancies but there wasn't, so I didn't really see it as prejudice.

Faced with likely discriminatory behavior, this Latino explicitly dismisses racial prejudice as a possible cause. It might seem that his interpretation was meant to protect his white wife's feelings. But she played a part in their investigation by asking the landlord if there were vacancies, and the landlord replied affirmatively. In spite of the evidence, he still gave the white landlord a rather significant benefit of the doubt.

Each of these responses to our interview vignettes illustrates social situations where Latinos identify with or give the benefit of the doubt to whites who have likely discriminated against Latinos. Their apparent submissive behavior is not extraordinary, for many Latinos and other people of color periodically view recurring racial events through the lens of some version of the widely circulated white racial frame and act accordingly.

## Enacting the White Racial Frame

Over the course of daily life, Latinos are sometimes substantial accomplices in reinforcing or implementing a white racial framing of a situation. Much of this conformity is unsurprising given the intensive pressures of the various white-normed environments that they must regularly traverse. Yet it does reinforce the continuing operation of the systemic racism that they also face. In this next example, a Mexican American student who works as a waiter in a restaurant gives a nuanced account of an incident involving his Mexican American manager:

> I was working at . . . a restaurant . . . owned by a Mexican American family. . . . I was talking to one of the chefs and it was getting kind of slow and . . . I had a sombrero and they [fellow workers] told me to put it on. So I put it on and I was walking away, ready to take it off, and a Mexican manager there told me to stop "acting like a spic and go check out that table." . . . *But you're telling me that he's Mexican American?* Yes. . . . *He obviously didn't think of himself as a "spic"?* No, because talking to him earlier before and among other people, he said he really wasn't Mexican, that he's "American" and his dad was born in Texas.

The racist epithet is hurled at the young waiter by his manager, a Mexican American who implicitly claims a white identity. The manager has in other contexts called himself "American," a term that he, like many other people, appears to use as a synonym for "white"—an identification practice right out of the dominant white frame. Notice that the manager did not say that he was white, only that he was American and not Mexican. Given the intensity of his reaction to the waiter, perhaps the latter's joking with the hat reminded the manager of an identity he wanted to disassociate himself with. Indeed, Latinos who insist that they are American may often just be saying to a larger audience that they are "not foreigners." By this insistence, however, they too are reinforcing certain anti-Latino biases and narratives of the white racial frame.

Interestingly, one female Mexican American respondent answers affirmatively when asked if Mexican Americans themselves mistreat newer Mexican immigrants:

> Yes, they do. . . . [If] a Mexican comes up to them [Mexican Americans] . . . and [speaks Spanish] . . . they're going to treat you differently. They start getting annoyed by it . . . and . . . start being rude toward you.

According to the experiences of numerous respondents, as demonstrated in Chapter 2, whites often react swiftly and disapprovingly when they hear Latino immigrants speak Spanish. This respondent notes that some Mexican Americans are similarly annoyed. It can be difficult to tell why some Latinos are vexed when other Latinos speak Spanish in their presence. Sometimes they do this because they are stating or following the tenet of "This is America, don't speak Spanish" in order to assert that their presence in the United States is justifiable and that they too are fully "American."

The nuances of this adaptation process are illustrated in the notes of the second author about an incident involving a friend:

> One of my friends from Cuba has a strong Spanish accent, and sometimes it is hard to understand her. She talks to her children in Spanish, although they speak to her in English. Once, her son stayed at a motel and complained to relatives that he couldn't understand the Latina clerk at the front desk because of *her* thick accent.

The young man's attitude is puzzling. His mother's English is strongly accented, yet this did not deter him from speaking derisively about the desk attendant's similarly accented speech. Indeed, among Cuban Americans, those who express this ethnocentric attitude are often called "Cubanos arrepentidos"—that is, Cubans who regret their origin.

Another respondent, a Mexican national who is also a documented resident of the United States, narrates an experience she had at the US-Mexico border:

I was crossing the border and I was by myself. And they [the border guards] told me to pull over. I got out of the car and they started taking everything out, inspecting everything. And I had to go use the restroom so bad; I had been holding it ever since I left town. And the white guy told me, yeah, go ahead and go. I was walking towards the restroom, I was inside the immigration office, and a Mexican American [guard] comes close and says, "Hey, hey where are you going? You can't go and use the restroom." And he makes me come back. I was about to walk into the restroom, he grabs me, and he makes me come back until they had finished inspecting the car, and then I could go. . . . *How much longer did it take?* About twenty-five minutes. . . . Yeah. I don't think I've ever been that upset before.

In this vignette the white border guard is more patient with the respondent than the Mexican American guard. Several of our respondents reported similar experiences with Mexican American border guards. In this and other such incidents, Mexican American guards apparently set out to be very strict with those who are Mexican. One can only speculate about the motivation behind these guards' harsh behavior, but it may be an effort to distance themselves from Mexican nationals in the eyes of the white guards or their often white superiors. Yet again, whatever the motivation, the dominant negative framing of Mexicans in the white racial frame is thereby reinforced.

In the following interview excerpt, another Mexican national, who was asked how he views his racial identity, responds by ignoring that question and instead giving this reply:

A lot of times discrimination comes from your own race. Sometimes it comes from whites, but it is from Mexican Americans that I have felt discrimination the majority of the time.

Although the interviewer's question was about the respondent's self-identity, the respondent is reminded of what he sees as a significant source of his everyday discrimination—Mexican Americans. He does not spell out what form this discrimination takes, but it is clear that he is disappointed and that he expects better treatment from what he views as his own group. Unfortunately, numerous members of the previous respondent's larger community periodically act as important conduits of white racism, perhaps in self-defense against possible white barriers they themselves fear they will face.

Indeed, other research suggests the kind of serious intragroup tensions that develop within Mexican American communities because of such acceptance of elements of the white anti-Latino subframe by one segment of the community. One study of a large number of undocumented Mexican farmworkers found that they were distrustful not only of whites but also of local Mexican Americans (Chavez, Wampler, and Burkhart, 2006). One likely reason is the attempts of many Mexican Americans to distance themselves from the group of Mexicans that whites often attack and derogate in their dominant racial framing—the undocumented. A related reason is that Mexican American subcontractors who work for white owners in agriculture and construction are often those with whom undocumented Mexican workers must deal on a daily basis as their employers (Molina, 2012). These subcontractors are sometimes reported by undocumented Mexican workers as stereotyping them and being unfair in wages, which creates significant tensions within the larger community. As researcher Hilario Molina (2012: n.p.) has argued, in these cases the "elite white male remains unseen but active in racializing the social and structural activities."

The portions of the interviews we analyzed above thus show instances in which Mexican Americans sometimes enforce the dominant white frame on other Latinos, sometimes with greater vigor than white antagonists. This odium is particularly keen when directed at Mexican nationals, those who evoke the common suspicion of being "illegals." The conventional white racial framing of Latinos is despicable but efficient: It makes some of the persecuted Latinos into instruments of further persecution. Not surprisingly, many whites are not only aware of this intragroup impact but encourage the thinking or actions that bring it about.

Our findings in this regard are not unique. As noted previously, several other research studies have shown how white racial hostility and discrimination directed against new immigrants from Latin America and Asia have periodically affected how the older, more established generations in these groups sometimes negatively view these more recent immigrants (Pyke and Dang, 2003; Saito, 1998; D. Gutierrez, 1995). Thus, the white hostility and discrimination have caused some native-born Latinos to articulate harsh white-framed resentment toward immigrants from Latin America, especially those who are working class or undocumented. It is likely that such intragroup divisions among Latinos make it harder to create significant Latino coalitions to fight the general problem of white racial discrimination confronted by all communities of those oppressed.

### More Internalized Oppression in Everyday Life

Recall that "symbolic violence" involves the social violence that a people suffer from their oppressors with their own complicity. In the next interview account, a Cuban American reports a very good example of this internalized oppression. He was singled out for adverse treatment by a border official at the US-Mexico border:

> We were . . . coming over at midnight on a ferry from Canada to the United States. I think, we had our passports. . . . So we show them [to border guards] . . . our passports, and this guy looked at them and said, "Oh, Miami passport Agency; so where do you guys live?" We said, "Miami." "So what do you do?" "I'm a banker and . . . the other guy is an optician." So they said move over, and they went and searched our car. Personally I thought that they thought we were bringing in drugs. Not that we were discriminated against because we were Hispanic. I thought it was because they thought we were bringing in drugs. . . . If I'm that border patrol guard, I see two guys with a Colorado license plate on a [rental] car coming in the middle of the night from Canada into the United States and they happened to be Hispanics from Miami, I'm thinking drugs.

The respondent knew that he was profiled because he is Latino, yet he explicitly insists that being searched was not an act of discrimination but a reasonable choice on the part of the border guard. Indeed, he actually seems to want to validate the white officer's discriminatory actions. He even asserts that if he had been in the officer's shoes, he would have been equally suspicious because they were Cubans from Miami. Chances are that his own racialized image will cause similar situations with whites and others in the future. No matter how he thinks of himself, he cannot stop being viewed by some whites as a Latino from a drug-infested area. Even though he's a certified financial adviser with a high income and has navigated the white-controlled economy well, he is still very vulnerable to being racially stereotyped and framed as being a person of color involved in the international drug trade.

When asked if she has observed whites stereotype Latinos as lazy, unintelligent, or undesirable, a Puerto Rican respondent reacts in this manner:

> Some Latinos are lazy for all the wrong reasons. They're being paid to be lazy. Welfare also does that. . . . If a person is not motivated to get educated, they won't get out of the rut to higher up in the line. And unfortunately that's just what a lot of people do. They just stay there. They like that comfort . . . sitting at home, watching soap operas.

This Latina's answer completely skips the query about whites' negative framing of Latinos, and she herself begins to voice the common, mostly white-generated racial stereotypes. Her derision of lower-income Latinos is built on the old white-framed fantasy accusing people of color of enjoying the comfort of welfare and television soap operas instead of extricating themselves out of their rut with educational or work efforts.

The following segment comes from an interesting interview with a Puerto Rican respondent. The question we asked taps her own economic and social situation, but she quickly moves to the topic of public assistance. Asked how she sees her situation in comparison with that of her parents, she responds in this distinctive way:

> I think it's a whole lot better. *Ok. What was your parents' economic situation?* Very bad. We lived on welfare. . . . I think my economic situation is about 300% better than theirs was. I have more things. I don't live on welfare. I never lived on welfare! I never intend to live on welfare!

It would seem that the respondent carries inside a feeling of shame for her parents' dependence on welfare. It appears too that she has internalized the stereotype and related narrative of the lazy Latino living on the dole and proclaims that she will never be in that situation. She may have experienced scorn as a younger member of a family on welfare and thus may want to avoid the pain of that often white-generated framing of poor Americans of color.

In the following account, a Puerto Rican respondent explains why she would not call her Mexican American husband a "Chicano":

> *You wouldn't call your husband a Chicano?* No, I would not. He doesn't behave that way. *Ok, so Chicano is somebody that behaves a certain way?* It's a different class and they treat people differently. They're more Americanized. . . . They're not into the culture as much. . . . I wouldn't raise my kid as a Chicano, because I do not think it's right. . . . They ride low-rider cars. . . . And they speak with slang like they're dragging their tongues. They're not that educated. They don't care what they look like.

This woman's pointed answer is loaded with certain racial stereotypes, imagery, and narratives targeting working-class Mexican Americans ("Chicanos" for her). She expresses disapproval of Chicanos by attributing to them pejorative traits that in her view have subcultural origins: uninvolved in important mainstream Latino traditions, uneducated, and speaking Spanish "slang." This is a rare instance in our interviews where a Latino respondent expresses such stereotypical white-frame condemnation of other Latinos in terms of strong in-group invectives. Whatever the medium, the same stereotyped message is delivered: Certain working-class Mexican Americans ("Chicanos") are too socially different and are thus defective.

The following interlocutor, a Mexican American, relates how members of his town's older generations judge the professional competence of Latino professionals:

> The older generation is into, like, this self-hatred. *Who do they hate?* Other Hispanics. This is the older generation who think that Hispanics are not good

enough as whites, and they don't want to see a Hispanic doctor or . . . a Hispanic lawyer. *Do you think that that's widespread?* I don't know if it is widespread or not, but I've seen it in my own home town: the older generation who doesn't want to go see a Hispanic doctor or dentist.

The discriminatory experiences of the older generation extend back to the time when a great many whites openly flaunted anti-Latino framing, mistreated Latinos with impunity, and brazenly limited their ability to pursue an adequate education, much less professional degrees. Mexican Americans, the white frame commonly held, were intellectually incapable of getting an advanced education. Their proper place was as manual laborers, such as those picking fruit and vegetables, or house maids. Although it is not possible to assess with certainty, it seems that these older Latinos were exposed to harsh anti-Latino elements of the white racial frame for so long that it has been difficult for them to think outside of it, as here in regard to Latino competency issues (see J. Gutiérrez, 2001).

The interview selections in this section generally reflect numerous respondents' internalization of significant elements of the dominant racial framing of both whites and Latinos. This symbolic violence manifests itself in a variety of ways, but the message is invariant: Latinos are defective in some key respects, and certain white views or folkways remain examples of white superiority that should be emulated.

Note too the issue of some Latinos choosing a personal identity that is "white" in the US sense. Recall from our discussion in Chapter 1 of a few surveys of US Latinos that revealed that a significant minority identify themselves as "white" when given a broad array of identity options. All Latinos, including recent immigrants, come to understand that being viewed by US whites as "not white" has serious negative consequences in this society. Similar to the responses of other Americans of color to this white-controlled society (see Chou and Feagin, 2008), some have responded with an "ethnic persona" strategy by means of which they seek to reduce white hostility by moving as far away as they can from being considered (especially by whites) as nonwhites like blacks or Indians. Indeed, in our interviews some respondents suppress viewing themselves and their communities as racially categorized and subordinated by emphasizing an "American" identity or a white-Hispanic ethnicity and cultural orientation. Some also play down the reality of anti-Latino racism. They seem to assume that such strategies will enable them to better operate in, or integrate into, important white-run institutions (Feagin, 2013; Gayle, 2007).

In important public settings, many Latinos try to speak or act in a way that conforms to what they think typical whites do. Such a strategy can periodically be successful in pleasing whites and thereby reduce some of the white hostility that typically goes with being assigned to lower rungs on the

US racial hierarchy. However, efforts to conform eagerly to white framing and folkways in order to please whites often do not work—or they are forestalled by the discriminatory conditions of the moment. For example, there is the proverbial case of a person of color being stopped by a white police officer in a secluded area at 2 a.m. when no one else is around. Most who are clearly identified as Mexican or black by the officer would think twice before insisting they are *not* what the officer identifies them as in such an isolated and racially hierarchical setting. Such situations make evident the point we have made before about the recurring imposition of racialized identities by whites with the *power* to do so.

Notice too that the US situation in regard to whiteness choices generally contrasts with racial identity choices in much of Latin America and the Caribbean. In numerous countries in those geographical areas, a person with both significant European ancestry and significant non-European ancestry can successfully assert a "white" (blanco) identity that would not be accepted as such by most European Americans in the United States. Given this home-country reality, many immigrants from Latin America who have significant European ancestry, even those who also have some non-European ancestry, often assert that they are "white" in US settings, and not just because they are trying to please US whites. As we noted in Chapter 1, they are simply identifying themselves as their families have for generations. Yet they are often surprised when this self-chosen white (blanco) identity is *not* accepted and is derided by native-born European Americans, especially those with significant power over them.

The societal power of European Americans frequently includes a conviction that virtually all people of Latin American ancestry are nonwhite, even though there is a great range of ancestry for Latin Americans. Despite how Latinos view themselves, European Americans commonly disregard that self-identity choice, and the white racialization and denigration of Latinos rules the day.

### Whitewashed Latino Views of African Americans

Along with Latinos, African Americans have a long history of racialized oppression. The dominant white racial frame has a major subframe that is full of negative and emotion-laden stereotypes, imagery, and narratives about African Americans that justify their centuries-old exploitation and often limited access to advancement in white-controlled institutions. When African Americans seek redress for this white racism, they are frequently accused of "playing the race card," depending too heavily on the federal government's help, or doing little themselves about their deprived socioeconomic situation.

Ironically, whites have long "played the race card" (a phrase created by whites to stereotype assertive black Americans) and over the centuries have secured the lion's share of federal government "affirmative action" programs providing racial emoluments and helping millions of white families into the comfortable middle class (see Katznelson, 2005; Feagin, 2010).

Unquestionably, antiblack messages from the centuries-old white frame are still widely and routinely disseminated in blatant and subtle ways, and it is impossible to live in the United States for long without being exposed to most of them. As a result, some Latinos in our sample periodically draw from this antiblack subframe of the dominant white frame to formulate their negative perceptions of African Americans. Indeed, many immigrants from Latin America, Asia, and other areas come into the United States with racially framed, negative views of African Americans, which they have picked up from the negative framing long present in their own country or from worldwide dissemination of antiblack framing by US movies and other US media over more than a century (Hsia, 1994). Indeed, one Latino scholar commented to us: "I have traveled to Guatemala and have seen theaters showing the same violent, racist movies we show here. When I asked one migrant in Houston why some migrants have antiblack attitudes, he responded that they first learn about blacks from U.S. movies" (N. Rodriguez, 1996). Clearly, the US media frequently provide premigration socialization into the US version of the white racial frame. Once they migrate, migrants' antiblack views are then reinforced by the antiblack framing commonplace throughout US society.

In the following excerpts, some middle-class respondents agree with the widely promoted white-framed belief that African Americans lack self-reliance and often expect others to fix their problems for them. The first respondent, a Mexican American, strongly admonishes black Americans. When asked what she thinks of the problems faced by them, she reacts in this stereotyped manner:

> I look at the [American] Indians and look at how much the government has helped them, and it really hasn't helped them. . . . And I think that the same thing with blacks; they keep getting all this help . . . and they're not going to advance as much. . . . Stop saying "give me, give me, give me," instead of "let's do, do, do."

Echoing a familiar theme, this respondent relies on very common white-framed stereotypes and associated narratives that blame African Americans for relying on the government dole instead of just helping themselves. To depend on government is futile, she avers, and she brings up Native Americans as another example of a group that has also relied on the government and as a result has not been successful.

The issue arises here as to the major culprits in the travails of Native Americans and African Americans. When modest or superficial government help is provided with no links to fully desegregating the US economy and political structure, such state assistance will ultimately prove futile. Indeed, it has been the mostly white-run government agencies that are responsible for support program failures, not usually those thus assisted. However, given the firm hold on many minds of the powerful white racial frame, it is difficult not to succumb to its age-old negative views of black Americans.

In the next vignette, the interlocutor, a Puerto Rican, again goes along with negative white-framed notions about African Americans. Asked how she views black Americans and their problems, she replies in a fashion similar to several others:

> I think that they do go through a lot of tough times. . . . I also think that some of them play off of that. I think they use that as an excuse sometimes. *An excuse for what?* To, to get out of problems or to, you know, complain.

In spite of her initial sympathy toward African Americans, this woman criticizes them in a standard, racially framed way. Notice the vagueness of her answer when the interviewer probes and asks her the purpose of African Americans' putative "excuse." Like others' claims, her condemnation of African Americans seems more than just verbal, but somewhat visceral.

One Puerto Rican respondent presented a more extensive and nuanced picture of the negative information he had gleaned from the mainstream media. When asked his view of African American problems, he provided this answer:

> I think they definitely do have some problems, and they are legitimate ones. But I also think that sometimes they over-squeak the wheel. They exaggerate the extent of their problems . . . because they use it as a tool to get things that otherwise wouldn't be coming their way to the same degree. *What kinds of things?* Well now we are talking about reparations for slavery. Well yeah, the Japanese got some reparations, things like that, but, come on, you know you gotta get over it. And you gotta move on. And I think they should, and again I am talking in general terms. I think that in a lot of instances you hear about the black family unit missing the father, for example. A lot of [the] time, you know, the inner-city schools are really poor, they are not good, not up to quality. . . . If their leadership would focus more on the quality of public schools and education within their inner cities, which are the blacks that are having the most problems . . . within a generation or two their problems would be much less.

Even this respondent, who seems at the beginning of his answer to be sympathetic to the African Americans' discriminatory plight, reiterates a familiar theme: Instead of solving their own problems, African Americans have been playing up their difficulties in order to get things. He reveals an awareness of the fact that some black Americans have in recent years raised issues of reparations for the long centuries of slavery that their ancestors endured. Like many whites, however, he has rejected that idea with the "get over it" response that he probably has heard white commentators articulate many times in the mainstream media (see Feagin, 2004).

When we replied to his comment with, "In other words, blacks have to help themselves a little bit?" he responded, "Correct," and further amplified the negative imagery and narratives of black families he had gleaned from the mainstream media. He links that stereotyped framing to the opportunity rhetoric central to much of the commonplace white framing of several subordinated groups in this society:

> If it's true what they say you hear in the media about black fathers missing in the family and all that stuff, then they need to get their act together there and then. Have a close family unit. Make sure their kids get educated and live. And the opportunity in this country is there. I mean, if you have the skills, I'm not saying you are not going to run into some problems, but by and large you are going to do reasonably well. You might run into racism here or there, but a skill is a skill and it's needed and you are going to get paid for it and that is probably the straightest act to solving your problems.

This interviewee seems unduly optimistic but more balanced than some other respondents in his sermonizing to black Americans about what their families need to be doing for societal success, for he recognizes the realities of racism "here or there." Yet he too has accepted uncritically the common white framing of US society as mostly providing great opportunities for people of color.

One Cuban American respondent was presented with the vignette portraying the hypothetical incident at the restaurant discussed earlier. Asked about a white patron ordering food who stalks out muttering "spics," he offers this pointed assessment:

> Only ignorant people react that way. I guarantee you that if it would have been a black kid that would have been speaking Ebonics, nothing would have been made out of it because everybody is so concerned about offending blacks. People here in the United States don't care about hurting our [Latinos'] feelings, but man they go out of their way backward not to offend a black person. You know, Jimmy the Greek lost his job because he said something that most

people believe is true, [that] blacks were bred to become stronger when they were slaves. . . . The other day Dusty Baker made a [similar] comment. Nothing came of it. . . . He would have been fired if he had been a white person.

In his evaluation of the incident and the anti-Latino epithet, this man quickly turned his attention to the unrelated topic of African Americans' supposed preferential treatment—a topic he was not asked about.

This interlocutor brings up widely commented upon incidents in which two public sports figures made comments about the physical abilities of black athletes. These involved the white television commentator Jimmy "the Greek" Snyder and the black baseball manager Dusty Baker. The respondent clearly disapproved of the "favoritism" that Dusty Baker had supposedly received at the hands of those with authority over him. Jimmy Snyder was fired by the CBS network for reportedly saying in 1988 that "the black is a better athlete to begin with because he's been bred to be that way, because of his high thighs," and continued with more biological-racial commentary along these lines (ESPN, 2009). Dusty Baker, years later in 2003, made less inflammatory but still stereotyped comments about black and Hispanic baseball players being "better suited to playing in the sun and heat than white players" because of their darker skin color (C. Johnson, 2003). Snyder was fired, while Baker was not so strongly disciplined.

In our view, the issue raised here is not as simple as that presented by this respondent—a racial contrast he had likely heard about from white and other commentators in the sports media. Dan Rather, a prominent CBS evening news anchor for years, at the time interpreted Jimmy Snyder's firing as a corporate decision that in a "crass business sense was an easy call." Rather went on to say that "networks don't like controversy, particularly controversy that involves race" (Goodwin, 1988). Baker's less flamboyant racial comment did not endanger corporate profits, the likely major reason for the differential responses to the incidents.

## Conclusion

We have previously discussed some popular and scholarly analysts of the situations of Latino immigrants who assess the immigrants and their descendants' paths toward various types of societal assimilation. In recent years we have heard frequent demands on the part of white and Latino analysts for these immigrants and their children to conform and assimilate in one-way fashion to the dominant white Anglo norms and folkways of US society. However, this sense of urgency that Latinos must assimilate and join the mainstream of US society is a call, however unwitting, for Latinos to learn their subordinated "place" in society. This typically includes learning to internalize certain essential aspects of this ongoing racial oppression.

The white-controlled racial system, including the dominant white framing, today has tremendous pressuring resources at its disposal in the form of most mass media, most educational curricula, and important political and economic positions, especially at the top echelons of this society. Whites with substantial media, socioeconomic, and political resources regularly transmit subtle and overt messages of racial imaging and interpretation of Latinos as, among other things, lazy, loud, criminal, deviant, and overly familistic. Such negative stereotypes, images, and associated narratives of Latinos seriously handicap them as they try to adapt and survive in the dominant institutions of US society. They often, as in this chapter, internalize some aspects of an anti-Latino framing. Symbolic violence, the violence "exercised upon a social agent with his or her complicity," is evident throughout the commentaries in this chapter.

In addition, yet other elements of the dominant white frame, such as those from the antiblack subframe, are pressed on Latinos from numerous white-controlled and other sources, and they have deleterious effects. As we suggested above, sometimes the US version of the antiblack frame reinforces the antiblack framing already embedded in the home-country culture of Latino immigrants, either from long contact with European-origin racist framing or from more recent racist imagery gleaned from the globalizing US mass media. Such antiblack framing expresses itself in various ways beyond those we examined previously. For example, in recent discussions with us, a Latina professor recounted that she once heard a Mexican American student say that when his parents found out that he was dating a black woman, apparently fearing he might marry her and have children, they admonished him in Spanish: "Tenemos que mejorar la raza." This Spanish saying signals the parents' strong concern that he not marry a black woman but instead marry to "better the race"—that is, in the direction of lightening the skin color, the overall phenotype of the family, and by implication people of Mexican descent.

Not surprisingly, the negative messages sent out by the omnipresent white racial frame about Americans of color easily penetrate Latino neighborhoods and communities, with noxious consequences for those thus targeted. One devastating consequence is to make intergroup coalitions against white racism much more difficult. Philosopher Ronald Sundstrom (2008: Kindle loc. 108–111) has argued that the growing demographic importance of people of color in the United States should be viewed by somewhat newer groups of Americans of color, such as Latinos,

> in a manner that does not support color-based racisms, or reverse progress on vital civil rights issues for African Americans and sovereignty claims for Native Americans. The groups that make up the browning of America have before

them a moral and political decision of national importance. They can seriously embrace anti-racism, or they can fail in their moral obligations.

We agree with Sundstrom that the groups of color, such as Latino and Asian Americans, that are fueling much of the demographic growth of Americans of color today must not operate out of the old antiblack and anti-Indian framing too easily picked up from the still-dominant white frame if they are to be an effective part of critical antiracism efforts, including important antiracist coalitions of Americans of color.

# 5

# Affirmative Action Programs: Latino Opposition and Support

The restriction of Mexican Americans and other Latinos to less desirable jobs and an extremely subordinated racial status in US society was a taken-for-granted state of affairs for the better part of US history. Under pressures from civil rights organizations and protests, a series of equal opportunity government measures that began to address these and other such racial injustices emerged during and after World War II. These efforts gradually evolved into what in the 1960s came to be termed "affirmative action." This official phrase originally meant just "positive action" by government agencies to reduce or end discrimination against Americans of color, but for several reasons it has come to mean much that is negative in its racialized framing by white Americans.

We begin here with a brief history of the public and private affirmative action programs created mostly by whites in authority, programs that appeared to aim at reducing or ending racial discrimination in various institutional spheres of society. This history reveals a lot about the highly racialized character of US society, today as in the past, and sets the background for understanding our respondents' diverse reactions to such programs.

## The Political Origins of Affirmative Action

Positive government action against racial discrimination began with executive orders issued by President Franklin Roosevelt during World War II. Responding to intensive pressure from African American civil rights leaders—and especially from A. Philip Randolph, then head of the Brotherhood of Sleeping Car Porters—in the 1940s, Roosevelt issued Executive Order 8802. This important order officially proscribed employment discrimination based on race, color, creed, and national origin in the US defense-related industries of World War II:

> As a prerequisite to the successful conduct of our national defense production effort, I do hereby reaffirm the policy of the United States that there shall be no discrimination in the employment of workers in defense industries or government because of race, creed, color, or national origin, and I do hereby declare that it is the duty of employers and of labor organizations, in furtherance of said policy and of this Order, to provide for the full and equitable participation of all workers in defense industries, without discrimination because of race, creed, color, or national origin. (Roosevelt, 1941)

Roosevelt added to these positive-action provisions of Executive Order 8802 by issuing Executive Order 9346 in 1943, which created the Committee on Fair Employment Practices and extended the nondiscrimination policy to "all departments and agencies of the government of the United States concerned with vocational and training programs for war production" (Roosevelt, 1943).

Not surprisingly, given this society's systemic racism, during and after World War II substantial majorities of whites in southern and border states, and countless whites in other regions, vigorously rejected government attempts to modestly remedy certain aspects of legal segregation in employment and education. At least since the Reconstruction era after the Civil War, white representatives in Congress, most of them from the southern states, had long been stalwart opponents of remedial actions for black oppression, even action in nascent forms. Their opposition in Congress and elsewhere in federal, state, and local governments had been very effective. Decade after decade, these white segregationists feared that other white federal officials would interfere with the white South's extensive system of Jim Crow segregation. From the 1930s to the 1960s they made a series of political deals that denied or restricted African American access to the numerous New Deal and subsequent social support programs and usually put their benefits very disproportionately in white pockets. As Katznelson puts it (2005: 23):

> Affirmative Action was then white. New national policies enacted in the pre-civil rights, last gasp era of Jim Crow constituted a massive transfer of quite specific privileges to white Americans. New programs produced economic and social opportunity for favored constituencies and thus widened the gap between white and black Americans in the aftermath of the Second World War.

Gradually, and hesitatingly, some government action against discrimination again emerged in the 1960s. A major reason, of course, was the growing number of black, Latino, and other civil rights protest movements of the

1950s and 1960s. In 1961, John F. Kennedy, another Democratic president, issued his momentous Executive Order 10925, which recognized that simply banning discrimination in the growing number of federal government contracts would not achieve equal opportunity for members of racialized groups. This important presidential order, the first to actually use the phrase "affirmative action," specified that government contractors had to be actively involved in the elimination of racial inequities in their federally linked businesses:

> Discrimination because of race, creed, color, or national origin is contrary to the Constitutional principles and policies of the United States. . . . The contractor will take affirmative action to ensure that applicants are employed, and that employees are treated during employment, without regard to their race, creed, color, or national origin. (Kennedy, 1961)

Kennedy's successor as president, Lyndon Johnson, greatly extended the scope of affirmative action by signing Executive Order 11246 in 1965. It added to the provisions of Kennedy's executive order the stipulation that federal contractors must practice "affirmative action" not only in government contracts but also in "all aspects of their employment" (Johnson, 1965a). Before issuing this executive order, Johnson had delivered a pathbreaking commencement address at Howard University in the summer of 1965. Therein he stated that it was unreasonable to expect black individuals who had not had access to real equality of opportunity before to venture into an unfamiliar economic world and soon succeed:

> You do not take a person who, for years, has been hobbled by chains and liberate him, bring him up to the starting line of a race and then say, "you are free to compete with all the others," and still justly believe that you have been completely fair. (Johnson, 1965b)

Influenced by advisers who had in mind an institutional approach to antiblack racism, Johnson went on to say that significant new institutional measures were needed to help black Americans strive for social and economic justice, including government job programs, housing programs, and programs to strengthen the family. Johnson's recognition that long-oppressed African Americans needed significant government help ran contrary to the deeply embedded axiom in US culture that economic success is strictly an individual achievement. Just as important was the fact that Johnson's statement contradicted the dominant racial frame's conception of African Americans as irresponsible and shiftless, and thus mostly responsible for their own economic fate (Oppenheimer, 1996; Feagin, 2012).

## White Opposition to Discrimination Remedies

Not surprisingly, given the past history of white resistance to racial change, these executive orders and other equal opportunity measures implemented or begun in the 1960s to remedy discrimination, especially those termed "affirmative action," elicited heated disputes and continuing pushback from a great many whites operating substantially out of the old racial framing of white superiority and nonwhite inferiority. Intensive white resistance to anything termed "affirmative action" has persisted now for several decades. Proponents have maintained that affirmative government action is necessary to rectify ongoing discrimination and racial injustices lingering from the highly inegalitarian US past. Opponents, on the other hand, have countered that this positive government action is unnecessary and has created unjust "quotas" that constitute "reverse discrimination" and "reverse racism"—the latter two phrases white-created terms designed to counter antidiscrimination efforts and preserve the racial status quo (Pincus, 2003). Notwithstanding their major differences, both proponents and opponents have regularly presented their positions using some equal opportunity discourse. For example, many a white person has insisted, "I am not a racist," "I don't see race," and "Why don't black people just get over slavery?" Using this type of rhetoric, many white Americans have insisted that we now live in a "post-racial society" and do not need affirmative action to end racial discrimination (Bonilla-Silva, 2006; Bush, 2004).

This "colorblind" discourse is a relatively new feature in the white racial framing that has accompanied the strong white pushback against affirmative action. Nonetheless, much in the white-resistance framing has not changed over the last century, because most whites have *never* supported major government action to fully eliminate the racial oppression and institutionalized inequality faced by Americans of color—not before, not during, and not after the 1960s civil rights movements (Bonilla-Silva, 2006; Feagin, 2012).

Such resistance has periodically come from the more conservative white political officials at or near the top of this society. Considering recent presidents, Ronald Reagan was a leading *opponent* of positive government action to end discrimination. He tended to operate, often rather openly, out of a strongly pro-white and antiblack framing of society. As a contender for the 1976 Republican presidential nomination, Reagan went so far as to propose a constitutional amendment that would end significant government affirmative action. Part of his white-oriented argument was that the government supposedly promoted discrimination against whites when it instituted numerical goals and timetables in hiring requirements for previously discriminatory employers doing business with the government. To back up his often specious claims, Reagan periodically narrated fanciful racist anecdotes in his speeches (Krugman, 2007). In one of his only modestly disguised racist stories, he related the great frustration supposedly experienced by certain hardworking men: "How upset workers must be to see an able-bodied man using food stamps at the grocery store." Knowing his general racial outlook and prior racist actions (Feagin, 2012: 93–108), we can assume that Reagan had in mind whites as the upset workers and blacks as the able-bodied men using food stamps. Another story that he used repeatedly was a thinly disguised attack on black women who supposedly lived on the government dole and cheated on social welfare programs. They were personified in his numerous speeches as a mythical black "welfare queen" whose success at exploiting public assistance knew no bounds:

> There's a woman in Chicago. . . . She has 80 names, 30 addresses, 12 Social Security cards. . . . She's got Medicaid, getting food stamps and she is collecting welfare under each of her names. Her tax-free cash income alone is over $150,000. (Rosenthal, 1989: B1)

Although crude and right out of the old white racist framing of black Americans, Reagan's phony anecdotes were effective in gaining or maintaining political support among many whites because they featured tried and true antiblack stereotypes and racialized narratives from the dominant racist framing still firmly held by many of his white followers.

Civil rights leaders were another of Reagan's racialized targets, as they have long been for many whites whose racial framing against change has needed such targets. He openly questioned civil rights leaders' integrity in a 1989 television interview in which he opined that some major civil rights leaders had overplayed the degree of racism and victimization to maintain their influence in their communities: "Sometimes I wonder if they really want what they say they want. Because some of those leaders are doing very well leading organizations based on keeping alive the feeling that they're victims of prejudice" (Rosenthal, 1989: B1).

Beyond Reagan's racialized rhetoric, his 1980s presidential administration played a central role in facilitating or accelerating the large-scale white conservative resurgence of recent decades. The Reagan political and administrative team often utilized and inspired much far-right social and political thinking and led a major right turn in the contemporary political era. They worked to weaken or eliminate numerous federal government programs aimed at reducing racial discrimination and, more generally, racial and class inequalities. Moreover, much of the Reagan era's attack on civil rights and other progressive domestic policies of the previous Democratic presidential administrations has persisted in various forms over recent decades—often as white-framed inspirations or procedural templates for implementing similarly restrictive efforts in conservative Republican administrations (George H. W. Bush and George W. Bush) and in Republican-controlled congresses since Reagan's terms as US president (Feagin, 2012: 93–168).

## Legal Assaults on Affirmative Action against Discrimination

Most of the organizational, legislative, and legal opposition to antidiscrimination programs of affirmative action has come, not surprisingly, from whites who have resisted most major changes in society's racial inequalities that, as a rule, have greatly favored whites. Early in this routinely white-framed pushback against the usually modest affirmative action programs to desegregate certain societal institutions were ideological attacks accenting aforementioned notions like "reverse discrimination" and "reverse racism," terms coined or accented by white conservatives in the 1970s (for example, Glazer, 1975) even before most significant affirmative action programs had been put in place. These attacks signaled that such opponents were operating out of a strong white racial framing, many elements of which date back well before the 1960s–1970s era of change in Jim Crow segregation.

A common white-framed charge made by opponents of affirmative action, from the Richard Nixon era of the late 1960s to the present, is that such programs discriminate against a great many deserving whites. This concept has formed the foundation of a series of political speeches by white politicians and a series of lawsuits filed by numerous white plaintiffs. For example, in the mid-1990s, then senator Bob Dole, the Republican presidential candidate, made some comments on *Meet the Press* that he was concerned about "displaced" white men who had to compete with black workers because of affirmative action. According to Dole, "people in America" (he meant "whites") should not be paying a price for discrimination that occurred "before they were born." Briefly acknowledging past discrimination, Dole (1995) added that he was not sure compensation for past discrimination was due from deserving whites today.

Many of the anti-affirmative-action efforts in the courts by white plaintiffs have targeted the more or less voluntary affirmative action programs developed by college and university administrators, most of them also white. For example, during the 1970s, one critical Supreme Court ruling on university affirmative action was the *Regents of the University of California v. Bakke* (1978) case. Allan Bakke, an older white male, applied for admission to the University of California (Davis) medical school but was turned down. One hundred places were available for new students, and sixteen were set aside for disadvantaged students. Most of those admitted under the latter program were students of color. Bakke claimed that the university screened him out of that disadvantaged group on the basis of his racial characteristics. The Supreme Court ruled that "race" could be considered to some degree in the selection for admission among well-qualified students, but it ruled against the particular practice followed by the Davis medical school that reserved seats for disadvantaged students. Bakke was thus admitted.

Some years later in 2003, another major university affirmative action lawsuit, *Grutter v. Bollinger* (2003), reached the Supreme Court. Again, a white plaintiff in the case claimed that she had been denied admission to the University of Michigan law school because its admission policies gave applicants of color a greater chance of being accepted than equally qualified whites. The university vigorously defended its use of a rather limited form of affirmative action as a lawful component of its mission to provide educational opportunity and intergroup experiences to a diverse student population. Significantly, in *Grutter v. Bollinger* (2003) the Supreme Court majority said it was constitutionally permissible for a law school to use student applicants' racial characteristics as one factor among several in admissions to increase diversity, including increasing the presence of "underrepresented minority groups." The author of the majority opinion, Justice Sandra Day O'Connor, suggested out of her optimistic white framing of these issues that government antidiscrimination efforts in higher education would not be needed twenty-five years in the future—a view contested only by liberal justices in the court majority.

More recently, two 2007 Supreme Court decisions knocked down voluntary affirmative action plans for the Seattle and Louisville public schools, thereby suggesting that Justice O'Connor's time estimate was wrong and that the court's more conservative majority sought an even faster move away from government affirmative action to remedy racial segregation in education (Feagin, 2010: 174–177). One recent Supreme Court case is crucial for the future of affirmative action in education. Abigail Fisher, a white Texas student, filed a lawsuit against the University of Texas, *Fisher vs. University of Texas at Austin* (2013), because she was denied admission to the law school on the basis of a formula using racial characteristics as a modest part of complex criteria for admission to diversify the university. Operating out of a version of the white frame, she and her lawyers contended that even this modest use of racial characteristics to remedy massive past discrimination violates the equal protection clause of the Fourteenth Amendment—which, ironically, was originally intended to knock down antiblack discrimination. Her case was decided in June 2013 by the Supreme Court, which argued that the district and appellate courts had not applied "strict scrutiny" to the university's admissions plan and sent the case back for "further proceedings" of that type.

We do not have the space to critically assess the many white-framed critiques of affirmative government action to end discrimination, but we can note a few points of relevance. Much opposition to remedial action in educational institutions on the high court and elsewhere holds to a white-conservative framing of affirmative action that is unsupported by empirical evidence. For example, contrary to much judicial, media, and popular belief, some 96 percent of college undergraduate scholarship money has in recent decades involved *no consideration* of racial characteristics (US General Accounting Office, 1994). Not surprisingly, thus, recent analyses show that among full-time undergraduates in four-year colleges and universities, students of color are about one-third of applicants for grants and scholarships, but get only about one-quarter of *private* scholarships. In addition, "Caucasian students receive more than three-quarters (76%) of all institutional merit-based scholarship and grant funding, even though they represent less than two-thirds (62%) of the student population" now at public and private colleges and universities (Kantrowitz, 2011: 1).

Recent surveys reveal that, in spite of continuing and huge racial inequalities, a substantial majority of white Americans are still opposed to forceful public and private action to racially desegregate US institutions. For instance, a *Newsweek* poll of whites reported that some 72 percent disapproved of giving "preferences to blacks and other minorities . . . [in] hirings, promotions, and college admissions." In addition, a bit more than that agreed affirmative action "preferences" were resulting in less qualified people being hired, promoted, or admitted to colleges ("Race and Ethnicity," 2009). In contrast, in similar polls most black Americans disagree, and the overwhelming majority still favor affirmative action programs (Jones, 2005). Thus, those who are very familiar with the reality and damage of contemporary racial discrimination disagree strongly with the prevailing view of whites who do not suffer such comprehensive discrimination.

Moreover, over the past two decades, numerous state governments and other government agencies, including public colleges and universities, have ended or significantly reduced their historically modest affirmative action programs. For example, in California a Proposition 209 campaign was successful and implemented a law eliminating public affirmative action programs for college students of color in that state, an action that hit Latino and black students the hardest. It is significant that there is still intense white opposition in many areas of the country to affirmative action programs that most assume, often incorrectly, are still in operation. Such intense white opposition today again suggests the emotional aspects of the common and negative white racial framing in regard to reparative action for past and persisting racial discrimination in the United States.

## Latinos Assessing Affirmative Action: Our Respondents

It is in this societal context, with its decades of intense rhetoric and conflict over affirmative action and other remedial programs for racial discrimination, that we asked our mostly middle-class Latino respondents about contemporary "affirmative action." As we will see, our respondents are divided in their views of such public and private remedial programs, indeed, often within their own minds. Recall the important point that all people are multiframers. They often hold several frames for understanding and interpreting particular aspects of society in their minds at the same time, some of which are contradictory frames. Thus, a common element in many of the following excerpts is the respondents' adherence to certain elements of the typical white racial frame's take on affirmative action. Some respondents ignore their own group's racialized experiences, or they have not learned the firm information or counter-framed concepts necessary to make full sense out of mainstream media and other public distortions of the reality of affirmative action. Others draw well on their own racialized experiences to tack away from these prevailing whitewashed understandings of affirmative action to deeper interpretations of this important topic of ongoing societal discussion.

### *Affirmative Action Jobs Are "Occupied by Incompetents"*

We first consider our respondents' arguments against what they consider to be affirmative action. Unquestionably, the dominance and intensity of the white racial frame make it difficult, if not impossible, for people of color to evade the suspicion that they themselves have violated the prevailing equal opportunity ideals, in at least two important ways. First, from the commonplace white-framed view, when Latinos get good jobs, it is presumably because of their nonwhite characteristics, not their substantial competence. Second, also from the white framing, in taking good jobs, people of color allegedly deprive presumably more competent whites of that solid employment. As described in the prevailing white framing, people of color are likely to be miscreants in the area of better-paying employment.

The first respondent is an economically successful Latino. He is highly regarded by his corporate employer, and his income is in the high six figures. We asked him what he thought about contemporary affirmative action programs in employment and education, and he reacts thus:

> I am more oriented toward achievement based, acceptance, results, and rewards. So affirmative action, I guess I don't have a negative reaction to it, but

I personally wouldn't want to be promoted because of affirmative action. *How would you know?* Probably if I got to the next level and my work responsibility was extremely watered down, and what I expected that responsibility to be would be pretty much with an empty job.

This respondent's answer is somewhat surprising. He is highly competent and very successful, and objectively it would be improbable that any employment promotion he received would be to an "extremely watered-down" position. He accepts the common white-framed view that jobs facilitated by affirmative action are sinecures for people of color and insists on "achievement based" rewards. He seems unaware of the fact that, if he is promoted, he may still be quite vulnerable to the white charge of being advanced over "more qualified" whites. It is very difficult for Latinos, even for someone as capable as he is, to escape certain racial stereotypes, imagery, and narratives of the white frame.

Consider too these comments from an interview with a Mexican American who is a computer technician. We asked him what he thought about affirmative action programs in employment and education, and he suggests a rather similar perspective:

I don't really think that people should get things when they do not deserve [them]. . . . I don't think that that door should be opened up undeservingly. . . . *What do you mean by undeservingly?* People that don't know skills.

Immediately, this Latino respondent links jobs associated with affirmative action as undeserved because in his stereotyped view their occupants are likely to be poorly skilled.

Another respondent, a self-employed Cuban American businessperson, accented a related negative image in reply to a question about affirmative action programs in employment. He views them as a source of recurring abuse:

I think they are a joke. I really do. Why? I see people abuse it all the time. The first thing out of someone's mouth when something doesn't go their way is [to complain about racism]. . . . I see right through it, I see, no he is wrong. He is not as good as this [white] guy in his job and that is why he will not get this position.

Unmistakably, this respondent views affirmative action jobs and those who hold them negatively. He focuses on perceived instances when the supposed "race card" is pulled, and he supposes successful affirmative action in employment to be commonplace and an instrument that people of color use to jump over more deserving whites. Operating substantially out of a white framing of affirmative action, these last few respondents do not even consider that most of those who have benefited from the mostly modest affirmative action programs once in place (many no longer exist) in employment settings have been highly qualified. Also missing from these critical assessments is any consideration of the many mediocre and unqualified whites who have held well-paying jobs in the US economy.

A Puerto Rican interviewee who is a city utility supervisor reacts to a question about affirmative action programs in employment and education in this conventional way:

> I think . . . it's kind of like reverse discrimination. . . . It could also be taken as a somewhat hypocritical approach because now by remedying the wrong that was done before, we're also doing the wrong to the people that were doing the wrong before. Like now, you know, we're either Hispanic or we're very black, or we'll give you the scholarship. What about the white kid that can't afford to go to school? You know, and he's not Hispanic or black; why doesn't he qualify for the scholarship too?

This respondent is also taking many of the white frame's traditional perspectives—in this case, of education. Right from the onset, the respondent assumes that affirmative action is "reverse discrimination," the white-coined term of the 1960s–1970s pushback against desegregation changes in the Jim Crow era. It is said to take opportunities away from more deserving whites. Yet, as we pointed out previously for higher education, merit-based scholarship and grant money has actually gone disproportionately to white students. Most students of color do not have more societal tracks and realistic opportunities for higher education than do white students. As with most whites who assert such stereotyped and mythical views, the evidence is not examined or even known by numerous Latino respondents who have bought into the white racial framing of affirmative action matters.

We asked another respondent, a Puerto Rican female, a similar question about affirmative action programs. She replies in a fashion like that of the previous respondents:

> If it's going to be given to a black guy and a white guy, if there's a choice and the black guy doesn't really know how to do it . . . then that's wrong. If it's going to be where the actual black guy can actually do the work, then OK. . . . Not just because he's black but because he actually does the work.

This important theme continues to appear: Affirmative action is fair only if the person of color knows how to "do the work." The unqualified-until-proven-differently assumption continues to haunt workers of color, a black man in this hypothetical instance. This interviewee does not appear to know, or is downplaying the fact, that often to prove his or her competence, a person of color has to surpass numerous vetting and credentialing obstacles in the workplace that a white person would not ordinarily face.

## Views of Quota Issues

The recurring, usually white-generated public discussion of affirmative action programs involving "quotas" (which many do not actually involve) has pressed this erroneous view into the minds of even many Americans of color (see Feagin, 2010). For instance, one Cuban American teacher answered our question about affirmative action programs in employment and education in this manner:

> I think that many times they are unfair to the other party. . . . Because . . . each school has to have a quota that they need. . . . A certain percentage of you know, Hispanic, black [teachers]. . . . [If] you are not meeting that quota with let's say . . . black teachers, then you make sure that you take one of the other races. . . . The administration gets into trouble. . . . I do believe that there should be jobs available for every race. . . . There could be many teachers that are Hispanic, and . . . [there] are not any good [ones]. And just because they need to fill a certain quota that they keep them, versus maybe keeping a black teacher that is maybe more efficient.

As she sees it, affirmative action often creates a situation where school administrators have to be concerned with filling specific "quotas," to the point that they have to hire or keep incompetent teachers of color. We have not seen any scholarly evidence that supports this claim of specific numerical percentages for particular groups of color, and while it may happen, we doubt that it is a commonplace occurrence. Like other respondents critical of affirmative action, she does not mention in her comments the role of white decision makers in limiting the employment of teachers of color for decades—and thus the need for affirmative action.

A Cuban American woman with a college degree who is currently a stay-at-home mother offers a more nuanced and historical view of affirmative action:

> I think when they first started affirmative action, years and years ago . . . yes, you needed it. To be honest with you, now I think it has been taken too far. . . . I think what affirmative action has done in some cases . . . is [that] people that can really do their jobs are being overlooked because they need to fill a quota.

Although she understands the need for some affirmative action to deal with discrimination, she seems to place that necessity in the past. Today, in her view, competent people—white people, one may presume—are kept from these jobs, again because of the putative quotas. Indeed, in our experience, one or two people of color hired by large university departments is sufficient to satisfy any affirmative action pressures, whether formal or informal. Today, there are few historically white organizational settings where contemporary pressures for a *critical mass* of employees of color are substantial and lasting (Feagin, 2010).

In the next commentary, a Mexican American woman who is a translator at a middle school replies to our question about affirmative action programs:

> I think we should move beyond that now. I would like to see it, everybody at the same equal value. You know, to value each other for what we know, what we can do, and whatever. Not because of our color. *How do you think we might be able to move beyond that?* . . . I only know that I moved; why can't they? *How did you move?* [I] pulled myself by my own bootstraps. . . . We didn't complain. We just worked harder.

Like the other respondents quoted in this chapter, this woman thinks the need to end affirmative action is now, but she too offers no critical understandings or commentary on the substantial discrimination still faced by employees of color in many historically white institutions. Instead, she accents the old individualistic framing that views hard work, including her own, as the answer to persisting racial barriers. Other researchers have found this heavy accent on hard work among Latinos, including Latino entrepreneurs (Valdez, 2011).

Accenting another problem with some affirmative action programs, as he sees it, a Cuban American with a construction business has this to say about certain shady white business practices:

> I am in the construction business. I can tell you from experience that in the construction business there are large white general contractors that are using affirmative action by having a black Hispanic female as the president of one of their companies. *You mean they are using this for their advantage?* For their advantage. *Well, are they doing this black Hispanic female any justice?* No. 'Cause the only reason she is in that position is because she is going to get them that contract. Because they are going to go with the affirmative action and not through the bidding process. *So when you have that type of situation, does affirmative action work?* No. There are too many abuses.

In this commentary the respondent points out how large white-run contractors have corrupted the modest affirmative action programs in some parts of the construction contracting business, which are often called business "set-aside" programs. These white-run contracting firms sometimes hire a person of color as a "front" to enable them to secure an even greater (and still unfair) share of public construction contracting than they already have.

Significantly, what this respondent does not mention in his complaint is that these business set-aside programs are usually modest in setting aside just a small percentage of government contracts for local construction projects, and that they are there to encourage the growth of women and minority contractors, who historically have faced, and currently face, prohibitive discrimination by white construction corporations (Feagin and Imani, 1994; Feagin and Hodge, 1995). Indeed, in many urban areas, the white contractors, who already hold a disproportionate and unfair share of much local contracting, quickly developed ways of corrupting these modest government programs designed to bring previously excluded Americans into the construction business. There is also no effort in this man's interview comments to hold these white contractors morally and legally accountable for corrupting these particular affirmative action programs.

These negative comments on affirmative action by our Latino interviewees often reproduce what they have picked up from conservative white political leaders, media commentators, and Supreme Court justices. For example, in a famous 1980s decision, *City of Richmond, Virginia v. J. A. Croson Co.* (1989), the conservative majority on the Supreme Court ruled that a modest Richmond, Virginia, program of business contract set-asides to assist those victimized by extensive past discrimination was unconstitutional. The white conservative majority insisted that the local government did not have a substantial reason for trying to remedy the historical discrimination faced by black residents for centuries, even though government statistics demonstrated that in a city that was half black, less than 1 percent of city business went to black-owned companies. The *Croson* case is important because it set the precedent for several later conservative Supreme Court decisions making a mockery of official efforts to provide modestly expanded business opportunities for firms owned by Americans of color in numerous economic sectors (Feagin, 2010).

The views of the previously quoted respondents are not just their own, for they are from time to time echoed in the comments of a few Latino leaders and media pundits. Frequently, these critics of affirmative action get more attention than they deserve because the mostly white media executives and other decision makers are glad to have their views parroted in regard to Americans in historically oppressed groups. For example, the conservative Latina activist Linda Chavez (2002: 34–35) has noted this about her former jobs:

Although I initially thought I had been hired because of my Capitol Hill experience, it became obvious on my first day at work that the NEA needed me to round out their "rainbow lobby." . . . I provided them with a "two-fer"; filling affirmative action slots as both a woman and a Mexican American. My first doubts had crept in just a few years earlier, while I was teaching in affirmative action programs myself at UCLA and the University of Colorado at Boulder. . . . Affirmative action was having devastating effects on academic standards and race relations. I learned, to my surprise, that the double standards these programs erect also badly hurt the intended beneficiaries—encouraging them to wallow in self-pity rather than improving their skills.

One observes here what we see in the comments of several respondents—the common response of looking at remedial actions for discrimination with no attention to the historical and contemporary contexts of racial oppression. The past and present reality of widespread discrimination does not figure significantly in her or our previous respondents' commentaries. Nor does she offer insight into why in these organizations the major white decision makers—people of color have rarely been involved in top decisions at major organizations—have set up remedial programs with the weaknesses alluded to. Indeed, these white decision makers have almost never been committed to the extensive actions needed to bring large-scale changes in discriminatory patterns in our historically white-run institutions.

Nor does Chavez seem to know the recent research showing whites' overwhelming opposition to *major* remedial actions for discrimination (see below). She also does not seem to be aware of the research on people who have desegregated white institutions (for example, research showing little self-pity), or the research showing that affirmative action has not changed academic standards and has improved to some degree the racial understandings of whites (see Massey, 2004; Feagin, 2010). Most of Chavez's critical comments appear to echo commonplace white-framed views she has heard from conservative whites or the conservative and other mass media.

## Positive Views of Affirmative Action

Numerous respondents in our middle-class sample disagreed with the negative views expressed by those opponents of affirmative action just quoted. These respondents accent the ways in which affirmative action offers protection against discrimination, provides new opportunities long blocked by whites, and fits well with the US rhetorical ideals of "liberty and justice for all."

For example, one Latina office worker at a nonprofit agency has this to say about the common negative views of affirmative action:

> I don't feel that it's reverse discrimination. . . . Because they're not just saying that because you're Hispanic we're gonna let you in. . . . There's other factors that that job and school are looking at. I mean, if you're going to Stanford, they're not just gonna let you in because you're Hispanic with an SAT score of 100. I mean, it's just not happening.

She rejects the white-crafted term and concept of reverse discrimination and accents the reality that most affirmative action in organizational settings involves qualified students and employees of color. When the interviewer asked a follow-up question about the common view that affirmative action means candidates of color are often unqualified, she adds this important point about the reality of most affirmative action:

> I don't think it's true. I don't think that companies just hire any dumb old Mexican or Hispanic or any minority just because they have to fill a quota for affirmative action. They may not be as qualified as maybe someone else, but I think what they are looking at is overall qualification. Sure, you may have all the education in the world but you don't have experience. They don't have education but they have experience, so that's why they get hired. I don't always think that they are getting hired because they are not qualified. In a way, they have to be qualified. If I had a business, and I was hiring people, why would you hire people that weren't qualified?

She is well aware that few profit-seeking companies would hire unqualified people just to fill a quota and thereby seriously risk their business success. Such racially framed, negative conceptions of people of color who are hired in organizations that may have had some sort of affirmative action program frequently appear to us to be more about white attempts to get rid of these remedial programs and reduce the number of employees of color than about the actual qualifications of those employed under such conditions.

In the following interview excerpt, a Mexican American university professor provides a supportive reply when asked his views on affirmative action programs in the workplace:

> I'm in favor of them. I see them as giving people an opportunity. I think it's giving people a chance to compete, to be employed. . . . I think that my career, getting into graduate school, getting the job here at the university was largely because of affirmative action.

Drawing on his own experiences, this respondent is well aware that even modest programs providing opportunities can have many favorable results. Note too that a person of color like this who secures a good position in the white-run economy can frequently serve as a model for other ambitious people of color to follow his or her example. Such an accumulating impact is one of the main benefits of the numerous affirmative action programs that are, or once were, in place across the country.

Another respondent, who is employed at a state agency, accents one more dimension to a realistic defense of affirmative action in historically white workplaces:

> Even though I would like to say that the time has come to do away with it, I still see a need for it. Because I see individuals that are Anglo that are not as qualified as some minorities that get the job because they are Anglo. And

it's racially based on the good ole boy attitude. . . . One of the complaints I [had] . . . how come there was no Hispanic on that board? I mean, there are a lot of Hispanics in the [name of agency], yet that board I went to was all white. *Did they give you a response as to why?* That nobody else was available at that time, which is a bunch of bull.

From this perspective, it is not time to get rid of these positive attempts to desegregate historically white institutions, in part because of the continuing reality of a built-in bias in many such institutions that regularly reproduces white dominance. Drawing on significant personal experience, this savvy respondent pointedly underscores the good-old-boy networks that significantly favor white employees, especially white men. These white networks are, indeed, still by far the most successful "affirmative action" programs in the US economy (Katznelson, 2005; Feagin, 2010).

In the next interview excerpt, a Latino business owner agrees with the previous respondent in regard to the best way to ensure opportunities. Questioned about affirmative action in employment and education, he answers with some specificity:

I think they are necessary. *Why is that?* Well . . . no one has showed me a better system to ensure that minorities and other people . . . [are] getting a fair shot at [opportunities]. . . . I think down here [in Miami], years ago . . . until the federal government enforced [affirmative action] in the police department and fire department, which have been pockets of good ole boy[s] . . . you are not getting in until the federal government forces the issue. . . . Not only Cubans, but everybody else.

Having a good historical memory, this Latino businessperson knows well that many white decision makers in historically white institutions, in both the past and present, will not take action to meaningfully desegregate their workplaces without significant outside pressures to take such reparative action. Indeed, many police and fire departments did not desegregate in terms of bringing in significant numbers of white women and people of color until they were forced to do so by antidiscrimination lawsuits and legislation (Feagin, 2010; Feagin and Feagin, 2011).

An office manager at a law firm discusses the benefits of affirmative action in his personal case some years back:

Generally, I support them. . . . I am certain that it helped me in growing up. *How did it help you?* Well, with admission to college. . . . I went through a program that took kids [of color] out of public schools and put them . . . through a program in private schools. . . . *And you were one of those kids?* Yeah. So, sure I benefited from affirmative action.

Several respondents noted that they had benefited from some type of positive action opening up formerly inaccessible avenues of personal achievement for them. This included the type of additive learning experiences that all children should have access to in order to enhance their individual talents and abilities. Expanding educational opportunities has been important in creating a larger Latino and black middle class, as this man strongly testifies from his own experience.

Major public and private cutbacks in such equal opportunity programs in recent years are creating much less opportunity for young people of color to make it into good colleges and subsequent white-collar jobs across the US economy. Indeed, a few of our respondents insisted on an expansion of such equal opportunity programs. One Mexican American interviewee reacts to our question about affirmative action with this strong reflective retort:

> I think there's not enough of it. I think there should be more. *Why?* Because there [still] is racism. . . . *So, in terms of affirmative action, how do you see that in the future?* I don't think it's something we should always need, because I believe with more education that everyone will learn to understand each other. *You mean more education for Hispanics?* More education for everybody. Affirmative action is not always for Hispanics . . . it's for all minorities. Typically it's been the whites, [the] male who's gone to college. . . . So I think affirmative action is still needed because it's our fight as minorities to get into upper- or middle-class society and not just be the low-end class. OK? *So what do you think about affirmative action programs in employment?* I think affirmative action programs are actually pretty good, because I think that a minority person can do just as good as a white person. . . . I don't think it should matter on what your freakin' color is, just as long as you get the work done.

Here we have another perceptive accent on whites, especially white men, having long had the social networks and other affirmative action programs that advantage them in education and most other sectors of society. Again, too, we see an accent on these programs in education and in employment as providing much opportunity for those who have the ability and work hard, but have long been disadvantaged by those whites in power in historically white institutions. In effect, more "education for everybody" is her ideal for society.

## Conclusion: The Realities of Affirmative Action

There is much that is ahistorical, ill-informed, and ironic in the public and private discussions of affirmative action efforts and programs in US society, including those of the more negative respondents quoted in this chapter. Let us highlight here, albeit briefly, some of the affirmative action realities that contradict public misperceptions of affirmative action, past and present.

One of our Latina acquaintances recently gave us this account of what happened to her when she was teaching at a high school while she was working on her master's degree. She was teaching under an internship teaching-credential program, but, as she recounts, a white male competitor for the position she held actually

> started a letter-signing campaign to have me removed because I was an "affirmative action hire" and therefore "not qualified." He got the head of the PTA to help him in his efforts. It got so toxic that my students were asking me if I was the affirmative action hire in class! I was totally undermined, in my 20s, working on my master's degree and trying to figure out how to go on for my PhD in order to leave all that behind me. Now that I think about it, I think people may not always act on the belief that I'm the affirmative action hire, but it is there. So, I've definitely benefited from affirmative action, but I also know I wouldn't have needed it if I hadn't been tracked in school from kindergarten on, because I am Latina and my father worked in the fields. I needed it because white men would kiss me on the cheek and say, "Aren't Latinos affectionate," and I stiffened in discomfort. I needed it because I didn't know the first thing about going to college, applying for college, or even paying for college—because my high school counselors and teachers made it very clear by their actions that they didn't think I would amount to anything.

In this remarkably revealing account, a very talented university professor destroys some of the anti-affirmative-action critique often parroted by whites and others operating out of an unreflective white framing of these matters. We observe that affirmative action is badly needed to even begin to compensate Latinos and other Americans of color for the racist tracking and other discrimination they have *regularly* faced in primary and secondary education in the United States. Positive government and private action is needed to support youth of color who have grown up in families where parents suffer harsh job conditions, low wages, and job discrimination. We also observe the sexualized racial framing at the hands of white men and the educational discrimination by white teachers and administrators that a young Latina had to constantly battle her way through just to get a good education and make a better life for herself and her family. And then, once she made it through college and into a graduate program with great effort, a privileged white male competitor intentionally targeted her and created a difficult teaching setting. She tells us, too, that she still experiences whites' negatively framing her substantial accomplishments and creating yet more barrier-filled environments in the historically white educational settings that she regularly traverses.

Ironically, the modest affirmative action secured by some Americans of color such as this Latina professor pales in comparison with that granted over the centuries to whites. Most white Americans, and many Americans of color, have never reflected on the well-documented fact that white Americans have long been by far the *greatest* recipients of affirmative government actions to facilitate their upward mobility as individuals and families, now over many (four to eighteen) generations of white residency in this country. Consider that from the seventeenth century to the early twentieth century, first the white colonists, and later white US citizens, were the recipients of substantial land grants that were inaccessible to almost all Americans of color. The famous US homestead laws in operation from the 1860s to the 1930s enabled the US government to provide tens of millions of acres of federal (originally Indian) land in the Midwest, South, and West almost exclusively to white families for homesteading and family wealth-building purposes. Jim Crow segregation implemented and maintained by white officials and organizations like the Ku Klux Klan kept most Americans of color in that long era, which lasted until the late 1960s, from access to federal land and many other important socioeconomic resources available to whites only (Feagin, 2010).

Indeed, during the 1930s–1940s New Deal era, whites were the primary or only beneficiaries of important federal socioeconomic mobility programs. These extraordinarily impactful new government subsidy programs, again overwhelmingly and disproportionately benefiting whites, included Federal Housing Administration loan insurance and other housing programs, along with the post–World War II veterans' educational and housing programs. With the great assistance of these government welfare programs, *many millions* of whites got college educations and/or bought their first homes and thereby built up significant family wealth over time in the form of home equity. This government-fostered family wealth was later utilized for such purposes as starting a new business or funding children's college educations. Sociologists Melvin Oliver and Thomas Shapiro (2007: A27) explain how powerful and discriminatory the housing equity programs since the 1950s have been:

> America's broad middle class accumulates two thirds of its wealth through homeownership enabled more by federal actions than private thrift, savings, and investments. The reach of these social-investment actions, however, by both intent and omission, has not been extended to low and moderate-income families, and only barely to Hispanics and African Americans.

The white descendants of the government-fostered middle-class families of the 1940s–1960s have been significantly assisted by yet more government programs and largesse in further moving up the socioeconomic ladder.

We should note too that since World War II, many white families have been greatly assisted in their upward mobility by the increasing scale of federal contracting programs. These significant government contracts, yet again, have been very disproportionately available to white-run firms of various sizes. With only rare exceptions, businesses owned by Americans of color were excluded by formal and informal Jim Crow segregation and other racial discrimination from almost all important federal contracts until the 1970s. As political scientist Ira Katznelson (2005) has underscored well, this long era of government land giveaways, housing programs, and other public programs used to support white families and enterprises has been one when "affirmative action was white." Today, much government affirmative action for individual and family mobility in this society still affirmatively, greatly, and disproportionately benefits white Americans.

# 6

# Melting Pot, or Not: Latinos and Whiteness

The roots of the white racial frame's central dictum that only whites are truly "American" are found as early as colonial times. During the first few decades of English colonization of North America in the seventeenth century, as we noted previously, the English colonizers and conquerors referred to themselves as "English" and "Christian," with few explicit references to their being "white." By the latter part of that century and the early part of the eighteenth century, however, there was a gradual shift to more frequent use of the term "white," especially with the significant growth in enslavement of many imported Africans. English Americans and other European Americans adopted a "superior" white racial identity for the express purpose of separating themselves diametrically from the enslaved African Americans and indigenous Native Americans, who were regarded as characteristically "uncivilized" and racially "inferior" (Feagin, 2013).

## The Strange Career of Mexican American "Whiteness"

Later on in the nineteenth century, with the dramatic colonization of Native American and Mexican lands in what became the western United States, this white identity principle and its associated white racist framing were constantly put into effect by an array of colonizers operating throughout what was gradually becoming the western United States. Its enforcement took a particular form in the southwestern area of the United States taken from Mexico in the 1840s by the US-Mexican War (discussed in Chapter 1), the war that coerced the first substantial group of Latinos into an ever-expanding US empire. Over time these new Mexican Americans became by far the largest Latino group in the United States, and they made up the overwhelming majority of the

US Latino population until the 1950s and 1960s, when they were joined with growing numbers of Puerto Ricans and Cubans. Today, they are a substantial 63 percent of the total Latino population.

Given this long era of Mexican American centrality to the Latino population, let us begin the discussion with a brief overview of the oscillating racial classifications applied by Anglo whites to Mexican Americans since the nineteenth century. This will help illuminate the past and present Latino positioning on the US racial ladder. The Treaty of Guadalupe Hidalgo formally ended the 1840s US-Mexican War. In a key article of that treaty, white officials specified the status of thousands of Mexicans forcibly brought into the United States: "Mexicans who shall prefer to remain [in the territory lost by Mexico] . . . may either retain the title and rights of Mexican citizens, or acquire those of citizens of the United States" (Anonymous, [1848] 2010; see Gonzalez and Fernandez, 2003). Since being "white" was a requirement for newcomers to the United States to secure US citizenship under federal law, it appeared that the Mexican citizens who chose US citizenship under the treaty provision had to be white, at least technically.

Nonetheless, white Anglo government and private attorneys argued in court over whether Mexican Americans should in fact be legally viewed as "white" because of that treaty provision. Strikingly, in 1897 a US federal judge ruled that a Mexican petitioner was white under the treaty provision and could become a naturalized US citizen. The white judge, however, indicated that he was forced to rule this way only because of this treaty with Mexico, even though he explicitly argued in the decision that "scientifically" the Mexican American petitioner "would probably not be classed as white" (I. López, 1996: 61). The commonplace white framing of Mexicans in that day as racially inferior and not white had unmistakably affected the judge's racist thinking. Indeed, from the nineteenth century to recent decades a great many white officials have agreed with this judge.

Over the decades after the US-Mexican War, the racialization process affecting Mexican Americans and other Latinos remained complex and sometimes confusing for those involved. For instance, the 1848 treaty's statement of Mexican Americans as officially white affected some federal and state government actions, such as the cataloging of Mexican Americans as "white" in US censuses from 1850 to 1920. Moreover, only when white government lawyers found it advantageous to protecting white-Anglo interests did they claim in court and a few other settings that Mexican Americans were "white." For example, in 1950 a Mexican American, Pete Hernandez, was convicted of murder by an all-white-Anglo jury in the then very racially segregated state of Texas, a court decision upheld by the Texas Court of Criminal Appeals. Some Mexican American lawyers appealed the Hernandez case to the US Supreme

Court. They argued that their client's constitutional rights had been violated because no Mexican Americans had been summoned to serve on any Texas jury in that era. Ironically, the lawyers for the state of Texas—white Anglos who defended the Jim Crow segregation of their day in other contexts—riposted that no legal rights had been violated, because Mexican Americans were officially white under that old 1848 treaty, and Hernandez had been convicted by whites. Their hypocritical argument did not convince the US Supreme Court justices who in their ruling in favor of Hernandez stated that "whether or not [Mexican Americans] were legally white, they had been treated as a 'separate class distinct from whites'" (Gross, 2007: 339).

Indeed, on most other official occasions, white Anglo local and state government officials found this historical Mexican American "whiteness" to be disadvantageous, and thus they would routinely define Mexican Americans as "colored" and treat them harshly. A flagrant example of this racist tack can be seen in the history of the city of El Paso, Texas. In 1936 Anglo officials in El Paso announced that henceforth the city government would classify Mexican Americans as "colored" instead of "white" in its birth and death records. Foley (1997: 210) explains the reason for the change:

> The main issue . . . was infant-mortality rates, which were embarrassingly high in a city attempting to market itself to the rest of the country as a major health resort. By classifying Mexicans as colored, city officials could realize a dramatic improvement in their white infant-mortality rates.

In addition, the explicit segregation of Mexican American children from white children in schools and other settings was long commonplace in the Southwest. Both white Anglos and Mexican Americans recognized this as racial segregation. Montejano (1987: 242) describes an example of this recognition and the pushback from Mexican Americans in Texas: "In the city of Kingsville in 1927, Mexican parents, by threatening a legal suit against the segregated system, pressured the school district into building a modern, well-equipped Mexican school." During this era before and after World War II, Mexican American children across the Southwest were often racially segregated, usually by local laws or gerrymandered school district lines. This school segregation was buttressed by widespread racial discrimination in housing and bank loans (Feagin and Feagin, 2011: 205–235).

Significantly, in a pathbreaking mid-1940s school segregation case, *Mendez et al. v. Westminster School District et al.* (1946), a white judge finally ruled that the racially segregated "Mexican schools" in the state of California were unconstitutional. Nonetheless, this judge's ruling represented only a very slow official movement toward reducing the overt racial oppression constantly directed at Mexican Americans. Most Anglo whites still pressed very hard for the segregation of Mexican Americans away from white schools and residential areas, as well as for aggressive one-way assimilation within their segregated schools into the Anglocentric core culture.

### Strong Assimilationist Reactions: Early Latino Organizations

The institutionalized machinations segregating Mexican Americans—and the growing population of other Latinos—on the part of white Anglo officials were unmistakably intended to solidify white dominance and ascendancy in the Southwest. Most such white officials, as well as most ordinary whites, ignored the 1848 treaty stipulation and did not view Mexican Americans, in their everyday framing and institutionalized practices, as "white" or even "American." This was true at all government levels. As Foley (1997: 19) has noted, whiteness "was inscribed in Texas law as the quintessential property for both citizenship rights and landownership."

In the face of the formal and informal racial segregation in southwestern areas, some Mexican American leaders decided that the only way that Mexican Americans could escape their discriminatory situation and their identity quandary was to become as "white" as they could. The establishment in 1929 of the League of United Latin American Citizens (LULAC) was a major addition to activist struggles in Texas and elsewhere. LULAC was a civil rights organization launched by middle-class Mexican Americans who carried a strong campaign insisting "on their status as whites in order to overcome the worst features of Jim Crow segregation" (Foley, 1997: 209). Additionally, as Foley (1997: 60) further explains, Mexican American achievement of white status would support their claim to Americanness, since whiteness and American identity were then, as now, inextricably linked.

As part of its campaign for Mexican Americans to be recognized as white, LULAC exhorted *them* to adopt behaviors that would make them more acceptable to the dominant white group. LULAC expected its members to assimilate to positive images of success in the prevailing white framing of society and "speak English, dress well, encourage education and be polite in race relations" (Montejano, 1987: 233). Other Mexican American organizations such as the American G.I. Forum and the Community Service Organization often joined with LULAC in this very assimilationist orientation. This is clearly observed in their naming themselves only in English and using English as their official organizational language, their emphasizing patriotic symbols like the US flag, and their accenting of US citizenship as an organizational membership requirement (J. Gutiérrez, 1985: 143). Efforts by LULAC and other Mexican American organizations to whiten Mexican Americans had some success at the federal level. For example, the 1930 US census had placed Mexican Americans in the "people of other races" category. However, LULAC opposed this racial classification, and its efforts and those of the Mexican government resulted in the 1940 census again placing Mexican Americans in the "white" category unless "they were definitely Indian or of other non-white race" (Gross, 2003: 198).

Despite LULAC's efforts, however, Anglo whites in Texas and other parts of the southwestern United States by and large did not change their view that Mexican Americans were racially inferior and not white. In reality, the views of whites in all classes were often viciously and very explicitly racist. One white member of the US Congress described Mexican-origin people as a mongrelized blending of Spanish ancestry, "low-grade Indians," and African slave "blood." In another revealing commentary, an expert witness at a House Immigration Committee hearing labeled the "Mexican race" as one that was very threatening to the "white race" (Cárdenas, 1975: 73–75; Guzmán, 1974: 22). Many white commentators were alarmed that the increasing presence of Mexican Americans would mean an increase in greatly feared "race mongrelization." Not being white, those of Mexican origin were also considered very alien and foreign. Foley (1997: 60) puts it succinctly: In Texas, Mexicans "might claim to be American and the law might regard them as Americans for the purpose of citizenship, but in everyday practice whites only referred to other whites as Americans." This, in turn, meant that in the 1940s–1950s era, Mexican Americans were still regularly and extensively racialized as not white and were thus treated in highly discriminatory ways by both elite and ordinary whites.

We should underscore the point made previously that these experiences of Mexican Americans with many decades of white oppression are relevant to understanding the racialized background and white framing that has affected all Latinos in various ways. For the long 1850–1950 era of very overt racial oppression, most Latinos in the United States were Mexican Americans, and it was their presence against which whites historically generated the anti-Latino framing that has endured in much white framing and discriminatory practice over recent decades.

## The 1960s–1990s Era: More Anti-Latino Framing

As we noted in Chapter 1, from the 1960s onward, and despite the rise of important local and national civil rights movements protesting white oppression, a great many prominent and rank-and-file whites still framed Latinos as quite inferior racially and very actively discriminated against them. Recall from previous discussions that hostile racial framing among whites appeared to be on the rise in various areas across the country. In the mid-1960s, for instance, one prominent white historian of the Southwest, Walter Prescott Webb, articulated well the commonplace hostile racist framing of Mexican Americans. He insisted that there is "a cruel streak in the Mexican nature," and this "doubtless should be attributed partly to the Indian blood" (Martinez, 1998: 178). In this 1960s–1990s era Mexican Americans and the growing number of other Latinos were not viewed as white or as a quaint US "ethnic group" but were still commonly racialized in the dominant white framing.

One serious sign of this routine racialization could be observed in the widespread use of "stop and frisk" or "arrest on suspicion" tactics by mostly white-run police agencies in a large number of Latino communities. Such antagonistic policing tactics have long resulted in the discriminatory treatment of Latinos, who are usually singled out by their physical appearance. Unsurprisingly, a substantial majority of Los Angeles Latinos reported in a 1991 opinion survey that police brutality was common in their urban area (Ford and Stolberg, 1991). This racial profiling by police agencies, as well as by many other white officials and whites in yet other societal settings, has persisted now over many decades (Feagin and Feagin, 2011: 217–231).

During the 1960s–1970s era, one result of continuing racist profiling and other discrimination at the hands of whites was a substantial increase among Mexican Americans (Chicanos) and some other Latinos of openly antiracist counter-framing and associated protests against oppression (see below). This antiracist counter-framing rejected earlier Latino organizations' accent on enthusiastic assimilation to whiteness for an assertive analysis focusing on white-imposed institutional racism and demands that such white racism must end (see Barrera, 1979; J. Gutiérrez, 1985). Indeed, civil rights activists in the 1960s–1970s era often suggested that integration "into a burning house"—that is, into racially troubled and discriminatory US institutions—should not be the ultimate goal of change-oriented civil rights movements among Americans of color. This critical antiracism perspective has been central to more overt Latino counter-framing to the present day.

## The Contemporary Era: Latinos and Whiteness

We can now return to issues of whiteness and Latino "assimilation" in the contemporary era. Remarkably, even in the face of the persisting and well-institutionalized racism documented throughout this book, some contemporary media commentators and social scientists have periodically been rather sanguine about some Latino and Asian American groups gradually becoming near-white or truly white and accepted as roughly equal in the mainstream institutions historically controlled by Anglo whites.

For example, in the late 1990s conservative sociologist Nathan Glazer (1997) described many Latinos and Asian Americans as becoming significantly like whites in economic status, place of residence, and attitudes—a societal situation that in his view would eventually result in just two US "nations," the "black and the others." The nonblack others become part of a blended-with-whites "nation." Since the 1990s, more liberal social scientists such as Andrew Hacker (1992: 16) have also argued that Latinos and Asian Americans are being "allowed," in his words, "to put a visible distance between themselves and black Americans." In his view, these nonblack "ethnicities" do not face the "presumptions of inferiority associated with Africa and slavery" that are faced by African Americans, and thus can become close to whiteness (Hacker, 1992: 16). Similarly, other assimilationist social science analysts, such as those discussed in Chapter 1, often accent this kind of moving toward whiteness on the part of certain Latino and Asian American groups.

Some media analysts have also articulated variations on this assimilation-into-whiteness perspective. Recently, several journalists published an article for a West Coast newspaper arguing that the significant growth in Latino numbers means that "being white is fading as a test of American-ness" (Yen, 2013). They conclude from their rather naive journalistic analysis that the speed of contemporary "assimilation for today's Latinos and Asian-Americans is often compared with that of the Poles, Irish, Italians and Jews who . . . eventually merged into an American white mainstream." Indeed, for some time now, a few public commentators have even insisted that some Latino and Asian American groups have already been accepted by older groups of whites as fully white (Lind, 1995: 115–119).

Some popular writers, mostly Americans of color, have even romanticized the demographic reality often called the "browning of America" as meaning much more intimacy, including intermarriage, across major racial groups in the near future, a process they suggest will facilitate full integration of people of color into the US mainstream and democracy (see R. Rodriguez, 2002). However, as philosopher Ronald Sundstrom (2008: Kindle loc. 121–127) has aptly underscored, this romantic view of the "browning of America . . . confuses the gritty realities of politics with soft-focused romantic fantasies." He reminds us that many years of intimate relationships between whites and other racial groups in Brazil and South Africa has created large numbers of mixed-race individuals but has not resulted in a vigorous multiracial democracy "through the simple magic of racial and ethnic intermarriage."

One aspect of these more optimistic arguments about Latinos being fully assimilated into the white-dominated culture and institutions should be noted here. Although it is often not clear in their arguments, these analysts may often have in mind certain middle-class Latinos who are light-skinned and "white looking" (to Anglo whites) and who have wholeheartedly assimilated to many white folkways. Indeed, "white looking" middle-class Latinos seem more likely than "Mexican looking" or "Indian looking" middle-class Latinos to be allowed by Anglo whites the option of more inclusion in some white-controlled institutions. While there is some empirical evidence in our data and in that of other researchers for this white Anglo differentiation among Latinos, there is also much evidence in these same sources for the substantial racialization of lighter-skinned Latinos on the basis of cues that go beyond phenotype, such as accent and name, to signal to Anglo whites the racial inferiority of these Latinos. As we have emphasized throughout this book, Anglo whites determine a person's racial status on the basis of real and imagined physical characteristics and associated cultural characteristics—for example, a supposed lack of intelligence that is signaled by a Spanish surname, commentary, or accent. As one of our lighter-skinned Latino colleagues has frequently noted, "I often get treated as white until I open my mouth." A Spanish accent or name is the cue, again and again, for white discrimination. Perception of a certain phenotype is often used by whites to establish Latino identity, but known Latino identity also influences and distorts whites' perception of the Latino phenotype.

## Additional Problems with "Assimilation" Theorizing

Recall from Chapter 1 the imagery of a US melting pot accented by playwright Israel Zangwill, just after 1900 and during the very large migration of Polish, Italian, and other European immigrants to the United States. In his idealistic vision, these European immigrant groups were blending together with British Americans already here into a melded composite with significant mutual adaptation. This enduring image of a thoroughly blended melting pot of groups has never happened, even for the southern and eastern European immigrant groups listed by Zangwill or by the contemporary analysts cited above. These southern and eastern European groups were forced to adapt to the Anglo-dominant core culture and institutions, for the most part, in a one-way assimilation process.

This mostly one-way character of US assimilation processes is recognized, although not critically called out or theorized, by the contemporary analysts discussed in the previous section. These analysts argue that Latinos (and Asian Americans) are engaging successfully in one-way assimilation to established white normativity, including important white folkways and framing of racial and class issues. Post-immigrant generations of Latinos are said to be gradually merging into the dominant white racial group through compliant conformity. As in the past, what is taking place in our contemporary era does not remotely resemble Zangwill's ideal of a mutually blended melting pot. Among other things, this underscores the substantial lack of critical analysis among these contemporary analysts of what "assimilation to whiteness" really means for those who are supposedly involved in this process.

We can ask, for instance, how accurate are the increasingly common assertions and theories about Latinos now whitening and moving well into the center of a historically white-controlled melting pot? We see several major empirical problems with this argument. First, there is the remarkably huge and continuing racial economic inequality between white Americans and Latinos. In recent federal data, the median net worth for white households was $113,149, which is *eighteen times* the median net worth of $6,325 for Latino households. As a Pew Research Center report concluded about this gap between whites and Latinos (and blacks), "These lopsided wealth ratios are the largest since the government began publishing such data a quarter century ago" (Kochhar, Fry, and Taylor, 2011). Not surprisingly, much of this wealth gap is made up of the housing equities that whites have built up over several generations of the white "affirmative action" discussed in Chapter 5 and of the related discrimination that has frequently limited access to homebuying (and better-paying jobs) for Latinos and other Americans of color.

This great and enduring wealth inequality means far more than just inequality in monetary assets. As we have suggested in earlier discussions, great racial inequality creates, or is associated with, much more access to *social* capital, such as networking and institutional-access capital, that further buttresses white position, power, and privilege. As one social scientist working on inequality issues has expressed it, the accumulated net worth of a family is central to its "class standing, social status, whether they own or rent housing, the kind of community they live in, and the quality of their children's schools" (Shapiro, 2004: 31).

Additionally, there is the central problem of continuing high levels of racist framing of Latinos by a majority of white Americans. We discussed this in Chapter 1, but we will reiterate and develop a few points of relevance here. Recall the research conducted by Feagin and Dirks (2004). Most of the 151 well-educated, relatively young whites surveyed did not view any Latino group as "white." Large majorities classified Mexican Americans, Puerto Ricans, and Cuban Americans as clearly not white. As we have observed throughout this book, the racial status and positioning of major societal groups are largely determined by whites, especially the whites with significant institutionalized power. Each group of color, including Latino immigrants and their descendants, has been placed by dominant whites somewhere on the centuries-old white-to-black status ladder, with a white-imposed racial position typically well down the ladder from whites and one indicating that group's subordinate societal status. Indeed, as we have already indicated, there is much evidence today in the mass media, popular books, and field research that many whites (and some others) now worry about the "browning of America" and conceptualize Latinos as a distinctive "brown" race. To note one example of this recent research, in a study of interactions at a large Anglo-run Mexican restaurant, Barrett (2006) discovered such "brown" categorizing of Latino workers in the language and decision making of the restaurant's white managers and servers.

While some opinion surveys suggest that whites are now publicly more accepting of Latinos than of African Americans as residential neighbors and in a few other settings, this is still a relative matter, since a majority of whites in these surveys are not fully accepting of Latinos into their residential neighborhoods. A few polls also show less publicly expressed resistance among whites to intermarriage between whites and Latinos. Still, fully positive acceptance of such intermarriages is usually well below a majority of whites (Golebiowska, 2007). In addition, other survey data suggest a much more troubling racial picture. One 2011 Associated Press survey found just over half of the non-Hispanic white respondents held significant anti-Latino views, with some *57 percent* also revealing negative reactions to Latino photos in an implicit association test (Ross and Agiesta, 2012). In a 2012 Associated Press survey of Americans, about two-thirds of whom were white, some 30 percent openly agreed with the strong racist stereotype of Latinos as lazy, and 36 percent agreed with the racist stereotype of them as irresponsible (Associated Press, 2012). Such percentages are likely underestimates, for research by Picca and Feagin (2007) demonstrates clearly how much white expression of a blatantly racist framing of Americans of color now takes place in the more private backstage settings where only whites are present.

Moreover, much of the data in this book and numerous other recent studies indicate that the view of major Latino groups being fully integrated into core white institutions in the near future is far too optimistic (see Telles and Ortiz, 2008: 283–287; M. Chavez, 2011). There is still widespread discrimination by whites out of the old anti-Latino framing. To take just one example, recall our discussion in Chapter 2 of a significant racialized affront experienced by Mexican American professionals at the hands of a white woman because they were speaking Spanish on an elevator. One of these professionals reported that "we were speaking Spanish. When she got off the elevator she commented, 'Well, you people have been here a long time in the United States. I don't know why you're still speaking Spanish.'" The arrogant white interlocutor felt entitled to scold the Mexican American professionals as though they were children because they were members of a racially tainted group. Witness to this fact is that she also employed the term "you people," a common white synonym for an "othered" racial group, when she spoke to them. Objectively speaking, she should not have been surprised when she saw them speaking Spanish. After all, the white frame sees not being white and being "foreign" as going together.

However, they were just being themselves and drawing on their comfortable home culture as millions of immigrants and their descendants have done for centuries. Major elements of the dominant white frame have never been subject to critical analysis among most whites, and these and many other middle-class Mexican Americans are still viewed as part of an inferior racial group in white eyes, indeed, probably in any societal circumstance.

We could continue summarizing these cases of discrimination from our interviews, of course, but let us note a few other research studies that also have recorded reports of the everyday discrimination encountered by middle-class and working-class Latinos in various settings. One national survey of Latinos and African Americans found that significant *majorities* reported much racial discrimination against their group (New America Media, 2007). Employment discrimination is a serious problem reported by Latinos in several recent studies, including Maria Chavez's (2011) study of Latino lawyers, from which we have quoted in previous chapters. In addition, a research study by Barrett (2006) of white and Latino workers in a large white-owned Mexican restaurant with mainly Anglo patrons found that the white management and staff "othered" and racialized Latino kitchen workers. The latter's paychecks were, for example, put into a "brown pile" for them to pick up, and white managers and servers "frequently referred to kitchen employees with phrases such as 'that one' or 'those two' rather than with personal pronouns such as 'him' or 'them,'" as they did for whites in the restaurant (Barrett, 2006: 176). This researcher discovered that discussions of racial matters by English-speaking white workers "almost universally involved stereotyped assessments of customers or negative attitudes toward Latino co-workers. In contrast, Spanish-language discussions [by Latino kitchen workers] often dealt with racist attitudes of individual English-speaking workers or the general problem of racism in the restaurant" (Barrett, 2006: 193). In this regard, the Latino workers discussed which whites were racist in their views and which were "good people," and such information was useful to them in navigating the racial hurdles of this workplace.

As we have argued in previous chapters, most European Americans have never envisioned even a partial (mutual) societal blending of their culture and families with those of immigrants of color and their descendants. Apart from the occasional and modest appropriations of certain elements of immigrant cultures, such as food or music, most European Americans continue to operate out of only a white framing of society, one in which whites remain dominant and the white Anglo core culture and whiteness are conventional standards of what and who are truly "American." Full, mutual, and egalitarian "assimilation" of immigrant groups of color into the core culture and institutions would doubtless require a re-creation of the whole society into one that is not pervasively white framed and white dominated.

## Accenting US Diversity: A Multiracial Melting Pot?

We now turn to how our middle-class respondents view the blending and mixing of Latinos into the contemporary US racial mixture. Not surprisingly, a great many immigrant Americans and their descendants still celebrate a hopeful version of an interactive blending of peoples within the United States. In their interviews, our middle-class respondents frequently seem to give credence to this idealistic imagery of a blending of racially and ethnically diverse peoples into one US melting pot.

### Assessing a Contemporary Melting Pot

In earlier discussions we touched on the current US demographic changes in the direction of an eventual white minority population, a trend that numerous scholars and media analysts have publicly assessed in recent decades. US census data unmistakably indicate that these demographic changes are well under way. European Americans are indeed decreasing in their proportion of the population (see Feagin, 2010). When we presented to our respondents the prediction of demographers that the United States will have a white minority in about forty years, quite a few explicitly named and accented the melting-pot concept in regard to the past, present, or future of the United States.

Unsurprisingly, our interviewees hold to a different view of the US melting pot from that of including just European groups that was accented a century ago by white immigrant advocates like Israel Zangwill (1909) in his famous play. One Latino respondent agrees with this demographic statement, responding:

> I think that it is changing, and that I don't think there is anything wrong with it. I mean the United States is the melting pot. That is what it was founded on—the people from different places—and it should be [a melting pot].

Here we see that the melting pot positively accented by our Latino respondents is usually one that emphasizes substantial national diversity and accents or implies significant cultural pluralism. A Cuban American respondent answers by including both North and South American continents in his dramatic cataloging of the relevant mixture:

> The Americas [are] a melting pot. Whether it was Latin America or English-speaking America, it's a melting pot. And that's basically what it is; you have whites, you have blacks, you have Asians, and there's a lot of Asian Latinos. I mean, there was a huge Chinese population in Cuba. There's a huge

Jewish population that lived in Cuba. . . . In the Americas everybody came here into a melting pot.

Again, we observe a view of the US melting pot that envisions the United States as including, respectfully, many groups of color, and not just European groups. All the continents are conspicuously accented in his broad and composite vision.

One Mexican American interviewee explicitly emphasized the melting-pot idea in response to our vignette about a white person's negative response to Latino professionals speaking Spanish at a bank. He responds with this pointed comment:

I heard that happen to people before, not like at a bank, but you know they'll be at somewhere, something like that would happen, and someone would say something. I think that's really kind of ignorant on the other person's part, for coming to conversation that is not included of him or her. And to, I mean, this is a country based for people of all nations, all races, all religions basically. And that was the foundation of this country, and I don't think anyone should have a problem with anyone else. . . . If they speak another language, if they can't understand it, how do they say: Learn it!

In his commentary about a diverse US foundation, there are echoes of important "liberty and justice for all" statements made by leading Americans over the centuries, often in reference to a complex array of immigrant groups. If older white immigrant groups' descendants are uncomfortable with the newer groups and their cultures, they can simply adopt a new "learning" mode. In contrast, the classical white approach has involved a missionary-type teaching mode emphasizing the "white man's burden" to bring civilization to people of color, one famously articulated in a late 1800s poem published under that title in an American magazine by the British poet Rudyard Kipling. We see this white "teaching," rather than listening and learning, mode in many of our middle-class respondents' accounts of interactions with Anglo whites throughout our chapters.

We do observe in these commentaries alluding to the United States as a melting pot that our respondents conspicuously include immigrants of color and their descendants in the mixture, in contrast to earlier idealistic images of it as all-white. It is also important to note that our respondents in these and other quotes often do not have a one-way assimilation process in mind as the national goal, but indicate or imply either a statistical US mix that is very diverse racially and culturally or some type of interactive blending of diverse groups that allows for significant cultural distinctiveness.

## *Favorable Views of Immigrants' Attempts at Assimilation*

Taken as a group, our middle-class respondents have a very good understanding of the immigration process and of the pain that racist whites impose on immigrants of color as they try to "fit in" in this historically racist society. For instance, in response to our vignette about a white woman getting angry over the accented English of a waitperson and using the "spic" epithet, one Cuban American reacts in this manner:

> I have actually seen that. . . . Not quite that derogatory a term, more like "why don't you learn to speak the language" type of comment. I think that is kind of close-minded for that individual. *For the person who reacted that way?* Yeah, yeah. It is probably a new immigrant, trying to make a living, and he is probably trying to learn the language. And I think that is what this country is about.

The close-mindedness of many whites is here emphasized, and there is a clear understanding of the significant difficulties that immigrants of color face in trying to adapt to US institutions. Similarly, a Mexican American respondent replies this way to the same vignette:

> Very arrogant of the Anglo-American to do that. Very uneducated about America's history as far as being the land of immigrants.

The last two respondents are emphasizing the old idealistic theme that the United States is indeed a land of immigrants. Unquestionably, most of our Latino respondents are closer to the immigration experience than many of their white critics. They can thus more easily spot and call out the close-mindedness, obstinacy, and arrogance that are frequently operative in maintaining the commonplace and negative white framing of Latino immigrants and their descendants.

Presented with the same vignette, another Cuban American respondent is similarly blunt in pointing out that the white woman using "spic" for a waitperson with a strong Spanish accent was an example of

> Racism. Definitely. *Why?* Just because they are in this country, and this country is predominately English speaking . . . and just because they have an accent and there is some difficulty with communicating is no reason to insult another person.

She is insistent about this attitudinal racism. In Chapter 2 we observed many excerpts from our interviews that illustrate white hostility to Spanish or Spanish-accented English. These last few respondents also put the negative white reaction into a larger framework of understanding the difficulties of many Latino immigrants who try hard to adapt to this English-dominant society, an understanding frequently missing in the majority white population. The pressured, one-way character of the actual assimilation process is also clearly recognized in these excerpts.

One Puerto Rican woman evaluates the restaurant vignette in this pointed way:

> That's, that's a wrong comment. Yeah, that's not right. She's, she's being racist. She's not racist, but she's . . . not understanding that the United States is becoming, is about all these different races.

While somewhat uncertain about terming the white woman's act as racist, this respondent is clear about the white failure to understand that the United States is becoming a country where whites are no longer as central, at least demographically, as they once were. The clear recognition of significant demographic and other social change can be observed throughout many of our interviews.

Assessing the restaurant incident, a Mexican American respondent likewise brings up the demographic change issue, and she adds a number of related issues about racial and ethnic diversity:

> I think it's really sad. And because we live . . . in the Southwest we have such a blend of so many different cultures that you have to be bilingual to be successful in the Southwest. The population has grown so much and there is such a great number of people coming over for work. And so you have to understand that you're going to have people of all different nationalities, of all different ethnicities. And they are going to speak with accents, whether it be a Spanish accent or an Arabic accent. You know we . . . have so many different people and that would make me think of the fact of how this country was founded on. It was founded upon immigrants, you know. Native Americans . . . this was their land. Everybody else invaded it. The English speakers came over and occupied all this territory, and so obviously the first thoughts would come into my head were, you know, who's speaking what? Who's speaking with an accent here? Whose land was this first?

Noting again that the United States is a land of immigrants, this savvy woman underscores the reality that all but Native Americans are actually immigrants to this country or their descendants. She celebrates the often unrecognized reality of *needing* a broad cultural awareness, and of knowing different languages, to be successful in areas of the contemporary Southwest. Her insights about cultural pluralism are, we suggest, increasingly applicable to many other areas of the United States.

Thinking more specifically about Latinos, she assesses an additional interview question about how Latinos are fitting into an increasingly multiracial society in this way:

> I think that they fit in a very important part. They're at the center because we will be the largest minority. We will be the largest ethnic minority group, which means that we will have a greater number of representation than African American or Pacific Asian-Islander or any other ethnic minority group . . . and we have to understand that we live in the United States and that's a very fluent place. As I said before, you know, the United States was founded by immigrants. You know the Europeans came across the sea. And they are the first immigrants, and so . . . they need to consider the fact that for much of the land in the Southwest area, you know, this was all part of Mexico. And so the people—for the most part, a lot of the Mexican American Chicanos—this is their native land, and so I think they should be at the center of it.

Not skipping a beat in her answer, she accurately underscores the reality and meaning of Mexican Americans plus other Latinos becoming the largest group of Americans of color. Indeed, in her comments this respondent is clearly emphasizing a country that is pluralistic and a respectful mixing together of people with different cultures who learn from each other, rather than just the process of continuing Anglo-conformity assimilation.

The old center of what became the US Southwest was, of course, Mexican. Today, Mexican Americans and other Latinos are becoming an even more centrally important population there, and gradually in other US regions. Yet another irony facing whites who are intensely hostile to Latinos, their Spanish language, and other aspects of their home cultures is this ancient anchoring of the parts of the Latino population in the Southwest *long* before many whites' ancestors arrived in North America. Unmistakably, this last respondent is much more perceptive about the history and reality of the Latino population than a great many non-Latino Americans.

## Multiracialism within Families

The increasingly diverse racial mixture that is the contemporary United States is accented in our interviews in yet other ways. For example, asked if she thought Hispanics/Latinos were now being welcomed by whites, a Mexican American teacher responds in this interesting way:

> I have a lot of white friends, and I have a white husband and white family members now. [I] think that there's a lot of multiracial families now; it's not just the white race . . . not just pure Mexican or pure white. . . . I'm hoping it

will become easier . . . for my children and their generation. And that's how it was before. That's what this country is. It's full of different races.

At the beginning of her commentary this woman sounds optimistic about the prospect of an ongoing fusion of whites with racially subordinated groups. However, she then suggests some uncertainties about the conditions faced by her biracial children in the United States in the future. Her apparent vacillation may reflect her own experiences and knowledge that whites can increase their distance from "othered" groups like these biracial children at any point and thereby make life harder for them. Notice too here, as throughout our interviews, the recurring language and easy conceptualization of whites and a Latino group as distinct "races."

As the last respondent noted, multiracial families are increasing across the United States, and this affects how Americans of color view themselves and how they view society generally. With a strong positive emphasis, one Cuban American respondent accents the interesting diversity of her own family in this fashion:

I'm Cuban, and I'm married to an Italian. . . . [He is third generation.] I look at my children and they are American. They were born in this country. You know, their background is Italian/Cuban, but they were born in this country. And . . . your wife is German and you're Hispanic, but your son was born in this country, so he is American. . . . The reality of it is that everybody comes from somewhere else. I know you do have those "Daughters of America" who came over on the Mayflower, OK. So you have those few people, but the reality of it [is] that generation which is our age group, they are marrying somebody that is not the "Daughter of America." They are marrying someone else from another culture. So . . . what are they telling me? That they are not going to have pure Anglo-Americans.

Like others among our middle-class respondents, she is very aware, personally and intellectually, of the significant impact that multiracial families are having on the racial mix that is the United States, and even on the current descendants of early English colonists. One sees here again an important framing of US society that unquestionably goes beyond the old Anglocentric version of the white racial frame.

Ever so slowly, perhaps, the generic "American" is coming to mean more than "white" for many people, and especially for those like this respondent. Nonetheless, the pace of this change seems rather slow. One 2000 research study that questioned Cuban American women found that most did not think that Anglo whites yet viewed them as "American" (Barlow, Taylor, and Lambert, 2000). Indeed, one 2011 Pew Hispanic Center survey of

US Latinos found that nationally only a modest minority (21 percent) currently use "American" for their own identity, and about half those interviewed said they still felt themselves to be "very different" from the "typical American" (Taylor, Lopez, Martínez, and Velasco, 2012).

Asked about the demographic predictions of a coming white minority population in the United States in future decades, one respondent notes affirmatively the importance of this increasing racial mixture already, at home and in her everyday work environment:

> Well, to begin with, I see it in our own family, OK. Our family's a complete mixture. We have German, Finland, Irish, mixture of Japanese-Hawaiian; we have African Americans in our family. We have everything. OK. So you have this mixture. My niece, one of my newest nieces is blond; of course, her father is Hispanic. Um, things are changing. . . . I'm . . . working on a project on my case load, and I cannot go by the name and indicate what their ancestry is: African American, Hispanic, Anglo. . . . The name just doesn't go with the person, you know. The person is white, speaks no Spanish whatsoever, but the name is Valdez. I have a person that surely is a Mexican national, brown, with a French name. So, I think in the long run, it will be good. I think everyone will end up this color or lighter. *Color meaning brown?* Um-hum.

A number of our respondents accent in positive ways the so-called browning of the United States, and they find the aforementioned demographic projection we presented to them as not only plausible but one that they frequently see evidence for in their daily lives. Not only are there more people who are immigrants of color or their descendants in the US population, but there are increasing numbers of interracial relationships and multiracial families like those noted in the last few respondent commentaries.

When one of our Mexican American respondents was asked what it is like being a Hispanic in a mostly white country, she answers in this way:

> I really haven't had any difficulties with [white] people. . . . It's just I concentrate on, more on me and don't worry about [what] other people think . . . [about] what I look like. . . . I just don't look at the United States as a white country. . . . *Why not?* I mean we have Asians here, Filipinos here; we have all these different races.

By trying to be inured to surrounding racist derision, this respondent seems to use a common strategy of Americans of color, one of isolating and insulating themselves as much as they can from the dominant group. In her interview she refuses to give in to the white frame's disapproval of her phenotype. Like numerous respondents, she additionally and explicitly challenges the white-framed view that the United States is a "white country." On the contrary, many racialized groups are now part of the national fabric. This strategy appears to be becoming more commonplace as the country becomes much less white in its demographic composition. Her determined opposition has thus confronted long-standing white racial frame dicta aimed at the subjugation of Americans of color.

## White Racism and the Range of Latino Resistance

Over the course of this book's chapters we have discussed a variety of resistance responses that Latinos employ as they fight the many types of blatant, subtle, and covert racist practices they encounter in their everyday lives. As we conclude this book, we can underscore some important examples of Latinos' resistance strategies. Such accounts show that Latinos are not just victims of recurring white discrimination but active agents who work as they can against everyday discrimination. As we have seen numerous times in previous chapters, resistance strategies are required for Latinos no matter what their social class is, where they live, or where they travel to.

Latino resistance strategies range over a spectrum of responses, some more subtle and others more overt and assertive. Sometimes, thus, the everyday resistance to racialized mistreatment takes the form of a quiet assertion of personal dignity. Recall, for example, the Argentinean American who overheard white clerks in a store saying that people like her looked "so innocent," implying that she might be shoplifting. She resisted such typification by not leaving but quietly continuing to shop.

Over several chapters we have also seen how important elements of Latino home cultures are frequently used in both passive and active resistance to white intrusions, insults, and other racialized discrimination. For example, in our interviews we observed numerous respondents defending their right and that of other Latinos to speak the Spanish language in most any setting. One Mexican American interviewee described speaking up forthrightly to her monolingual white supervisor, who was insisting that bilingual employees in that workplace must not speak Spanish. Similarly, another Mexican American woman openly defended some Latinos speaking Spanish in a store to a white man insisting they did not have a right to speak Spanish there. Recall, too, the Mexican American respondent who noted that he had countered his white employee's complaint about Latino employees speaking Spanish by reminding him that they were US veterans who had fought for the right to speak as they desired.

Other researchers have also documented the importance of Latino home cultures. In her study of Latino professionals on the West Coast, social scientist

Maria Chavez (2011: 43) interviewed a lawyer who pointedly underscored the importance of framing his experiences from the viewpoint of his Mexican American subculture, especially in dealing with injustices in business arenas:

> I think that I've given it my best good effort trying to deal with all these white groups and I gave up! . . . It's just uncomfortable and I don't like it. . . . I play it because it's business. I have business things I gotta do, and I can eat cheese and crackers like anybody else, a little wine. But I miss that Budweiser with carnitas. And I just want to go in, do my thing, and get the hell out of there. . . . I'm tired of that bullshit game where I have to be a white guy. Why don't they become Mexicans?

Many Latinos make use of a home-culture frame in their choosing of traditional Latino cultural preferences over those pressed on them by the dominant white culture and society. In this case, modest aspects of a Mexican American home culture help this lawyer in dealing with the barriers and pains of white-controlled business settings. Recall too the numerous examples in previous chapters where speaking Spanish, whether or not whites are present, is one way that many Latinos assert the importance of the home culture and thereby perpetuate it. Speaking Spanish at home has also been a way that many Latino immigrant parents have pressed their US-born children to stay in touch with their ancestral country's culture and also to have a useful tool to deal with certain everyday barriers. These various home-cultural resources are often extraordinarily important for Americans of color in navigating the everyday shoals involved in adapting to dominant white folkways, privately and quietly as in the quote above, or more overtly and forcefully in other societal settings.

Dealing with white-imposed conceptions of who one is requires exceptional alertness and preparation for a variety of white assaults, whether verbal or nonverbal, and whether they are expected or not. In previous chapters we saw numerous examples of such Latino alertness and the variety of their openly challenging responses as well. For example, there is the Cuban American husband and wife who went shopping for an expensive car at a local dealership but were treated poorly by a white salesperson. The husband was confrontational as he conspicuously tore up the salesperson's business card and then left with his wife without making a purchase. Then there is the Mexican American respondent who, when bypassed by a discriminatory white server in a restaurant, directly protested the obvious discrimination to that server and left without a purchase. One Puerto Rican respondent recounted an incident in a store where a white customer insisted that a Mexican farmworker to whom the respondent was talking should get out of the country; the respondent told the white man that if that happened, he would have to pick farm produce for himself. Also recall that the second author's French teacher in high school marked him down for his Spanish-accented French but had to back off and change his grade when the assertive Cuban American teenager pointed out that white students in the class spoke French with a strong English accent.

A few other researchers have provided some examples of confrontational resistance to whites' racist framing or actions. For example, reflections by faculty of color for educational researcher Christine Stanley included this poignant account from a Latino professor at a historically white institution. He describes with probing insights his experiences teaching in often difficult college settings:

> Typical of the initial questions posed by both [white] graduate and undergraduate students are, "Oh, Professor Bonilla, but you don't look Latino" or, "How long have you been in this country? You don't even have an accent!" Today, these kinds of questions present opportunities to enlighten them that not all Latinos look or sound alike. . . . Early in my teaching, my frosty reply to such questions tended to be the not so noble, "How many Latinos do you know?" or, "Well that's nice, I can barely tell you have an accent either." I took their inquiries as unwelcome reminders of my relative isolation. . . . They can be so immersed in the "normality" of their White cultural milieu that they neither see it nor understand it. (Bonilla, 2007: 70)

Again, whites like these college students have the power to put an experienced Latino professor "in his place" by making clear that they define him as racially and culturally different. Their variety of arrogant or condescending responses to him are those that many of our middle-class respondents have encountered, one of which is this "exception to your race" interpretation from whites at varying social-class levels. Whites here assume *their* way of stereotyping and framing Latinos and their way of framing themselves as superior agents of racial interpretation are normal and unproblematic. As we have often seen described by our interviewees, whites in this case have decided that most Latinos are unable to speak "good English" or have a too-heavy Spanish accent. Research by Daniel Solórzano (1998) and his colleagues has demonstrated similar types of recurring discrimination faced by Latino staff and students at yet other universities. Describing many such discriminatory acts as "microaggressions," a term coined by Charles Pierce (1995), they too have described a range of assaulting verbal commentaries such as "You're different," "I don't think of you as a Mexican," "You speak such good English," and "But you speak without an accent" (Solórzano, 1998: 125; Yosso, Smith, Ceja, and Solórzano, 2009).

Note too that in the account above, the Latino professor does not stand still for such white insults and other discrimination and over the years has developed not only a significant counter-framing but several strategies of resistance. He has used sharp sarcastic responses, as well as challenging thought questions, to create teaching moments for younger whites obviously operating out of a commonplace white racial framing of Latinos.

As we have seen in previous chapters, numerous respondents signal the importance of sometimes engaging in more overt and forceful responses to anti-Latino insults and other discrimination. One Mexican American woman expresses her view this way:

> That's what this country is made out of, different races; that's why it makes it so special here. To be mistreated within our own country, people should not stay quiet. They need to stand up and fight for what's right.

Recall the Cuban American father at Disneyworld who did just that. When his son was called a "spic" by a white person in the crowd, the respondent was very assertive in response and insisted that the "motherfucker" step forward and confront him, but no one was willing to do so. Consider too the Cuban American respondent whose mother was speaking Spanish in a store and was admonished by a white woman to speak English. Her mother asked if the white woman was an American Indian. When the latter stated that she was Polish, the respondent's mother capped her resistance to such white framing with a comment that the white woman too was a type of immigrant "refugee."

One Mexican American respondent provided an account of his very vigorous countering response in a dramatic example of white racist framing and associated white action. When he was in the US Army, he recounted in his interview, he and his family were on their way home one night:

> One of my headlights was burnt out, so I had to turn on my brights. . . . [A white driver was upset because] we were with our brights behind [him]. . . . He got behind us and turned on his brights. . . . [At the next red light] I explained to the guy . . . that the headlight was bad so we had to turn on the brights, sorry about that. . . . [He called me] . . . "wetback." . . . [I was wearing my Army uniform] and got out . . . and approached his car. . . . I said, "What did you say? Don't you see right here [on my uniform] I have United States Army? . . . He goes, "I don't care." [We started] fighting in the street. . . . I said, "You started all of this. Do I look like a wetback to you?" And he said, "Yes." And I told myself . . . it doesn't matter if I am a professor at a university, it doesn't matter if I'm a doctor of medicine, to some people my phenotype will always be nothing but a wetback.

This vignette vividly illustrates the racist nexus between whiteness and Americanness. The fact that the respondent was a US soldier willing to sacrifice his life for *his* homeland did not alter the white driver's negative perception of him as a racialized "wetback." He was framed as undeserving of the respect that a white—that is, truly "American"—soldier would likely have received. The respondent's closing words are poignant: Regardless of achievements, he remains a racialized outsider, a "wetback." Very significant too in this event is the Mexican American soldier's strong response to the white racist targeting and action. Not only has he fought overseas for the United States, but he has also had to fight, like many other people of color for centuries, for his freedom and rights within the United States.

As we have seen throughout this book, the relationship between whites and Mexican Americans in numerous areas of the United States has frequently been marred by the former's unabashed racist framing of the latter. This racist framing manifests itself in numerous ways, including in the overarching theme of Mexican Americans and other Latinos as distinctive "aliens" who will never qualify as real Americans. We can reiterate here a point we made previously that such racist framing appears frequently in the media and can be observed at all levels of white America. Indeed, as we were writing this section, an important member of the US House of Representatives from Alaska, Don Young, gave a radio interview in which he blithely described tomato workers on his father's ranch as "wetbacks," thereby revealing the racialized thinking about Mexican Americans that he shares with many ordinary whites like the man in the incident above (Adams, 2013). Young later apologized for his "commonly used" terminology, insisting he "meant no disrespect," yet he did not apologize for his casual but serious racist framing of Latinos. Moreover, as we have noted before, there is now a substantially greater number of Latinos in many US towns and cities, and their encounters with the "alien" and "wetback" framing, sometimes as part of violent attacks, seems to be on the increase across the country (see Ortega, 2013).

## Conclusion: Organized Resistance

Our respondents were not asked about their participation in organized movements of resistance to anti-Latino discrimination, but doubtless a number of them have been involved in various Latino organizations that seek social justice for Latinos. We can note briefly in conclusion that there has been a long history of organized resistance utilizing elements from Latino home-culture frames or from more developed antiracist counter-frames. There was a resurgence of these protests in the 1960s–1970s era. In the civil rights era of the 1960s–1970s, younger Mexican Americans, both working class and middle class, engaged in numerous protests against anti-Latino discrimination in various southwestern cities. Chicano organizations like the Brown Berets protested recurring police brutality and other officials' malpractice. These and other protest movements in turn sometimes provoked yet more police brutality, such as the attacks by police on the summer 1970 National Chicano Moratorium on the Vietnam War and on protests by Chicano groups during Mexican Independence Day parades in this era. In turn, these police responses to usually peaceful Latino protests provoked yet more protestation against police and other official discrimination (Morales, 1972).

Also during this era, numerous Mexican Americans joined in a southwestern political movement associated with the La Raza Unida Party (LRUP). Many in this movement operated out of an explicit Chicano counter-frame and sought to replace white control of local politics in a few southwestern areas where Mexican Americans were a substantial part of the population yet had little political power. Success in the Texas town of Crystal City, to cite one important example, brought significant Mexican American representation to the local school board and city council, which was in turn followed by a white political backlash (Shockley, 1974). Nonetheless, this political organization among southwestern Mexican Americans helped to restart a movement to further democratize Texas politics and the politics of other southwestern areas—one that persists, albeit often intermittently, in the present day.

Numerous civil rights groups have developed and become very important in the struggle to counter continuing discrimination against Latinos. Groups like LULAC have become more militant over the decades, and other increasingly influential groups like the Mexican American Legal Defense and Education Fund (MALDEF) have emerged since the protest era of the 1960s. A leading Latino social justice organization, MALDEF has worked with other Latino organizations to press for the expansion and protection of Latino voting rights and has worked against anti-Latino discrimination in other areas such as jury representation, employment, housing, and schools. Similarly, the National Council of La Raza (NCLR) is the largest national organization of Latinos in the United States, one that grew out of the civil rights movements of the 1960s. NCLR's statement of its organization and policies suggests the rapidly growing importance of Latino rights organizations across the United States:

> Through its network of nearly 300 affiliated community-based organizations, NCLR reaches millions of Hispanics each year in 41 states, Puerto Rico, and the District of Columbia. To achieve its mission, NCLR conducts applied research, policy analysis, and advocacy, providing a Latino perspective in five key areas—assets/investments, civil rights/immigration, education, employment and economic status, and health. ("About Us," 2013)

These various Latino groups often operate out of a strong counter-frame targeting and assertively critiquing anti-Latino racism in the United States and pressing forcefully for the expansion of social justice for Latinos and other Americans of color.

# 7

# The Great Demographic Shift and the US Future

In this and previous chapters we have tracked the oscillating and sometimes conflicting conceptions of what is meant by "assimilation" of Latinos to the core culture and institutions of this society. We have seen the importance of the more idealistic view of a melting pot that involves respectful cultural diversity and/or mutual blending versus, more centrally, the actual assimilation "pot" that means that new groups must mostly assimilate in a conforming and one-way fashion to the white-Anglo core culture and institutions. Our middle-class respondents often seem more hopeful about the cultural pluralism view, and most are aware that elements of one-way assimilation can be quite harmful, while Anglo whites in this society have long overwhelmingly supported the one-way view. Additionally, as we have seen, the historical and contemporary data indicate that the one-way view has mostly been the one put into practice by its white controllers and implementers now over several centuries.

## A Major Demographic Transition Today

The ongoing demographic changes in the composition of the US population will likely provide major challenges to the continuing dominance of this white core culture and associated white-run institutions. Whites are decreasing in their proportion of the US population. In recent decades the white population has had relatively low birth and immigration rates and has increased more slowly than the Latino, Asian, and African American populations. Indeed, in 2012 a majority of the babies born in the United States were to families of color. Assuming birth and immigration rates stay near current levels, half the US population will be Americans of color by no later than the 2040s. Whites are already a statistical minority in the populations of California, Texas,

New Mexico, Hawaii, and the District of Columbia. By about 2020 the states of Arizona, Nevada, Florida, Georgia, Mississippi, New York, and New Jersey are expected to join this important demographic list (Yen, 2013). No later than the early 2040s, moreover, a majority of the labor force is forecast to be workers of color, with a large proportion being Latinos. Additionally, according to US Census Bureau projections, by 2020 the US public education system will have a majority of students of color. Many local school systems, such as large ones in Texas and California, have already reached this demographic distribution (Feagin, 2010; Yen, 2013).

Unquestionably, changes in educational and employment demography, as well as in the voting population, will have significant implications for historical white dominance in this society. Some evidence on the impact of the demographic changes has been discussed previously, but we can note a couple of other possible political impacts. In addition to the scrambling of the conservative Republican Party for Latino voters, a substantial majority of whom have recently voted for the Democratic Party, there is the potential for the growing Latino population to bring more (small "d") democratic politics to the United States. As Parenti (2011) and Feagin (2012), among others, have shown in detail, the United States has never been truly democratic in its political structure—and especially in regard to the US Congress and state legislatures. The membership of these political bodies has until recently been overwhelmingly (elite) white and male, and they are still very dispro-portionately that way. The growing and relatively progressive Latino voting population—together with the voting populations of other groups of color and certain white demographic groups—has the *potential* to generate much more democratic representation in the US Congress and numerous state legislatures. Although we certainly realize that there are other less democratic trajectories that might result from this demographic change, it could conceivably mean that no longer will elite white men rule so substantially over these supposedly representative and democratic political bodies.

Some of this potential political impact can already be seen in contemporary California politics, where the Latino vote buttressed the vote of other voters of color and liberal whites in 2012 to provide the Democratic Party with an overwhelming two-thirds majority in both houses of the state legislature (also one-fifth Latino). Today, numerous city councils in our largest state have Latino majorities, all statewide offices (including both US senators) are held by Democrats, and President Obama won California twice in electoral landslides. Recent state elections have resulted in significantly greater legislative support for pro-immigrant and certain other progressive legislation, support likely to increase as the state economy further improves (J. Lopez, 2013). What will the future of US politics look like when a majority of voters are the generally more progressive voters of color? California *may* be the "time machine" that signals a more democratic future for the United States as a whole.

How are elite and ordinary whites responding to the demographic changes that signal a continuing increase in the Latino population and in US racial diversity in coming years? As we observed in our respondents' experiences, many whites view such a demographic transition rather negatively and routinely from a white racial framing. The majority do not seem to want a United States that is highly diverse with a white minority. Some of this white perspective was dramatically documented in the 1996 book *The Coming White Minority*, by journalist Dale Maharidge. In it he discusses how white Californians are already dreading a "not-so-distant tomorrow when a statistical turning point will be reached that could have very bad consequences for them" (Maharidge, 1996: 11). His interviews indicate that many whites are fearful not only of losing jobs but also of changes that might be coming for the dominant culture. Today, these white fears of, and consequent reactions to, the increase in Latino political and union power—including white movement away from diversifying urban areas—have apparently accelerated in California and elsewhere. We previously discussed how upset many white political and intellectual leaders are. Influential arch-conservatives like Peter Brimelow (1995), Samuel Huntington (2004), and Patrick Buchanan (2008) have been joined by liberals like Arthur Schlesinger (1991) in their often wildly stated fears of immigrants of color, especially Latin American immigrants, and their descendants bringing about a supposed decline and fall of US or Western civilization.

Numerous analysts from various political and academic backgrounds are now critical of Latino immigration and population growth. For example, in a 2007 op-ed article in an elite Washington, DC, newspaper, influential Yale professor and racial-ethnic policy analyst Amy Chua, the daughter of Pacific Islander immigrants, penned a substantially white-framed analysis that seems to resonate with much non-Latino thinking about Latino immigrants in the nation's capital and elsewhere. While rejecting the most extreme anti-immigrant nativism of people like Samuel Huntington, Chua (2007) nonetheless accents Latin American immigrants as problematic for the country:

> That the 11 million to 20 million illegal immigrants are 80 percent Mexican and Central American is itself a problem. . . . If the U.S. immigration system is to reflect and further our ethnically neutral identity, it must itself be ethnically neutral, offering equal opportunity to [all immigrants]. . . . The starkly disproportionate ratio of Latinos . . . is inconsistent with this principle.

Again, it is *who* the immigrants are that is the problem, and Chua says nothing about how US corporations' destruction of farming economies in Latin

America ultimately lies behind much of this working-class Latin American immigration. Note too her contention, refuted by much data in this book, that the United States has an "ethnically neutral identity." Chua's solutions are also, to a significant degree, out of a white racial framing. She agrees with nativistic organizations that English should be the "official national language."

Without a doubt, there is much illiteracy in the United States about the US Latino population and its long history, an issue we have examined throughout this book. The first European language spoken frequently in what came to be named North America was Spanish, not English, and this North American area had numerous Spanish residents long before there were English residents. In addition, the incorporation of the first Latinos into the United States came after an unjust imperialistic war tore off the northern half of Mexico. This background history is ignored by or unknown to most of the chauvinistic critics of today's Latin American immigration to the United States. In addition, the Spanish language is currently the second most important language in the United States, and the US economy, among other important institutions, would not operate well if speaking Spanish was suddenly and completely prohibited in all work arenas.

Significantly, too, most critics of undocumented Mexican and other Latin American immigrants do *not* note the courage of these workers who cross a difficult US-Mexico border and then face substantial discrimination at the hands of whites (and others) across the United States. In contrast, the millions of European immigrants who came to the United States just before and after 1900 have long been lauded for their bravery in coming to the "land of opportunity" and overcoming many obstacles in search of a better life for themselves and their families. Undocumented Latino immigrants have often incurred even more risks on their frequently dangerous trips to the "land of opportunity" in search of that same better life for themselves and their families. Moreover, if they have children born in this country (as many do), they are often accused by white immigration critics of giving birth to racially framed "anchor babies," who by virtue of their US citizenship supposedly can ease their mother's attainment of citizenship status. However, most critics of these immigrant women have ignored the fact that most are building families just as European immigrant women have long done. In addition, few seem to understand that US babies of undocumented mothers do not have the legal status to help their mothers with citizenship options until they are 21—a very long wait that makes the stereotyped baby-anchoring strategy both very difficult and rare (see Lacey, 2011). In addition, the racialization indicated by the harsh "anchor baby" language is clear in that virtually none of the white critics single out for criticism the numerous babies born to undocumented immigrant mothers from countries not in Latin America.

Numerous racial stereotypes and narratives about Latino immigrants in the conventional white racial frame are increasingly discredited by recent interviews with or surveys of Latino immigrants, both those who are unauthorized and those who are authorized (see Telles and Ortiz, 2008; Valdez, 2011). For instance, one recent Latino Decisions national survey of undocumented Latino immigrants found that most are long-term residents, have US families, and desire US citizenship (Lilley, 2013). More than two-thirds have been US residents for at least ten years, and most of the rest have been residents for at least five years. Three-quarters said they came to work and create a better economic situation for themselves and their families; most of the rest came to unify families. The overwhelming majority currently have close relatives who are US citizens, and a substantial majority have US-born children. In addition, 87 percent indicated that they would seek US citizenship if that were permitted (Lilley, 2013). Clearly, most of these unauthorized Latino immigrants have quite significant family ties and roots in the United States and are committed to raising good families and contributing much hard work to the US economy and larger society.

In addition, recent demographic research has found that Mexican migration (over recent decades a little more than half undocumented) to the United States has been dropping over the last few years, to the point that from 2005 to 2010 there was a net zero migration—that is, out-migration at least offset in-migration. Demographers at the Pew Hispanic Center have summarized the following reasons for this: "the weakened U.S. job and housing construction markets, heightened border enforcement, a rise in deportations, the growing dangers associated with illegal border crossings, the long-term decline in Mexico's birth rates and broader economic conditions in Mexico" (Passel, Cohn, and Gonzalez-Barrera, 2012). Indeed, the total number of undocumented Mexican immigrants living in the United States *declined* over this time period.

The nativistic and Anglocentric critics of Latino immigration and assimilation noted in this book usually ignore these data on undocumented immigrants, as well as on other immigrants, and tend to operate out of a pro-white and anti-Latino racial framing of US society. This should not be surprising. As we have demonstrated throughout this book, this society is still systemically racist in many ways. Systemic oppression by whites of Latinos and other Americans of color continues to involve many aspects of US society—this dominant white racial framing, significant discrimination in most institutions, and numerous related white-generated societal problems. In our view, breaking down the racial oppression affecting Latinos into some of its complex and diverse component parts and understanding its operation and impact better, as we have tried to do in this book, are essential first steps for the significant social changes necessary for making US society more just and democratic.

## Is Multiracial Democracy Possible?

In conclusion, we can consider some analysis of US society that has managed an optimistic view of a multiracial US future, one envisioned as having much less institutional racism and substantial movement toward a truly egalitarian and just society. This more egalitarian society will necessarily involve abandonment by whites of significant racial privileges and a much more respectful and mutual blending of US group cultures and interests.

Today we live in an increasingly global and interconnected world, one that is predominantly not white. In many ways the US Latino population is one of the most interconnected of all US umbrella groups. Educated estimates indicate that close to *half* the adult population of Mexico has relatives in the United States, and this is likely true for at least a third of adult Cuban and Puerto Rican Americans (Rumbaut, 1997). If there is ever to be an egalitarian multiracial United States, it is likely to be one that is globally interconnected and one in which people of color—who make up about 83 percent of the planet's population—are taken much more seriously by people of European descent as equal partners in global progress. If this is the case, these people of color must be much better resourced to improve their lives and societies and must not continue to suffer the theft of their land, resources, or labor by people of European descent whom they have faced now for nearly five centuries.

Is a country that is closer to the more respectful, just, and pluralistic multiracial society that is accented or implied by numerous Latino respondents in this and previous chapters actually possible? Some early twentieth-century US immigration theorists explored models of non-British immigrant adjustment that departed very significantly from the Anglo-conformity assimilation perspective in the direction of real racial-ethnic pluralism. One of these was a Jewish immigrant of Polish-German origin, Horace Kallen, who became an important US philosopher. He authored a famous *Nation* magazine article in 1915 arguing that new immigrant groups should have a guaranteed right to maintain their own distinctive cultures without being forced to assimilate in one-way fashion into the British American core culture and institutions dominant then as now (Kallen, 1915).

Opposed to the intensive British-Americanization pressure of his time, Kallen coined the term "cultural pluralism" for an approach insisting that each distinctive European ethnic group had a democratic right to maintain, accent, and live by its cultural heritage (Kallen, 1915; Gordon, 1964). At that time, Kallen had in mind the impoverished and inferiorized European immigrants then coming in from southern and eastern Europe—from places like Poland, Italy, and Russia—and was a pioneer in accenting the legitimacy and importance of what has come to be called "multiculturalism." Kallen and other immigrant defenders of his era accented a key reality that a number of our Latino respondents have also emphasized—that there is great value and security in a country having diverse linguistic and other cultural traditions that are important, mutually understood, and valued.

As these early immigrant defenders viewed it, one of the great strengths of the United States was its substantial diversity in national origins and immigrant cultures. As we see it, this is still true, and especially so today in regard to languages and other cultural elements of those Americans with origins in Latin America, Africa, Asia, and the Middle East. The much maligned home cultures of immigrants and other Americans of color, as well as their sociocultural intelligence and persistent hard work, must be recognized as sources for continuing cultural and social creativity for the United States. In our view, as a country, we must greatly extend Kallen's pluralistic ideas to include all racial and ethnic groups herein, and with a *real* multiracial democracy in mind, as we hear Kallen's (1915: 20) ringing metaphorical language about a truly democratic country with

> a multiplicity in a unity, an orchestration of mankind. As in an orchestra, every type of instrument has its specific timbre and tonality, founded in its substance and form; as every type has its appropriate theme and melody in the whole symphony, so in society each ethnic group is the natural instrument, its spirit and culture are its theme and melody, and the harmony and dissonances and discords of them all make the symphony of civilization, with this difference: a musical symphony is written before it is played; in the symphony of civilization the playing is the writing, so that there is nothing so fixed and inevitable about its progressions as in music, so that within the limits set by nature they may vary at will, and the range and variety of the harmonies may become wider and richer and more beautiful. But the question is, do the dominant classes in America want such a society?

Indeed, this is the big question: Will the dominant white American group, and especially its ruling elite, allow the creation of such a democratic multiracial society?

At a minimum, real multiracial democracy requires an *end* to the suppression of the civil and other human rights of all subordinated people of color, most especially the *persisting reality of systemic racism* in the case of the United States. As we have seen, this racial oppression for Latinos ranges across an array of white-generated discrimination in workplaces, educational settings, stores and public streets, and other public and private social spaces. Persisting racialized oppression includes the suppression of languages and other home-culture elements that are essential to the self-worth and prosperity of Latinos and other

Americans of color. Indeed, a respectful view of group cultures has become an international human rights standard (Skutnabb-Kangas, 2000). The right of a subordinated racial or ethnic group to maintain its distinctive cultural values and folkways—so long as they do not suppress the rights of others—is also important to a slowly developing, yet very incomplete democratic country like the United States. The reasons include the provision of a home-culture base for resisting the persisting societal oppression and for pressing for much greater fairness and justice in this society.

Political philosopher Will Kymlicka (1996, 2001) has argued that multiculturalism, including expanded societal and government recognition of the important cultures of subordinated groups, is a very necessary step to pursuing real democracy. A fair society "must express a commitment to its immigrant citizens, and to adapt its institutions to accommodate their identities and practices" (Kymlicka, 2001: 171). Social scientist Ron Schmidt (2000: Kindle loc. 2371–2375), drawing on Kymlicka, has underscored the reality that each individual develops a self, including self-worth and self-esteem, *within* a particular cultural community of a society. A person's well-being, range of values, and action options—as well as those of her or his family—are normally rooted in a particular cultural community. Since people do not get to choose the cultural context in which they are raised, *fairness values* dictate that cultural differences should be respected and recognized and not regularly or harshly suppressed by the dominant racial group and its dominant culture.

Thus, local, state, or national governments that adopt an official language, or make one nearly official, do more than greatly bias government and other institutional operations toward that language and its native speakers. They greatly help to institutionalize the foundation for the dominant cultural community even as they suppress the foundations for the cultural "others." Such government action violates the international human rights standard of "elemental fairness" that requires that individuals' real cultural choices be made on a relatively level playing field. From this perspective, elemental fairness requires that a government like that of the United States support the language and other cultural orientations and values of people of color as it does for the dominant group (Schmidt, 2000: Kindle loc. 2392–2400).

Full recognition and egalitarian support of the diversity of languages and cultures in a society is a very important step toward a more respectful and cosmopolitan society. Cesar Chavez, the great organizer of US Latino and other farmworkers, frequently underscored the importance of keeping one's eye on societal justice as a goal and, thus, of pressing the white elites by means of "counterpower, or through a change in their hearts and minds, or change will not come" (Moyer, 1974: 253). In 1972, while he was fasting for weeks on behalf of farmworkers' rights, Chavez and Dolores Huerta, cofounder of the United Farm Workers (UFW), coined the famous phrase "¡Si, se puede!" as the motto for the UFW. Translated by the UFW into English as "Yes, it can be done," it fits well the hard work and family-building of millions of Latin American immigrants who have come to the United States in search of better economic opportunities for themselves and their families. Indeed, it also fits well the hard tasks ahead for those Americans of all backgrounds who are committed to equality and justice for all—and thus for real multiracial democracy in the United States.

# References

"About Us." *National Council of La Raza*, http://www.nclr.org/index.php/about_us (accessed April 15, 2013).

"About U.S. English." *U.S. English*, http://www.us-english.org (accessed February 26, 2013).

Acuña, Rodolfo. 1996. *Anything but Mexican: Chicanos in Contemporary Los Angeles*. London: Verso.

Adams, Eric Christopher. 2013. "Don Young: Calling Hispanics 'Wetbacks' No Longer Appropriate." *Alaska Dispatch*, http://www.alaskadispatch.com/article/20130328/don-young-calling-hispanics-wetbacks-no-longer-appropriate (accessed March 29, 2013).

Alba, Richard. 2009. *Blurring the Color Line: The New Chance for a More Integrated America*. Cambridge: Harvard University Press.

Allen, Walter R., and Daniel Solórzano. 2001. "Affirmative Action, Educational Equity and Campus Racial Climate: A Case Study of the University of Michigan Law School." *La Raza Law Journal* 12:237–277.

Almaguer, Tomás. 1994. *Racial Fault Lines*. Berkeley and Los Angeles: University of California Press.

Anonymous. [1848] 2010. "Treaty of Guadalupe Hidalgo." *Monterey County Historical Society*, http://www.mchsmuseum.com/treaty.html (accessed April 9, 2013).

Anonymous. 2000. "The Mixture as Never Before." *The Economist*, http://www.economist.com/node/289800 (accessed April 9, 2013).

Anonymous. 2008. "Ruben Salazar Remembered." *Los Angeles Times*, http://www.latimes.com/news/custom/scimedemail/la-oew-rubenremembered22apr22,0,7285266.story?page=15 (accessed February 15, 2013).

Anonymous. 2013. "James K. Polk." *Britannica Concise Encyclopedia*, http://www.answers.com/topic/james-polk (accessed April 23, 2013).

Associated Press. 2007. "Teen Survivor of Hate Crime Attack at Texas Party Jumps from Cruise Ship, Dies." *Fox News*, http://www.foxnews.com/story/0,2933,287721,00.html#ixzz2OwLsXdoI (accessed March 29, 2013).

Associated Press. 2012. "Racial Attitudes Survey." http://surveys.ap.org (accessed March 19, 2013).

Associated Press. 2013. "Forest Service Warning Called Racial Profiling." *MSNBC.com*, http://tinyurl.com/aargkny (accessed January 25, 2013).

Barlow, Kelly M., Donald M. Taylor, and Wallace E. Lambert. 2000. "Ethnicity in America and Feeling 'American.'" *Journal of Psychology* 134:581–600.

Barrera, Mario. 1979. *Race and Class in the Southwest*. Notre Dame, IN: University of Notre Dame Press.

Barrett, Rusty. 2006. "Language Ideology and Racial Inequality: Competing Functions of Spanish in an Anglo-Owned Mexican Restaurant." *Language in Society* 35:163–204.

Bell, Derrick. 1993. *Faces at the Bottom of the Well.* New York: Basic Books.

Bonilla, James F. 2007. "'Are You Here to Move the Piano?': A Latino Reflects on Twenty Years in the Academy." Pp. 68–79 in Christine A. Stanley (ed.), *Faculty of Color: Teaching in Predominantly White Colleges and Universities.* Bolton, MA: Anker Publishing Company.

Bonilla-Silva, Eduardo. 2006. *Racism without Racists: Color-Blind Racism and the Persistence of Racial Inequality in the United States.* New York: Rowman and Littlefield.

Bourdieu, Pierre. 1977. "The Economics of Linguistic Exchanges." *Social Science Information* 16:645–668.

Bourdieu, Pierre. 1991. *Language & Symbolic Power.* Cambridge, MA: Harvard University Press.

Bracey, Glenn. 2013. E-mail discussion with the author on institutional enabling.

Brimelow, Peter. 1995. *Alien Nation: Common Sense about America's Immigration Disaster.* New York: Random House.

Buchanan, Patrick J. 2002. *Death of the West.* New York: St. Martin's Griffin.

Buchanan, Patrick J. 2008. "A Brief for Whitey." http://www.buchanan.org (accessed March 31, 2008).

Burns, Walter N. 1999. *The Saga of Billy the Kid.* Albuquerque: University of New Mexico Press.

Bush, Melanie. 2004. *Breaking the Code of Good Intentions: Everyday Forms of Whiteness.* Lanham, MD: Rowman and Littlefield.

Calhoun, John C. [1848] 2007. "Conquest of Mexico." *Teaching American History,* http://teaching americanhistory.org/library/index.asp?document=478 (accessed December 13, 2007).

Cárdenas, Gilberto. 1975. "United States Immigration Policy toward Mexico." *Chicano Law Review* 2:66–91.

Chavez, Linda. 2002. "No Thanks to Affirmative Action." *The American Enterprise* 7:34–35.

Chavez, Maria. 2011. *Everyday Injustice: Latino Professionals and Racism.* Lanham, MD: Rowman and Littlefield.

Chavez, Maria L., Brian Wampler, and Ross E. Burkhart. 2006. "Left Out: Trust and Social Capital among Migrant Seasonal Farmworkers." *Social Science Quarterly* 87:1012–1029.

Cheskin Company. 2002. *Hispanic Trends.* Redwood Shores, CA: Cheskin.

Chin, Steven A. 1994. "KFRC Deejay Draws Suspension for On-Air Derogatory Remarks." *San Francisco Examiner,* December 6, A2.

Chou, Rosalind, and Joe R. Feagin. 2008. *The Myth of the Model Minority: Asian Americans Facing Racism.* Boulder, CO: Paradigm Publishers.

Chua, Amy. 2007. "The Right Road to America?" *Washington Post,* http://www.washington post.com/wp-dyn/content/article/2007/12/14/AR2007121401333_pf.html (accessed March 15, 2013).

*City of Richmond, Virginia v. J. A. Croson Co.* 1989. 488 U.S. 469.

Cobas, José A., and Joe R. Feagin. 2008. "Language Oppression and Resistance: The Case of Middle Class Latinos in the United States." *Ethnic and Racial Studies* 31:390–410.

Conklin, Nancy Faires, and Margaret A. Lourie. 1983. *A Host of Tongues: Language Communities in the United States.* New York: Free Press.

Cornelius, Wayne. 2002. "Ambivalent Reception: Mass Public Responses to the 'New' Latino Immigration to the United States." Pp. 165–189 in Marcelo M. Suárez-Orozco and Mariela M. Páez (eds.), *Latinos: Remaking America.* Berkeley: University of California Press.

Crawford, James. 1992. "Editor's Introduction." Pp. i–ii in *Language Loyalties: A Source Book on the Official English Controversy.* Chicago: University of Chicago Press.

Daniels, Jessie. 2009. *Cyber Racism*. Lanham, MD: Rowman and Littlefield.

Davis, Angela. 1971. "Reflections on the Black Woman's Role in the Community of Slaves." *Black Scholar* 3:2–15.

De Crèvecœur, J. Hector St. John. [1782] 1997. *Letters from an American Farmer*. Oxford: Oxford University Press.

De Genova, Nicholas, and Ana Y. Ramos-Zayas. 2003. *Latino Crossings: Mexicans, Puerto Ricans, and the Politics of Race and Citizenship*. New York: Routledge.

Delgado, Richard. 1996. *The Coming Race War?: And Other Apocalyptic Tales of America after Affirmative Action and Welfare*. New York: New York University Press.

Delgado, Richard, and Jean Stefancic. 2012. *Critical Race Theory: An Introduction*. 2nd ed. New York: New York University Press.

Devos, Thierry, Brian A. Nosek, and Mahzarin R. Banaji. 2007. "Aliens in Their Own Land? Implicit and Explicit Ascriptions of National Identity to Native Americans and White Americans." Research paper presented at the SPSP Groups and Intergroup Relations Pre-Conference, Memphis, Tennessee.

DMIer. 2006. "Reaction to Lou Dobbs Town Hall on Broken Borders." *MyDD*, http://www.mydd.com/story/2006/10/27/112734/61 (accessed February 1, 2013).

Dole, Bob. 1995. Interview, *Meet the Press*, NBC Television, February 5.

Du Bois, W. E. B. [1935] 1992. *Black Reconstruction in America 1860–1880*. New York: Atheneum.

ESPN. 2009. "The Legend of Jimmy the Greek." *30 for 30 Series*, November 10.

Essed, Philomena. 1991. *Understanding Everyday Racism*. Newbury Park, CA: Sage.

Feagin, Joe R. 2002. "White Supremacy and Mexican Americans: Rethinking the 'Black-White Paradigm.'" *Rutgers Law Review* 54:959–989.

Feagin, Joe R. 2004. "Documenting the Costs of Slavery, Segregation, and Contemporary Discrimination: Are Reparations in Order for African Americans?" *Harvard BlackLetter Law Journal* 20:49–80.

Feagin, Joe R. 2006. *Systemic Racism: A Theory of Oppression*. New York: Routledge.

Feagin, Joe R. 2010. *Racist America*. 2nd ed. New York: Routledge.

Feagin, Joe R. 2012. *White Party, White Government: Race, Class, and U.S. Politics*. New York: Routledge.

Feagin, Joe R. 2013. *The White Racial Frame*. 2nd ed. New York: Routledge.

Feagin, Joe R., and Danielle Dirks. 2004. "Who Is White? College Students' Assessments of Key US Racial and Ethnic Groups." Unpublished manuscript, Department of Sociology, Texas A&M University, College Station, Texas.

Feagin, Joe R., and Clairece B. Feagin. 1978. *Discrimination American Style: Institutional Racism and Sexism*. Englewood Cliffs, NJ: Prentice-Hall.

Feagin, Joe R., and Clairece B. Feagin. 2011. *Racial and Ethnic Relations*. 9th ed. Upper Saddle River, NJ: Prentice-Hall.

Feagin, Joe R., and Michael Hodge. 1995. "African American Entrepreneurship and Racial Discrimination: A Southern Metropolitan Case." Pp. 99–120 in Michael P. Smith and Joe R. Feagin (eds.), *The Bubbling Cauldron: Race, Ethnicity and the Urban Crisis*. Minneapolis: University of Minnesota Press.

Feagin, Joe R., and Nikitah Imani. 1994. "Racial Barriers to African American Entrepreneurship: An Exploratory Study." *Social Problems* 41:562–584.

Feagin, Joe R., and Karyn McKinney. 2003. *The Many Costs of Racism*. Lanham, MD: Rowman and Littlefield.

Feagin, Joe R., and Eileen O'Brien. 2003. *White Men on Race*. Boston: Beacon Press.

Feagin, Joe R., and Melvin Sikes. 1995. *Living with Racism: The Black Middle-Class Experience.* Boston: Beacon Press.

Feagin, Joe R., Hernan Vera, and Nikitah Imani. 1996. *The Agony of Education: Black Students in White Colleges and Universities.* New York: Routledge.

Fischer, David Hackett. 1989. *Albion's Seed: Four British Folkways in America.* New York: Oxford University Press.

*Fisher v. University of Texas at Austin et al.* 570 U.S. ____ (2013).

Fishman, Joshua A. 1989. *Language and Ethnicity in Minority Sociolinguistic Perspective.* Clevedon, Avon, England: Multilingual Matters Ltd.

Foley, Neil. 1997. *White Scourge: Mexicans, Blacks, and Poor Whites in Texas Cotton Culture.* Berkeley: University of California Press.

Ford, Andrea, and Sheryl Stolberg. 1991. "Latinos Tell Panel of Anger at Police Conduct." *Los Angeles Times*, May 21, A1.

Franklin, Benjamin. 1753. "Letter to Peter Collinson." *Teaching American History*, http://teaching americanhistory.org/library/index.asp?document=472 (accessed March 12, 2013).

Freeman, Douglas Southall. 1992. *Washington.* New York: First Collier Books Edition.

Frey, William H. 1997. "Domestic and Immigrant Migrants: Where Do They Go?" *Current* (January): 22–23.

Gans, Herbert J. 1979. "Symbolic Ethnicity." *Ethnic and Racial Studies* 2:1–20.

Gayle, Brenda (ed.). 2007. *Window on Freedom: Race, Civil Rights, and Foreign Affairs, 1945–1988.* Chapel Hill: University of North Carolina Press.

Glazer, Nathan. 1975. *Affirmative Discrimination: Ethnic Inequality and Public Policy.* New York: Basic Books.

Glazer, Nathan. 1997. *We Are All Multiculturalists Now.* Cambridge, MA: Harvard University Press.

Gleason, Philip. 1964. "The Melting Pot: Symbol of Fusion or Confusion?" *American Quarterly* 16:20–46.

Golebiowska, Ewa A. 2007. "The Contours and Etiology of Whites' Attitudes toward Black-White Interracial Marriage." *Journal of Black Studies* 38:268–287.

Gonzalez, Gilbert G. 1990. *Chicano Education in the Era of Segregation.* Philadelphia: Balch Institute Press.

Gonzalez, Gilbert, and Raul A. Fernandez. 2003. *A Century of Chicano History: Empire, Nations, and Migration.* New York: Routledge.

Gonzalez, Juan. 2000. *Harvest of Empire: A History of Latinos in America.* New York: Penguin Books.

Goodwin, Michael. 1988. "CBS Dismisses Snyder." *New York Times*, http://www.nytimes.com/1988/01/17/sports/cbs-dismisses-snyder.html (accessed February 14, 2013).

Gordon, Milton M. 1964. *Assimilation in American Life: The Role of Race, Religion, and National Origins.* New York: Oxford University Press.

Gramsci, Antonio. [1932] 1975. *Letters from Prison: Antonio Gramsci.* Lynne Lawner (ed.). New York: Harper Colophon.

Gramsci, Antonio. 1971. *Selections from the Prison Notebooks.* Quintin Hoare and Geoffrey Nowell Smith (eds.). New York: International Publishers.

Gramsci, Antonio. 1988. *The Antonio Gramsci Reader: Selected Writings 1916–1935.* David Forgacs (ed.). London: Lawrence and Wishart.

Gross, Ariela J. 2003. "Texas Mexicans and the Politics of Whiteness." *Law and History Review* 21:195–205.

Gross, Ariela J. 2007. "The Caucasian Cloak: Mexican Americans and the Politics of Whiteness in the Twentieth-Century Southwest." *Georgetown Law Journal* 95:338–392.

*Grutter v. Bollinger.* 2003. 539 U.S. 306.

Gutierrez, David. 1995. *Walls and Mirrors: Mexican Americans, Mexican Immigrants, and the Politics of Ethnicity.* Berkeley: University of California Press.

Gutiérrez, José Ángel. 1985. "Sondas y Rollos: The Ideology of Contemporary Chicano Rhetoric." Pp. 121–162 in John C. Hammerback, Richard Jay Jensen, and José Ángel Gutiérrez (eds.), *A War of Words: Chicano Protest in the 1960s and 1970s.* Westport, CT: Greenwood Press.

Gutiérrez, José Ángel. 2001. *A Gringo Manual on How to Handle Mexican Americans.* 2nd ed. Houston, TX: Arte Público Press.

Guzmán, Ralph. 1974. "The Function of Anglo-American Racism in the Political Development of Chicanos." Pp. 22–25 in F. Chris Garcia (ed.), *La Causa Politica.* South Bend, IN: University of Notre Dame Press.

Hacker, Andrew. 1992. *Two Nations: Black and White, Separate, Hostile, Unequal.* New York: Scribner's.

Hill, Jane H. 1999. "Language, Race, and White Public Space." *American Anthropologist* 100:680–689.

Hill, Jane H. 2008. *The Everyday Language of White Racism.* New York: Wiley-Blackwell.

Hing, Julianne. 2011. "Luis Ramirez's Attackers Get Nine Years in Prison for Deadly Beating." *Colorlines,* http://colorlines.com/archives/2011/02/luis_ramirezs_attackers_get_nine_years_in_prison_for_deadly_hate_crime.html (accessed March 29, 2013).

Hofstadter, Richard. 1955. *Social Darwinism in American Thought.* Rev. ed. Boston: Beacon Press.

Horsman, Reginald. 1981. *Race and Manifest Destiny: The Origins of American Racial Anglo-Saxonism.* Cambridge, MA: Harvard University Press.

Horton, John. 1995. *The Politics of Language Diversity: Immigration, Resistance, and Change in Monterey Park, California.* Philadelphia: Temple University Press.

Hsia, Hsiao-Chuan. 1994. "Imported Racism and Indigenous Biases: The Impacts of the U.S. Media on Taiwanese Images of African Americans." Paper presented at the Annual Meeting of the American Sociological Association, Los Angeles, California, August.

Hunt, Kasie. 2007. "Gingrich: Bilingual Classes Teach 'Ghetto' Language." *Washington Post,* http://www.washingtonpost.com/wp-dyn/content/article/2007/03/31/AR2007033100992.html (accessed April 25, 2013).

Huntington, Samuel P. 2004. *Who Are We?: The Challenges to America's National Identity.* New York: Simon and Schuster.

Jackson, Linda A. 1995. "Stereotypes, Emotions, Behavior, and Overall Attitudes toward Hispanics by Anglos." Research Report 10, Julian Samora Research Institute, Michigan State University.

Jacobson, Matthew Frye. 1998. *Whiteness of a Different Color: European Immigrants and the Alchemy of Race.* Cambridge, MA: Harvard University Press.

Jefferson, Thomas. [1785] 1999. *Notes on the State of Virginia.* Frank Shuffelton (ed.). New York: Penguin.

Johnson, Chuck. 2003. "Baker Stands by Heat Comments." *USA Today,* http://www.usatoday.com/sports/baseball/nl/cubs/2003-07-07-baker_x.htm (accessed October 2, 2011).

Johnson, Lyndon. 1965a. Executive Order 11246, http://www.eeoc.gov/eeoc/history/35th/thelaw/eo-11246.html (accessed April 10, 2013).

Johnson, Lyndon. 1965b. "Commencement Address." Howard University, http://www.lbjlib.utexas.edu/johnson/archives.hom/speeches.hom/650604.asp (accessed April 9, 2013).

Jones, Jeffrey M. 2005. "Race, Ideology, and Support for Affirmative Action: Personal Politics Has Little to Do with Blacks' Support." Gallup Poll.

Kallen, Horace M. 1915. "Democracy versus the Melting-Pot: A Study of American Nationality." *Nation*, February 25, 20.

Kant, Immanuel. [1775] 1950. "On the Distinctiveness of the Races in General." Pp. 16–24 in Earl W. Count (ed.), *This Is Race: An Anthology Selected from the International Literature on the Races of Man*. New York: Henry Shuman.

Kantrowitz, Mark. 2011. "The Distribution of Grants and Scholarships by Race." *Finaid: Student Financial Aid Policy Analysis*, http://www.finaid.org/scholarships/20110902race scholarships.pdf (accessed April 8, 2013).

Katznelson, Ira. 2005. *When Affirmative Action Was White: An Untold History of Racial Inequality in Twentieth-Century America*. New York: W. W. Norton.

Kennedy, John F. 1961. Executive Order 10925, http://www.eeoc.gov/eeoc/history/35th/thelaw/eo-10925.html (accessed April 10, 2013).

Kochhar, Rakesh, Richard Fry, and Paul Taylor. 2011. "Wealth Gaps Rise to Record Highs between Whites, Blacks, Hispanics Twenty-to-One." *Pew Research Center*, http://pewsocialtrends.org/2011/07/26/wealth-gaps-rise-to-record-highs-between-whites-blacks-hispanics (accessed August 18, 2011).

Krugman, Paul. 2007. "Republicans and Race." *New York Times*, November 19, http://www.nytimes.com/2007/11/19/opinion/19krugman.html?_r=0 (accessed May 25, 2013).

Kymlicka, Will. 1996. *Multicultural Citizenship: A Liberal Theory of Minority Rights*. New York: Oxford University Press.

Kymlicka, Will. 2001. *Contemporary Political Philosophy: An Introduction*. 2nd ed. Oxford: Oxford University Press.

Lacey, Marc. 2011. "Birthright Citizenship Looms as Next Immigration Battle." *New York Times*, January 4, 1.

Lemons, Stephen. 2010. "SB 1070 Shooter Gary Kelley Sentenced to 27.5 Years in White-on-Brown Slaying." *Phoenix New Times Blogs*, http://blogs.phoenixnewtimes.com/bastard/2011/07/sb_1070_shooter_gary_kelley_se.php (accessed March 29, 2013).

Leonhardt, David. 2013. "Hispanics, the New Italians." *New York Times Sunday Review*, http://www.nytimes.com/2013/04/21/sunday-review/hispanics-the-new-italians.html?pagewanted=all&_r=1& (accessed April 23, 2013).

Lewis, Sam. 2011. "Patchogue Plus Three." *Metrofocus*, http://www.thirteen.org/metrofocus/2011/09/patchogue-plus-three-a-look-back-at-a-fatal-hate-crime (accessed March 29, 2013).

Liddy, G. Gordon. 2008. "Gordon Liddy Show." *Radio America*, http://kickinitwithcg.blogspot.com/2008/07/mediafail-liddy-edition.html (accessed February 4, 2013).

Lilley, Sandra. 2013. "Poll: 9 out of 10 Undocumented Latinos Would Pursue Citizenship." *NBCLatino*, http://nbclatino.com/2013/04/15/poll-9-out-of-10-undocumented-latinos-would-pursue-citizenship (accessed April 15, 2013).

Lind, Michael. 1995. *The Next American Nation: The New Nationalism and the Fourth American Revolution*. New York: Free Press.

Lippi-Green, Rosina. 1997. *English with an Accent: Language, Ideology, and Discrimination in the United States*. London: Routledge.

Lippi-Green, Rosina. 2012. *English with an Accent: Language, Ideology and Discrimination in the United States*. 2nd ed. New York: Routledge. Kindle edition.

Livermore, Abiel A. [1850] 2009. *War with Mexico Reviewed*. Bedford, MA: Applewood Books.

López, Ian F. Haney. 1996. *White by Law: The Legal Construction of Race*. New York: New York University Press.

Lopez, Juan. 2013. "Latinos Helping Transform California and Nation." *People's World Blog*, February 26, http://peoplesworld.org/latinos-helping-transform-california-and-nation (accessed April 22, 2013).

MacKinnon, Catharine A. 1989. *Toward a Feminist Theory of the State*. Cambridge, MA: Harvard University Press.

Maharidge, Dale. 1996. *The Coming White Minority: California's Eruptions and America's Future*. New York: Random House.

MALDEF. 2009. "MALDEF Urges Texas Secretary of State to Re-Issue Language Assistance Guidance to County Election Officials in Light of Recent Comments." *MALDEF The Latino Legal Voice for Civil Rights in America*, http://maldef.org/news/releases/TX_election_11122009 (accessed January 27, 2013).

*Maldonado v. City of Altus*. 2006. 433 F.3d 1294.

Martinez, George A. 1998. "Mexican Americans and Whiteness." P. 178 in Richard Delgado and Jean Stefancic (eds.), *The Latino/a Condition: A Critical Reader*. New York: New York University Press.

Massey, Garth. 2004. "Thinking about Affirmative Action: Arguments Supporting Preferential Policies." *Review of Policy Research* 21:783–797.

McIntosh, Peggy. 1988. "White Privilege and Male Privilege: A Personal Account of Coming to See Correspondences through Work in Women's Studies." Unpublished paper, Wellesley College Center for Research on Women, Wellesley, MA.

Means, Russell. 1980. "For America to Live, Europe Must Die!" Black Hills International Survival Gathering, Black Hills, South Dakota, http://www.russellmeans.com (accessed September 19, 2008).

Means, Russell. 1995. "Free to Be Responsible." *Navajo Community College*, http://www.russellmeans.com (accessed September 19, 2008).

*Mendez et al. v. Westminster School District et al*. 1946. 64 F.Supp. 544 (C.D. Cal. 1946), aff'd, 161 F.2d 774 (9th Cir. 1947) (en banc).

Millard, Ann V., and Jorge Chapa. 2004. *Apple Pie and Enchiladas: Latino Newcomers in the Rural Midwest*. Austin: University of Texas Press.

Mindiola, Tatcho, Nestor Rodriguez, and Yolanda Flores-Niemann. 1996. "Intergroup Relations between African Americans and Hispanics in Harris County." Unpublished report, Center for Mexican American Studies, University of Houston, Texas.

Molina, Hilario II. 2012. "Racializing the Migration Process: An Ethnographic Analysis of Undocumented Immigrants in the United States." Unpublished doctoral dissertation, Texas A&M University, College Station, Texas.

Montejano, David. 1987. *Anglos and Mexicans in the Making of Texas, 1836–1986*. Austin: University of Texas Press.

Montoya, Margaret E. 1998. "Law and Language(s)." Pp. 574–578 in Richard Delgado and Jean Stefancic (eds.), *The Latino/a Condition: A Critical Reader*. New York: New York University Press.

Morales, Armando. 1972. *Ando Sangrando*. Fair Lawn, NJ: R. E. Burdick.

Moyer, John R. 1974. "A Conversation with César Chávez." Pp. 253–254 in Matt S. Meier and Feliciano Rivera (eds.), *Readings on La Raza: The Twentieth Century*. New York: Hill and Wang.

Mujica, Mauro. 2012. "Testimony before the Subcommittee on the Constitution of the Committee of the Judiciary House of Representatives One Hundred Twelfth Congress Second Session on H.R. 997." Serial No. 112–141.

NALEO. 2006. "Newcomers Eager to Learn English Face Waiting Lines across the Nation."

*National Association of Latino Elected and Appointed Officials*, http://www.naleo.org/pr100606.html (accessed October 17, 2006).

Navarrette, Ruben. 2006. "Calm Down, It's Not an Assault on America." *Realclearpolitics Blog*, http://www.realclearpolitics.com/articles/2006/05/calm_down_its_not_an_assault_o.html (accessed October 26, 2006).

Navarro, Mireya. 2000. "Complaint to Spanish TV: Not Enough Americans; Few U.S. Plots for Growing U.S. Audience." *New York Times*, August 21.

Nee, Victor, and Richard Alba. 2009. "Assimilation as Rational Action." P. 8 in Rafael Wittek, Tom Snijders, and Victor Nee (eds.), *Handbook of Rational Choice Social Research*. New York: Russell Sage Foundation.

New America Media. 2007. *Deep Divisions, Shared Destiny: A Poll of African Americans, Hispanics, and Asian Americans on Race Relations*. San Francisco: New America Media.

Noriega, Jorge. 1992. "American Indian Education in the United States." Pp. 371–383 in M. Annette Jaimes (ed.), *The State of Native America: Genocide, Colonization, and Resistance*. Boston: South End Press.

Oliver, Melvin L., and Thomas M. Shapiro. 2007. "Creating an Opportunity Society." *American Prospect* 18:A27.

Oppenheimer, David Benjamin. 1996. "Understanding Affirmative Action." *Hastings Constitutional Law Quarterly* 23:921–997.

Orfield, Gary, and Chugmei Lee. 2006. *Racial Transformation and the Changing Nature of Segregation*. Cambridge, MA: Harvard Civil Rights Project.

Ortega, Frank. 2013. "When Whites Attack: The Deadly Consequences of Anti-Latina/o Violence." *RacismReview*, http://www.racismreview.com (accessed March 19, 2013).

O'Sullivan, John Louis. 1980. "*United States Magazine and Democratic Review*, July–August 1845." P. 522 in Emily M. Beck et al. (eds.), *Bartlett's Familiar Quotations*. 15th ed. New York: Little, Brown and Co.

Parenti, Michael. 2011. *Democracy for the Few*. 9th ed. Belmont, CA: Wadsworth.

Park, Robert, and Ernest Burgess. 1924. *Introduction to the Science of Society*. Chicago: University of Chicago Press.

Passel, Jeffrey, D'Vera Cohn, and Ana Gonzalez-Barrera. 2012. "Net Migration from Mexico Falls to Zero—and Perhaps Less." *Pew Research Hispanic Center*, http://www.pewhispanic.org/2012/04/23/net-migration-from-mexico-falls-to-zero-and-perhaps-less (accessed April 26, 2013).

Perea, Juan F. (ed.). 1997. *Immigrants Out!: The New Nativism and the Anti-immigrant Impulse in the United States*. New York: New York University Press.

Pew Hispanic Center and Kaiser Family Foundation. 2002. *National Survey of Latinos*. Pew Hispanic Center/Kaiser Family Foundation.

Picca, Leslie H., and Joe R. Feagin. 2007. *Two-Faced Racism: Whites in the Backstage and Frontstage*. New York: Routledge.

Pierce, Charles M. 1995. "Stress Analogs of Racism and Sexism: Terrorism, Torture, and Disaster." Pp. 277–293 in C. V. Willie, P. P. Rieker, B. M. Kramer, and B. S. Brown (eds.), *Mental Health, Racism, and Sexism*. Pittsburgh: University of Pittsburgh Press.

Pincus, Fred L. 2003. *Reverse Discrimination: Dismantling the Myth*. Boulder, CO: Lynne Rienner Publishers.

*Plessy v. Ferguson*. 1896. 163 U.S. 537, 551.

Portes, Alejandro, and Min Zhou. 1993. "The New Second Generation: Assimilation and Its Variants." *Annals of the American Academy of Political and Social Science* 530:74–96.

Pyke, Karen, and Tran Dang. 2003. "'FOB' and 'Whitewashed': Identity and Internalized Racism among Second Generation Asian Americans." *Qualitative Sociology* 26:168–172.

"Race and Ethnicity." 2009. Race and Ethnicity Polling Report, http://www.pollingreport.com/race.htm (accessed February 27, 2009).

*Regents of the University of California v. Bakke.* 1978. 438 U.S. 265.

Rodríguez, Clara E. 2009. "Counting Latinos in the U.S. Census." Pp. 37–53 in José A. Cobas, Jorge Duany, and Joe R. Feagin (eds.), *How the United States Racializes Latinos: White Hegemony and Its Consequences.* Boulder, CO: Paradigm Publishers.

Rodriguez, Nestor. 1996. Personal communication, March.

Rodriguez, Richard. 2002. *Brown.* New York: Viking-Penguin.

Roosevelt, Franklin D. 1941. Executive Order 8802, http://www.eeoc.gov/eeoc/history/35th/thelaw/eo-8802.html (accessed April 10, 2013).

Roosevelt, Franklin D. 1943. Executive Order 9346, http://www.archives.gov/federal-register/executive-orders/1943.html (accessed April 10, 2013).

Rosenthal, Andrew. 1989. "Reagan Hints Rights Leaders Exaggerate Racism to Preserve Cause." *New York Times*, January 14, B1.

Ross, Sonya, and Jennifer Agiesta. 2012. "AP Poll: Majority Harbor Prejudice against Blacks." *Associated Press*, October 27, http://bigstory.ap.org/article/ap-poll-majority-harbor-prejudice-against-blacks (accessed March 19, 2013).

Rumbaut, Rubén G. 1997. "Paradoxes (and Orthodoxies) of Assimilation." *Sociological Perspectives* 40:483–511.

Russell-Brown, Katherine. 1998. *The Color of Crime: Racial Hoaxes, White Fear, Black Protectionism, Police Harassment and Other Macro Aggressions.* New York: New York University Press.

Saito, Leland. 1998. *Race and Politics: Asian Americans, Latinos, and Whites in a Los Angeles Suburb.* Urbana: University of Illinois Press.

Santa Ana, Otto. 1994. "'Like an Animal I Was Treated': Anti-immigrant Metaphor in U.S. Public Discourse." *Discourse & Society* 10:194–224.

Santa Ana, Otto. 2002. *Brown Tide Rising: Metaphors of Latinos in Contemporary American Public Discourse.* Austin: University of Texas Press.

Santa Ana, Otto. 2013. *Juan in a Hundred: The Representation of Latinos on Network News.* Austin: University of Texas Press.

Schlesinger, Arthur. 1991. *The Disuniting of America: Reflections on a Multicultural Society.* New York: W. W. Norton and Company.

Schmidt, Ron. 2000. *Language Policy and Identity in the United States.* Philadelphia: Temple University Press. Kindle edition.

Shafir, Gershon. 1995. *Immigrants and Nationalists: Ethnic Conflict and Accommodation in Catalonia, the Basque Country, Latvia, and Estonia.* Albany: State University of New York Press.

Shannon, Sheila. 1999. "The Debate on Bilingual Education in the U.S." Pp. 171–199 in Jan Blommaert (ed.), *Language Ideological Debates.* Berlin: Mouton de Gruyter.

Shapiro, Thomas M. 2004. *The Hidden Cost of Being African American: How Wealth Perpetuates Inequality.* New York: Oxford University Press.

Shockley, John S. 1974. *Chicano Revolt in a Texas Town.* Notre Dame, IN: University of Notre Dame Press.

Shore, Bradd. 2000. "Human Diversity and Human Nature." Pp. 81–104 in Neil Roughley (ed.), *Being Humans: Anthropological Universality and Particularity in Transdisciplinary Perspective.* Berlin: Walter de Gruyter.

Silverstein, Michael. 1996. "Monoglot 'Standard' in America: Standardization and Metaphors of Linguistic Hegemony." Pp. 284–306 in Donald Brenneis and Ronald K. S. Macaulay (eds.), *The Matrix of Language: Contemporary Linguistic Anthropology*. Boulder, CO: Westview Press.

Simmel, Georg. [1908 ] 1964. "The Stranger." Pp. 402–408 in Kurt H. Wolff (ed.), *The Sociology of Georg Simmel*. New York: Free Press.

Skutnabb-Kangas, Tove. 2000. *Linguistic Genocide in Education, or Worldwide Diversity and Human Rights?* Mahwah, NJ: Lawrence Erlbaum Associates.

Solórzano, Daniel G. 1998. "Critical Race Theory, Racial and Gender Microaggressions, and the Experiences of Chicana and Chicano Scholars." *International Journal of Qualitative Studies in Education* 11:121–136.

Steele, Claude M., and Joshua Aronson. 1995. "Stereotype Threat and the Intellectual Test Performance of African Americans." *Journal of Personality & Social Psychology* 69:797–811.

Stellar, Tim. 2012. "Border Patrol Faces Little Accountability." *Arizona Daily Star*, http://azstarnet.com/news/local (accessed March 11, 2013).

Sundstrom, Ronald R. 2008. *The Browning of America and the Evasion of Social Justice*. Albany, NY: SUNY Press. Kindle edition.

Tafoya, Sonya. 2004. "Shades of Belonging." *Pew Hispanic Research Center*, http://www.pewhispanic.org/files/reports/35.pdf (accessed March 24, 2013).

Tanaka, Janice D. 1999. "When You're Smiling: The Deadly Legacy of Internment." Documentary produced and directed by Janice D. Tanaka, Visual Communications.

Taylor, Paul, Mark Hugo Lopez, Jessica Hamar Martínez, and Gabriel Velasco. 2012. "When Labels Don't Fit: Hispanics and Their Views of Identity." *Pew Hispanic Research Center*, http://www.pewhispanic.org/2012/04/04/iv-language-use-among-latinos (accessed February 1, 2013).

Telles, Edward, and Vilma Ortiz. 2008. *Generations of Exclusion: Mexican Americans, Assimilation, and Race*. New York: Russell Sage Foundation.

Thielman, Sam. 2012. "Hispanic Networks Rebrand en Masse." *Adweek*, http://www.adweek.com/news/television/hispanic-networks-rebrand-en-masse-145833 (accessed March 17, 2013).

Tuan, Mia. 1998. *Forever Foreigners or Honorary Whites?: The Asian American Experience Today*. New Brunswick, NJ: Rutgers University Press.

Ture, Kwame [Stokely Carmichael], and Charles V. Hamilton. 1967. *Black Power: The Politics of Liberation in America*. New York: Vintage.

Urciuoli, Bonnie. 1996. *Exposing Prejudice: Puerto Rican Experiences of Language, Race, and Class*. Boulder, CO: Westview Press.

US Census Bureau. 2010. "Table QT-P10, Hispanic or Latino by Type: 2010."

US Census Bureau. 2011. "Table 1, Hispanic or Latino Origin Population by Type: 2000 and 2010." *The Hispanic Population 2010 Census Brief*.

US General Accounting Office. 1994. *Information on Minority Targeted Scholarships*. Washington, DC: U.S. Government Printing Office.

Valdez, Zulema. 2011. *The New Entrepreneurs: How Race, Class and Gender Shape American Enterprise*. Palo Alto, CA: Stanford University Press.

Varela, Julio R. 2013. "The Troubling Study on U.S. Latinos CNN Didn't Want You to See." *Latino Rebels*, http://www.latinorebels.com/2013/04/11/the-troubling-study-on-u-s-latinos-cnn-didnt-want-you-to-see (accessed April 12, 2013).

Wood, Nicholas. 2005. "In the Old Dialect, a Balkan Region Regains Its Identity." *New York Times*, February 24, A4.

Wu, Frank. 1995. "Neither Black nor White: Asian Americans and Affirmative Action." *Boston College Third World Law Journal* 15:249–250.

Yen, Hope. 2013. "Rise of Latino Population Blurs US Racial Lines." http://news.yahoo.com/rise-latino-population-blurs-us-racial-lines-114944593.html (accessed March 18, 2013).

Yosso, Tara J., William A. Smith, Miguel Ceja, and Daniel G. Solórzano. 2009. "Critical Race Theory, Racial Microaggressions, and Campus Racial Climate for Latina/o Undergraduates." *Harvard Educational Review* 79:659–690.

Zangwill, Israel. 1909. *The Melting-Pot, Drama in Four Acts*. New York: Macmillan.

# Further Readings

## Racial Theory

Back, Les, and John Solomon (eds.). 2009. *Theories of Race and Racism: A Reader*. 2nd ed. London: Routledge.

Curry, Tommy J. 2011. "Shut Your Mouth When You're Talking to Me: Silencing the Idealist School of Critical Theory through Culturalogical Turn in Jurisprudence." *Georgetown Law Journal of Modern Critical Race Studies* 3:1–38.

Feagin, Joe R. 2006. *Systemic Racism: A Theory of Oppression*. New York: Routledge.

Feagin, Joe R. 2013. *The White Racial Frame*. 2nd ed. New York: Routledge.

Feagin, Joe R., and José A. Cobas. 2008. "Latinos/as and the White Racial Frame." *Sociological Inquiry* 78: 39–53.

Feagin, Joe R., and Eileen O'Brien. 2003. *White Men on Race*. Boston: Beacon.

Horsman, Reginald. 1981. *Race and Manifest Destiny: The Origins of American Racial Anglo-Saxonism*. Cambridge, MA: Harvard University Press.

## Immigration

Duany, Jorge. 2011. *Blurred Borders: Transnational Migration between the Hispanic Caribbean and the United States*. Chapel Hill: University of North Carolina Press.

Menjívar, Cecilia. 2000. *Fragmented Ties: Salvadoran Immigrant Networks in America*. Berkeley: University of California Press.

Portes, Alejandro, and Rubén Rumbaut. 2001. *Legacies: The Story of the Immigrant Second Generation*. Berkeley: University of California Press.

Suárez-Orozco, Carola, and Marcelo M. Suárez-Orozco. 2002. *Children of Immigration (Developing Child)*. Cambridge, MA: Harvard University Press.

## Language

Bourdieu, Pierre R. 1991. *Language & Symbolic Power*. Cambridge, MA: Harvard University Press.

Cobas, José A., and Joe R. Feagin. 2008. "Language Oppression and Resistance: Latinos in the United States." *Ethnic and Racial Studies* 31: 390–410.

Hill, Jane H. 2008. *The Everyday Language of White Racism*. New York: Wiley-Blackwell.

Lippi-Green, Rosina. 2012. *English with an Accent: Language, Ideology and Discrimination in the United States*. 2nd ed. New York: Routledge.

Santa Ana, Otto. 2002. *Brown Tide Rising: Metaphors of Latinos in Contemporary American Public Discourse*. Austin: University of Texas Press.

## Whiteness and Color-Blind Racism

Bonilla-Silva, Eduardo. 2008. *Racism without Racists: Color-Blind Racism and Racial Inequality in Contemporary America*. 3rd ed. Lanham, MD: Rowman and Littlefield.

Carr, Leslie. 1997. *"Color-Blind" Racism*. Thousand Oaks, CA: Sage.

Feagin, Joe R., and Eileen O'Brien. 2003. *White Men on Race*. Boston: Beacon.

Lipsitz, George. 2006. *The Possessive Investment in Whiteness: How White People Profit from Identity to Politics*. Philadelphia: Temple University Press.

López, Ian F. Haney. 1996. *White by Law: The Legal Construction of Race*. New York: New York University Press.

Roediger, David R. 2007. *The Wages of Whiteness: Race and the Making of the American Working Class*. London: Verso.

Roediger, David R. 2005. *Working toward Whiteness: How America's Immigrants Became White*. New York: Basic Books.

## Latin Americans and Latinos

Acosta-Belén, Edna, and Carlos E. Santiago. 2006. *Puerto Ricans in the United States: A Contemporary Portrait*. Boulder, CO: Lynne Rienner Publishers.

Carr, Raymond. 1984. *Puerto Rico: A Colonial Experiment*. New York: Vintage.

Cobas, José A., and Jorge Duany. 1997. *Cubans in Puerto Rico: Ethnic Economy and Cultural Identity*. Gainesville: University Press of Florida.

Cobas, José A., Jorge Duany, and Joe Feagin (eds.). 2009. *How the United States Racializes Latinos: White Hegemony and Its Consequences*. Boulder, CO: Paradigm Publishers.

Gómez, Laura E. 2007. *Manifest Destinies: The Making of the Mexican American Race*. New York: New York University Press.

Gonzalez, Gilbert. 2007. *Guest Workers or Colonized Labor?: Mexican Labor Migration to the United States*. Boulder, CO: Paradigm Publishers.

Greenbaum, Susan D. 2002. *More than Black: Afrocubans in Tampa*. Gainesville: University Press of Florida.

Grenier, Guillermo J., Lisandro Pérez, and Nancy Foner. 2002. *The Legacy of Exile: Cubans in the United States*. Boston: Allyn and Bacon.

Hames-García, Michael, and Ernesto J. Martínez (eds.). 2011. *Gay Latino Studies: A Critical Reader*. Durham, NC: Duke University Press.

Hernández, Ramona. 2002. *The Mobility of Workers under Advanced Capitalism: Dominican Migration to the United States*. New York: Columbia University Press.

Masud-Piloto, Félix. 1996. *From Welcomed Exiles to Illegal Immigrants: Cuban Migration to the U.S., 1959–1995*. Lanham, MD: Rowman & Littlefield.

Ramos-Zayas, Ana Y. 2003. *National Performances: The Politics of Class, Race, and Space in Puerto Rican Chicago*. Chicago: University of Chicago Press.

Rosales, F. Arturo. 1999. *Pobre Raza!: Violence, Justice, and Mobilization among México Lindo Immigrants, 1900–1936*. Austin: University of Texas Press.

Samora, Julian, and Patricia Vandel Simon. 1977. *A History of the Mexican American People*. Notre Dame, IN: University of Notre Dame Press.

Telles, Edward, and Vilma Ortiz. 2009. *Generations of Exclusion: Mexican Americans, Assimilation, and Race*. New York: Russell Sage Foundation.

---

An expanded Further Readings list will be available at http://www.paradigmpublishers.com/resrcs/chapters/1612055540_otherchap.pdf.

# Index

Acuña, Rodolfo, 90
Adaptation and conformity, by Latinos, 89–106; acceptance of elements of racial frame, 91–93; active enactment of racial frame, 93–96; and dominant white racial frame, 90–104; symbolic/internalized violence, 90–91, 96–100; whitewashed Latino views of African Americans, 100–104
Affirmative action programs, 107–127; aiding white families, 101, 126–127, 137; benefits of, 121–124; competency criteria, viewpoints on, 115–118; experiences of survey respondents, 115–124; legal assaults on, 112–114; political origins of, 107–109; quotas, viewpoints on, 118–122; realities of, 124–127; white opposition to discrimination remedies, 110–114
African Americans: antiblack framing of in other countries, 101; average family wealth, comparison to whites, 9; early systemic racism impacts, 7, 8, 15–16; and Jim Crow segregation, 15, 108, 112, 126; and myth of economic success ties to English proficiency, 41; oppressed group status of, 20; support for affirmative action, 114; whitewashed Latino views of, 100–104
Alba, Richard, 4
American G.I. Forum, 132
Anchor babies, use of term, 156
Anglo-conformity assimilation, x, 3–6, 8
"Anglo-Saxon race," viewed superiority of, 12, 15, 18–19, 34–35, 73

Anti-oppression counter-frame, 12–13, 26–27, 43–46, 147–152. *See also* Home-culture resistance frame
Arizona, 31, 65, 73, 154
Asian Americans: during 1870–1920 immigration era, 5; attempts to preserve languages, 43; as constructive blacks, 20–21; early systemic racism impacts, 8, 9; hostile mocking of speech, 42–43; internalized oppression among, 91; racial barriers for, 5; social scientists on blending-with-whites concept, 134–136
Assimilation, as unidirectional, x, 5, 8, 10–11, 105, 132, 136–137, 153, 158
Assimilation tradition and US immigration, 3–11; assimilation analyses, flaws in, 4–6; full assimilation, 8–10; impacts of unidirectional assimilation pressures, 10–11; institutionally enabled white racial status, 8–9; segmented assimilation, 4–5. *See also* Melting-pot perspective, Latinos and whiteness
Assimilation-into-whiteness perspective, 134–137
Aztlan, 85

Baker, Dusty, 103–104
Bakke, Allan, 112–113
Barrera, Mario, 20
Barrett, Rusty, 138, 139
Beaner hopping, use of term, 86
Bell, Derrick, 13
Border patrol: discriminatory treatment of Latinos crossing US-Mexico border, 82–85, 95–97; US agent shootings

# About the Authors

**Joe R. Feagin**, Ella C. McFadden Professor in the Sociology Department at Texas A&M University, has done much research on racism issues in the United States. He has written 61 scholarly books and 200-plus scholarly articles and reports in his research areas of sociology of racism and sexism and urban sociology. Feagin's books include *Systemic Racism* (Routledge, 2006); *Liberation Sociology*, with Hernán Vera (2nd ed., Paradigm Publishers, 2008); *White Party, White Government* (Routledge, 2012); and *The White Racial Frame* (2nd ed., Routledge, 2013). He is the recipient of a 2012 Soka Gakkai International–USA Social Justice Award, the 2013 American Association for Affirmative Action's Arthur Fletcher Lifetime Achievement Award, and the 2013 American Sociological Association's W. E. B. Du Bois Career of Distinguished Scholarship Award and Section on Racial & Ethnic Minorities' Founder's Award. He was the 1999–2000 president of the American Sociological Association.

**José A. Cobas** is Professor Emeritus of Sociology in the T. Denny Sanford School of Social and Family Dynamics at Arizona State University. He has published in the areas of Cubans in Puerto Rico as a Middleman Minority, racism against Latinos, Latinos and health, and Latinos' mate selection. He is the author of *Cubans in Puerto Rico: Ethnic Economy and Cultural Identity*, with Jorge Duany (University Press of Florida, 1997), and *How the United States Racializes Latinos: White Hegemony and Its Consequences*, with Jorge Duany and Joe Feagin (Paradigm Publishers, 2009).